JOHN GREEN

CORNELSEN SENIOR ENGLISH LIBRARY

Looking for Alaska

Cornelsen

John Green **Looking for Alaska**

Herausgegeben von:
Birgit Ohmsieder

Verlagsredaktion:
Neil Porter

Technische Umsetzung:
Ingo Ostermaier

Umschlaggestaltung:
Cornelsen Verlag Design

Umschlagfoto:
© Shutterstock Images/Indmila Yilmaz

Herausgeber der Cornelsen Senior English Library:
Prof. Dr. Albert-Reiner Glaap

www.cornelsen.de

1. Auflage, 7. Druck 2014

Alle Drucke dieser Auflage sind inhaltlich unverändert
und können im Unterricht nebeneinander verwendet werden.

Druck: Offizin Andersen Nexö Leipzig

ISBN 978-3-06-031125-5

Inhalt gedruckt auf säurefreiem Papier aus nachhaltiger Forstwirtschaft.

Contents

To my family:
Sydney Green, Mike Green, and Hank Green

"I have tried so hard to do right."
(last words of President Grover Cleveland)

Abbreviations and Annotations

adj	adjective	**jdm./jdn.**	jemandem/en
adv	adverb	**n**	noun
AE	American English	**p., pp**	page, pages
cf.	confer; see	**pl**	plural
derog	derogatory	**sb.**	somebody
e.g.	exempli gratia; for example	**sl**	slang
esp.	especially	**sth.**	something
fml	formal	**usu.**	usually
i.e.	id est; in other words	**v**	verb
infml	informal		

The annotations are arranged chronologically; the first time a word is used is where you will find it explained.

before

one hundred thirty-six days before

THE WEEK BEFORE I left my family and Florida and the rest of my minor life to go to boarding school in Alabama, my mother insisted on throwing me a going-away party. To say that I had low expectations would be to underestimate the matter dramatically. Although I was more or less forced to invite all my "school friends," i.e., the ragtag bunch of drama people and English geeks I sat with by social necessity in the cavernous cafeteria of my public school, I knew they wouldn't come. Still, my mother persevered, awash in the delusion that I had kept my popularity secret from her all these years. She cooked a small mountain of artichoke dip. She festooned our living room in green and yellow streamers, the colors of my new school. She bought two dozen champagne poppers and placed them around the edge of our coffee table.

And when that final Friday came, when my packing was mostly done, she sat with my dad and me on the living-room couch at 4:56 P.M. and patiently awaited the arrival of the Good-bye to Miles Cavalry. Said cavalry consisted of exactly two people: Marie Lawson,

2 **minor** (adj): not very important 4 **underestimate sth.**: think that sth. is smaller than it really is 5 **ragtag** (infml): (here) having no real connection with each other 6 **geek** (infml): person who is boring 7 **cavernous** (fml): very large and often empty and/or dark 8 **persevere** [ˌpɜːsəˈvɪr]: continue trying to do sth. despite difficulties 8 **be awash in sth.**: *schwimmend in etwas* 8 **delusion**: *Irrglaube* 10 **festoon sth.**: decorate sth. (e.g. a room) for a party 12 **champagne popper**: *Flasche gefüllt mit Konfetti* 17 **said cavalry**: (here) those who came to save the day

a tiny blonde with rectangular glasses, and her chunky (to put it charitably) boyfriend, Will.

"Hey, Miles," Marie said as she sat down.

"Hey," I said.

"How was your summer?" Will asked.

"Okay. Yours?"

"Good. We did *Jesus Christ Superstar*. I helped with the sets. Marie did lights," said Will.

"That's cool." I nodded knowingly, and that about exhausted our conversational topics. I might have asked a question about *Jesus Christ Superstar*, except that *1*. I didn't know what it was, and 2. I didn't care to learn, and *3*. I never really excelled at small talk. My mom, however, can talk small for hours, and so she extended the awkwardness by asking them about their rehearsal schedule, and how the show had gone, and whether it was a success.

"I guess it was," Marie said. "A lot of people came, I guess." Marie was the sort of person to guess a lot.

Finally, Will said, "Well, we just dropped by to say good-bye. I've got to get Marie home by six. Have fun at boarding school, Miles."

"Thanks," I answered, relieved. The only thing worse than having a party that no one attends is having a party attended only by two vastly, deeply uninteresting people.

They left, and so I sat with my parents and stared at the blank TV and wanted to turn it on but knew I shouldn't. I could feel them both looking at me, waiting for me to burst into tears or something, as if I hadn't known all along that it would go precisely like this. But I *had* known. I could feel their pity as they scooped artichoke dip with chips intended for my imaginary friends, but they needed pity more than I did: I wasn't disappointed. My expectations had been met.

"Is this why you want to leave, Miles?" Mom asked.

1 **chunky**: (here) having a short strong (here: fat) body   12 **excel at sth.**: be very good at sth.   14 **rehearsal** [rɪˈhɜːrsl]: the act of practising a play for a performance   18 **drop by**: visit sb. for a short period of time   27 **scoop sth.**: *(hier) etwas schaufeln*

I mulled it over for a moment, careful not to look at her. "Uh, no," I said.

"Well, why then?" she asked. This was not the first time she had posed the question. Mom was not particularly keen on letting me go to boarding school and had made no secret of it.

"Because of me?" my dad asked. He had attended Culver Creek, the same boarding school to which I was headed, as had both of his brothers and all of their kids. I think he liked the idea of me following in his footsteps. My uncles had told me stories about how famous my dad had been on campus for having simultaneously raised hell and aced all his classes. That sounded like a better life than the one I had in Florida. But no, it wasn't because of Dad. Not exactly.

"Hold on," I said. I went into Dad's study and found his biography of François Rabelais. I liked reading biographies of writers, even if (as was the case with Monsieur Rabelais) I'd never read any of their actual writing. I flipped to the back and found the highlighted quote ("NEVER USE A HIGHLIGHTER IN MY BOOKS," my dad had told me a thousand times. But how else are you supposed to find what you're looking for?).

"So this guy," I said, standing in the doorway of the living room. "François Rabelais. He was this poet. And his last words were 'I go to seek a Great Perhaps.' That's why I'm going. So I don't have to wait until I die to start seeking a Great Perhaps."

And that quieted them. I was after a Great Perhaps, and they knew as well as I did that I wasn't going to find it with the likes of Will and Marie. I sat back down on the couch, between my mom and my dad, and my dad put his arm around me, and we stayed there like that, quiet on the couch together, for a long time, until it seemed okay to turn on the TV, and then we ate artichoke dip for dinner and watched the History Channel, and as going-away parties go, it certainly could have been worse.

1 **mull sth. over**: think carefully about sth. 10 **raise hell** (infml): cause trouble 11 **ace classes**: (here) be very good at school 14 **François Rabelais**: French author (1483–1553) 25 **the likes of** (infml): used to refer to sb. who is considered a type

one hundred twenty-eight days before

FLORIDA WAS PLENTY HOT, certainly, and humid, too. Hot enough that your clothes stuck to you like Scotch tape, and sweat dripped like tears from your forehead into your eyes. But it was only hot outside, and generally I only went outside to walk from one airconditioned location to another.

This did not prepare me for the unique sort of heat that one encounters fifteen miles south of Birmingham, Alabama, at Culver Creek Preparatory School. My parents' SUV was parked in the grass just a few feet outside my dorm room, Room 43. But each time I took those few steps to and from the car to unload what now seemed like far too much stuff, the sun burned through my clothes and into my skin with a vicious ferocity that made me genuinely fear hellfire.

Between Mom and Dad and me, it only took a few minutes to unload the car, but my unair-conditioned dorm room, although blessedly out of the sunshine, was only modestly cooler. The room surprised me: I'd pictured plush carpet, wood-paneled walls, Victorian furniture. Aside from one luxury – a private bathroom – I got a box. With cinder-block walls coated thick with layers of white paint and a green-and-white-checkered linoleum floor, the place looked more like a hospital than the dorm room of my fantasies. A bunk bed of unfinished wood with vinyl mattresses was pushed against the room's back window. The desks and dressers and bookshelves were all attached to the walls in order to prevent creative floor planning. *And no air-conditioning.*

I sat on the lower bunk while Mom opened the trunk, grabbed a stack of the biographies my dad had agreed to part with, and placed them on the bookshelves.

"I can unpack, Mom," I said. My dad stood. He was ready to go.

2 **scotch tape**: *Klebeband* 8 **SUV**: *eine Art Geländewagen* 9 **dorm = dormitory** (AE) room where students sleep in a boarding school 12 **vicious** (infml): (here) bad or severe 12 **ferocity** [- '- -]: violence, aggressiveness 12 **genuine** ['dʒənjuɪn]: real 15 **modestly:** (here) slightly 16 **plush** (adj; infml): luxurious 18 **cinder-block**: *Schlackenstein* 18 **coat with sth.**: cover with sth. 21 **vinyl** ['vaɪnl]: strong plastic 26 **part with sth.**: give sth. to sb. else, esp. sth. that you would prefer to keep

"Let me at least make your bed," Mom said.

"No, really. I can do it. It's okay." Because you simply cannot draw these things out forever. At some point, you just pull off the Band-Aid and it hurts, but then it's over and you're relieved.

"God, we'll miss you," Mom said suddenly, stepping through the minefield of suitcases to get to the bed. I stood and hugged her. My dad walked over, too, and we formed a sort of huddle. It was too hot, and we were too sweaty, for the hug to last terribly long. I knew I ought to cry, but I'd lived with my parents for sixteen years, and a trial separation seemed overdue.

"Don't worry." I smiled. "I's a-gonna learn how t'talk right Southern." Mom laughed.

"Don't do anything stupid," my dad said.

"Okay."

"No drugs. No drinking. No cigarettes." As an alumnus of Culver Creek, he had done the things I had only heard about: the secret parties, streaking through hay fields (he always whined about how it was all boys back then), drugs, drinking, and cigarettes. It had taken him a while to kick smoking, but his badass days were now well behind him.

"I love you," they both blurted out simultaneously. It needed to be said, but the words made the whole thing horribly uncomfortable, like watching your grandparents kiss.

"I love you, too. I'll call every Sunday." Our rooms had no phone lines, but my parents had requested I be placed in a room near one of Culver Creek's five pay phones.

They hugged me again – Mom, then Dad – and it was over. Out the back window, I watched them drive the winding road off campus. I should have felt a gooey, sentimental sadness, perhaps. But mostly I just wanted to cool off, so I grabbed one of the desk chairs and sat down outside my door in the shade of the overhanging eaves, waiting for a breeze that never arrived. The air outside sat as still and

3–4 **Band-Aid**: *Pflaster* 10 **trial**: *Versuchs-, Probe-* 15 **alumnus**: former student 17 **streak**: run naked 19 **badass**: not obeying the rules 29 **gooey** ['gu:i] (infml): sweet and soft 31 **eaves** [i:vz]: *Dachgesims*

oppressive as the air inside. I stared out over my new digs: Six one-story buildings, each with sixteen dorm rooms, were arranged in a hexagram around a large circle of grass. It looked like an oversize old motel. Everywhere, boys and girls hugged and smiled and walked together. I vaguely hoped that someone would come up and talk to me. I imagined the conversation:

"Hey. Is this your first year?"

"Yeah. Yeah. I'm from Florida."

"That's cool. So you're used to the heat."

"I wouldn't be used to this heat if I were from Hades," I'd joke. I'd make a good first impression. *Oh, he's funny. That guy Miles is a riot.*

That didn't happen, of course. Things never happened like I imagined them.

Bored, I went back inside, took off my shirt, lay down on the heat-soaked vinyl of the lower bunk mattress, and closed my eyes. I'd never been born again with the baptism and weeping and all that, but it couldn't feel much better than being born again as a guy with no known past. I thought of the people I'd read about – John F. Kennedy, James Joyce, Humphrey Bogart – who went to boarding school, and their adventures – Kennedy, for example, loved pranks. I thought of the Great Perhaps and the things that might happen and the people I might meet and who my roommate might be (I'd gotten a letter a few weeks before that gave me his name, Chip Martin, but no other information). Whoever Chip Martin was, I hoped to God he would bring an arsenal of high-powered fans, because I hadn't packed even one, and I could already feel my sweat pooling on the vinyl mattress, which disgusted me so much that I stopped thinking and got off my ass to find a towel to wipe up the sweat with. And then I thought, *Well, before the adventure comes the unpacking.*

1 **digs** (pl; infml): room(s) you rent to live in 3 **hexagram**: star shape made from two triangles 10 **Hades** ['heɪdi:z]: ancient Greek underworld 11 **riot** (old-fashioned, infml): person or an event that is very amusing and enjoyable
18–19 **John F. Kennedy**: US President (1917–1963) 19 **James Joyce**: Irish author (1882–1941) 19 **Humphrey Bogart**: US actor (1899–1957) 20 **prank**: trick that is played on sb. as a joke 25 **arsenal**: collection (usu. of weapons)

I managed to tape a map of the world to the wall and get most of my clothes into drawers before I noticed that the hot, moist air made even the walls sweat, and I decided that now was not the time for manual labor. Now was the time for a magnificently cold shower.

The small bathroom contained a huge, full-length mirror behind the door, and so I could not escape the reflection of my naked self as I leaned in to turn on the shower faucet. My skinniness always surprised me: My thin arms didn't seem to get much bigger as they moved from wrist to shoulder, my chest lacked any hint of either fat or muscle, and I felt embarrassed and wondered if something could be done about the mirror. I pulled open the plain white shower curtain and ducked into the stall.

Unfortunately, the shower seemed to have been designed for someone approximately three feet, seven inches tall, so the cold water hit my lower rib cage – with all the force of a dripping faucet. To wet my sweat-soaked face, I had to spread my legs and squat significantly. Surely, John F. Kennedy (who was six feet tall according to his biography, my height exactly) did not have to *squat* at *his* boarding school. No, this was a different beast entirely, and as the dribbling shower slowly soaked my body, I wondered whether I could find a Great Perhaps here at all or whether I had made a grand miscalculation.

When I opened the bathroom door after my shower, a towel wrapped around my waist, I saw a short, muscular guy with a shock of brown hair. He was hauling a gigantic army-green duffel bag through the door of my room. He stood five feet and nothing, but was well-built, like a scale model of Adonis, and with him arrived the stink of stale cigarette smoke. *Great*, I thought. *I'm meeting my roommate naked*. He heaved the duffel into the room, closed the door, and walked over to me.

"I'm Chip Martin," he announced in a deep voice, the voice of a radio deejay. Before I could respond, he added, "I'd shake your hand, but I think you should hold on damn tight to that towel till you can get some clothes on."

4 **magnificent** [-'- - -]: fantastic 7 **faucet** (AE): *Wasserhahn* 19 **beast** (infml) (here): thing of a particular kind 25 **duffel bag**: *Matchbeutel*

I laughed and nodded my head at him (that's cool, right? the nod?) and said, "I'm Miles Halter. Nice to meet you."

"Miles, as in 'to go before I sleep'?" he asked me.

"Huh?"

"It's a Robert Frost poem. You've never read him?"

I shook my head no.

"Consider yourself lucky." He smiled.

I grabbed some clean underwear, a pair of blue Adidas soccer shorts, and a white T-shirt, mumbled that I'd be back in a second, and ducked back into the bathroom. So much for a good first impression.

"So where are your parents?" I asked from the bathroom.

"My parents? The father's in California right now. Maybe sitting in his La-Z-Boy. Maybe driving his truck. Either way, he's drinking. My mother is probably just now turning off campus."

"Oh," I said, dressed now, not sure how to respond to such personal information. I shouldn't have asked, I guess, if I didn't want to know.

Chip grabbed some sheets and tossed them onto the top bunk. "I'm a top bunk man. Hope that doesn't bother you."

"Uh, no. Whatever is fine."

"I see you've decorated the place," he said, gesturing toward the world map. "I like it."

And then he started naming countries. He spoke in a monotone, as if he'd done it a thousand times before.

Afghanistan.

Albania.

Algeria.

American Samoa.

Andorra.

And so on. He got through the A's before looking up and noticing my incredulous stare.

5 **Robert Frost**: US poet (1874–1963) 9 **mumble**: speak or say sth. in a quiet voice 14 **La-Z-Boy**: (brand name) kind of sofa 32 **incredulous**: not willing or able to believe sth.

"I could do the rest, but it'd probably bore you. Something I learned over the summer. God, you can't imagine how boring New Hope, Alabama, is in the summertime. Like watching soybeans grow. Where are you from, by the way?"

"Florida," I said.

"Never been."

"That's pretty amazing, the countries thing," I said.

"Yeah, everybody's got a talent. I can memorize things. And you can … ?"

"Um, I know a lot of people's last words." It was an indulgence, learning last words. Other people had chocolate; I had dying declarations.

"Example?"

"I like Henrik Ibsen's. He was a playwright." I knew a lot about Ibsen, but I'd never read any of his plays. I didn't like reading plays. I liked reading biographies.

"Yeah, I know who he was," said Chip.

"Right, well, he'd been sick for a while and his nurse said to him, 'You seem to be feeling better this morning,' and Ibsen looked at her and said, 'On the contrary,' and then he died."

Chip laughed. "That's morbid. But I like it."

He told me he was in his third year at Culver Creek. He had started in ninth grade, the first year at the school, and was now a junior like me. A scholarship kid, he said. Got a full ride. He'd heard it was the best school in Alabama, so he wrote his application essay about how he wanted to go to a school where he could read long books. The problem, he said in the essay, was that his dad would always hit him with the books in his house, so Chip kept his books short and paperback for his own safety. His parents got divorced his sophomore year. He liked "the Creek," as he called it, but "You have to be careful here, with students and with teachers. And I do hate being careful." He smirked. I hated being careful, too – or wanted to, at least.

10 **indulgence**: something that you do even though it is not essential
30 **sophomore**: second year at college or university 32 **smirk**: *blöd grinsen*

He told me this while ripping through his duffel bag, throwing clothes into drawers with reckless abandon. Chip did not believe in having a sock drawer or a T-shirt drawer. He believed that all drawers were created equal and filled each with whatever fit. My mother would have died.

As soon as he finished "unpacking," Chip hit me roughly on the shoulder, said, "I hope you're stronger than you look," and walked out the door, leaving it open behind him. He peeked his head back in a few seconds later and saw me standing still. "Well, come on, Miles To Go Halter. We got shit to do."

We made our way to the TV room, which according to Chip contained the only cable TV on campus. Over the summer, it served as a storage unit. Packed nearly to the ceiling with couches, fridges, and rolled-up carpets, the TV room undulated with kids trying to find and haul away their stuff. Chip said hello to a few people but didn't introduce me. As he wandered through the couch-stocked maze, I stood near the room's entrance, trying my best not to block pairs of roommates as they maneuvered furniture through the narrow front door.

It took ten minutes for Chip to find his stuff, and an hour more for us to make four trips back and forth across the dorm circle between the TV room and Room 43. By the end, I wanted to crawl into Chip's minifridge and sleep for a thousand years, but Chip seemed immune to both fatigue and heatstroke. I sat down on his couch.

"I found it lying on a curb in my neighborhood a couple years ago," he said of the couch as he worked on setting up my Play-Station 2 on top of his footlocker. "I know the leather's got some cracks, but come on. That's a damn nice couch." The leather had more than a few cracks – it was about 30 percent baby blue faux leather and 70 percent foam – but it felt damn good to me anyway.

2 **with reckless abandon**: in a very careless and unorganized way 14 **undulate**: move gently up and down like waves 17 **maze**: *Irrgarten* 24 **fatigue**: tiredness 24 **heatstroke**: *Hitzschlag* 26 **curb**: *Bordkante* 28 **footlocker**: small kind of chest

"All right," he said. "We're about done." He walked over to his desk and pulled a roll of duct tape from a drawer. "We just need your trunk."

I got up, pulled the trunk out from under the bed, and Chip situated it between the couch and the PlayStation 2 and started tearing off thin strips of duct tape. He applied them to the trunk so that they spelled out COFFEE TABLE.

"There," he said. He sat down and put his feet up on the, uh, coffee table. "Done."

I sat down next to him, and he looked over at me and suddenly said, "Listen. I'm not going to be your entrée to Culver Creek social life."

"Uh, okay," I said, but I could hear the words catch in my throat. I'd just carried this guy's couch beneath a white-hot sun and now he didn't like me?

"Basically you've got two groups here," he explained, speaking with increasing urgency. "You've got the regular boarders, like me, and then you've got the Weekday Warriors; they board here, but they're all rich kids who live in Birmingham and go home to their parents' air-conditioned mansions every weekend. Those are the cool kids. I don't like them, and they don't like me, and so if you came here thinking that you were hot shit at public school so you'll be hot shit here, you'd best not be seen with me. You did go to public school, didn't you?"

"Uh …" I said. Absentmindedly, I began picking at the cracks in the couch's leather, digging my fingers into the foamy whiteness.

"Right, you did, probably, because if you had gone to a private school your freakin' shorts would fit." He laughed.

I wore my shorts just below my hips, which I thought was cool. Finally I said, "Yeah, I went to public school. But I wasn't hot shit there, Chip. I was regular shit."

"Ha! That's good. And don't call me Chip. Call me the Colonel."

2 **duct tape**: very strong tape that is often used for repairing things 11 **entrée to sth.** (fml): right or ability to enter a social group or institution 17 **boarder**: student who lives at a boarding school 20 **mansion**: large impressive house

I stifled a laugh. *"The Colonel?"*

"Yeah. The Colonel. And we'll call you … hmm. Pudge."

"Huh?"

"Pudge," the Colonel said. "Because you're skinny. It's called irony, Pudge. Heard of it? Now, let's go get some cigarettes and start this year off right."

He walked out of the room, again just assuming I'd follow, and this time I did. Mercifully, the sun was descending toward the horizon. We walked five doors down to Room 48. A dry-erase board was taped to the door using duct tape. In blue marker, it read: *Alaska has a single!*

The Colonel explained to me that *1.* this was Alaska's room, and that *2.* she had a single room because the girl who was supposed to be her roommate got kicked out at the end of last year, and that *3.* Alaska had cigarettes, although the Colonel neglected to ask whether *4.* I smoked, which *5.* I didn't.

He knocked once, loudly. Through the door, a voice screamed, "Oh my God come in you short little man because I have the best story."

We walked in. I turned to close the door behind me, and the Colonel shook his head and said, "After seven, you have to leave the door open if you're in a girl's room," but I barely heard him because the hottest girl in all of human history was standing before me in cutoff jeans and a peach tank top. And she was talking over the Colonel, talking loud and fast.

"So first day of summer, I'm in grand old Vine Station with this boy named Justin and we're at his house watching TV on the couch – and mind you, I'm already dating Jake – actually I'm still dating him, miraculously enough, but Justin is a friend of mine from when I was a kid and so we're watching TV and literally chatting about the SATs or something, and Justin puts his arm around me and I think, *Oh that's nice, we've been friends for so long and this is totally comfortable*, and we're just chatting and then I'm in the middle of a sentence about analogies or something and like a hawk he reaches down and

2 **Pudge** from **pudgy**: slightly fat 31 **SAT = Scholastic Aptitude Test**: university entrance test

he honks my boob. *HONK.* A much-too-firm, two- to three-second *HONK.* And the first thing I thought was *Okay, how do I extricate this claw from my boob before it leaves permanent marks?* and the second thing I thought was *God, I can't wait to tell Takumi and the Colonel.*"

The Colonel laughed. I stared, stunned partly by the force of the voice emanating from the petite (but God, curvy) girl and partly by the gigantic stacks of books that lined her walls. Her library filled her bookshelves and then overflowed into waist-high stacks of books everywhere, piled haphazardly against the walls. If just one of them moved, I thought, the domino effect could engulf the three of us in an asphyxiating mass of literature.

"Who's the guy that's not laughing at my very funny story?" she asked.

"Oh, right. Alaska, this is Pudge. Pudge memorizes people's last words. Pudge, this is Alaska. She got her boob honked over the summer." She walked over to me with her hand extended, then made a quick move downward at the last moment and pulled down my shorts.

"Those are the biggest shorts in the state of Alabama!"

"I like them baggy," I said, embarrassed, and pulled them up. They had been cool back home in Florida.

"So far in our relationship, Pudge, I've seen your chicken legs entirely too often," the Colonel deadpanned. "So, Alaska. Sell us some cigarettes." And then somehow, the Colonel talked me into paying five dollars for a pack of Marlboro Lights I had no intention of ever smoking. He asked Alaska to join us, but she said, "I have to find Takumi and tell him about The Honk." She turned to me and asked, "Have you seen him?" I had no idea whether I'd seen Takumi, since I had no idea who he was. I just shook my head.

"All right. Meet ya at the lake in a few minutes, then." The Colonel nodded.

*

1 **honk sth.**: *hupen* 1 **boob** (sl): woman's breast 2 **extricate sth.**: (here) remove sth. unpleasant 5 **stunned**: very surprised or shocked 9 **haphazard** [ˌhæp'hæzəd]: with no particular order 11 **asphyxiate sb.** [æs'fɪksieɪt]: *jdn. ersticken*
23 **deadpan** (v): say sth. without any expression or emotion

At the edge of the lake, just before the sandy (and, the Colonel told me, fake) beach, we sat down in an Adirondack swing. I made the obligatory joke: "Don't grab my boob." The Colonel gave an obligatory laugh, then asked, "Want a smoke?" I had never smoked a cigarette, but when in Rome …

"Is it safe here?"

"Not really," he said, then lit a cigarette and handed it to me. I inhaled. Coughed. Wheezed. Gasped for breath. Coughed again. Considered vomiting. Grabbed the swinging bench, head spinning, and threw the cigarette to the ground and stomped on it, convinced my Great Perhaps did not involve cigarettes.

"Smoke much?" He laughed, then pointed to a white speck across the lake and said, "See that?"

"Yeah," I said. "What is that? A bird?"

"It's the swan," he said.

"Wow. A school with a swan. Wow."

"That swan is the spawn of Satan. Never get closer to it than we are now."

"Why?"

"It has some issues with people. It was abused or something. It'll rip you to pieces. The Eagle put it there to keep us from walking around the lake to smoke."

"The Eagle?"

"Mr. Starnes. Code name: the Eagle. The dean of students. Most of the teachers live on campus, and they'll all bust you. But only the Eagle lives in the dorm circle, and he sees all. He can smell a cigarette from like five miles."

"Isn't his house back there?" I asked, pointing to it. I could see the house quite clearly despite the darkness, so it followed he could probably see us.

2 **Adirondack swing**: *Hollywoodschaukel* 5 **When in Rome (do as the Romans do)**: proverb saying that if you go abroad you should behave like the people who live there 8 **wheeze**: breathe noisily and with difficulty 9 **vomit**: bring food from the stomach back out through the mouth 17 **spawn**: child 24 **dean**: teacher in charge of student discipline 25 **bust sb.**: (here) punish sb.

"Yeah, but he doesn't really go into blitzkrieg mode until classes start," Chip said nonchalantly.

"God, if I get in trouble my parents will kill me," I said.

"I suspect you're exaggerating. But look, you're going to get in trouble. Ninety-nine percent of the time, your parents never have to know, though. The school doesn't want your parents to think you became a fuckup here any more than you want your parents to think you're a fuckup." He blew a thin stream of smoke forcefully toward the lake. I had to admit: He looked cool doing it. Taller, somehow. "Anyway, when you get in trouble, just don't tell on anyone. I mean, I hate the rich snots here with a fervent passion I usually reserve only for dental work and my father. But that doesn't mean I would rat them out. Pretty much the only important thing is never never never never rat."

"Okay," I said, although I wondered: *If someone punches me in the face, I'm supposed to insist that I ran into a door?* It seemed a little stupid. How do you deal with bullies and assholes if you can't get them into trouble? I didn't ask Chip, though.

"All right, Pudge. We have reached the point in the evening when I'm obliged to go and find my girlfriend. So give me a few of those cigarettes you'll never smoke anyway, and I'll see you later."

I decided to hang out on the swing for a while, half because the heat had finally dissipated into a pleasant, if muggy, eighty-something, and half because I thought Alaska might show up. But almost as soon as the Colonel left, the bugs encroached: no-see-ums (which, for the record, you can see) and mosquitoes hovered around me in such numbers that the tiny noise of their rubbing wings sounded cacophonous. And then I decided to smoke.

Now, I did think, *The smoke will drive the bugs away*. And, to some degree, it did. I'd be lying, though, if I claimed I became a smoker to

2 **nonchalant**: casual as if not important 7 **fuckup** (n; sl): person who behaves badly or fails 11 **snot** (sl): *Scheißkerl* 11 **fervent**: showing strong feelings 13 **rat sb. out** (sl): *jdn. verraten/verpetzen* 23 **dissipate**: gradually become weaker until it disappears 23 **muggy**: (of weather) warm and damp in an unpleasant way 25 **bug**: small insect 25 **encroach**: slowly begin to cover more and more of an area 25 **no-see-um**: small insect 28 **cacophonous**: producing a mixture of loud unpleasant sounds

ward off insects. I became a smoker because *1.* I was on an Adirondack swing by myself, and 2. I had cigarettes, and 3. I figured that if everyone else could smoke a cigarette without coughing, I could damn well, too. In short, I didn't have a very good reason. So yeah, let's just say that *4.* it was the bugs.

I made it through three entire drags before I felt nauseous and dizzy and only semipleasantly buzzed. I got up to leave. As I stood, a voice behind me said:

"So do you really memorize last words?"

She ran up beside me and grabbed my shoulder and pushed me back onto the porch swing.

"Yeah," I said. And then hesitantly, I added, "You want to quiz me?"

"JFK," she said.

"That's obvious," I answered.

"Oh, is it now?" she asked.

"No. Those were his last words. Someone said, 'Mr. President, you can't say Dallas doesn't love you,' and then he said, 'That's obvious,' and then he got shot."

She laughed. "God, that's awful. I shouldn't laugh. But I will," and then she laughed again. "Okay, Mr. Famous Last Words Boy. I have one for you." She reached into her overstuffed backpack and pulled out a book. "Gabriel García Márquez. *The General in His Labyrinth.* Absolutely one of my favorites. It's about Simón Bolívar." I didn't know who Simón Bolívar was, but she didn't give me time to ask. "It's a historical novel, so I don't know if this is true, but in the book, do you know what his last words are? No, you don't. But I am about to tell you, Señor Parting Remarks."

And then she lit a cigarette and sucked on it so hard for so long that I thought the entire thing might burn off in one drag. She exhaled and read to me:

"'He' – that's Simón Bolívar – 'was shaken by the overwhelming revelation that the headlong race between his misfortunes and his

2 **figure sth.**: decide that sth. is true 6 **nauseous** ['nɔːʃəs; BE 'nɔːsiəs]: feeling as if you want to vomit 7 **buzzed** (infml): *benebelt* 22 **Gabriel García Márquez**: Colombian novelist (born 1927) 23 **Simón Bolívar**: general who fought for the independence of Spanish colonies in South America (1783–1830) 32 **revelation**: *Enthüllung, Offenbarung*

dreams was at that moment reaching the finish line. The rest was darkness. "Damn it," he sighed. "How will I ever get out of this labyrinth!"' "

I knew great last words when I heard them, and I made a mental note to get ahold of a biography of this Simón Bolívar fellow. Beautiful last words, but I didn't quite understand. "So what's the labyrinth?" I asked her.

And now is as good a time as any to say that she was beautiful. In the dark beside me, she smelled of sweat and sunshine and vanilla, and on that thin-mooned night I could see little more than her silhouette except for when she smoked, when the burning cherry of the cigarette washed her face in pale red light. But even in the dark, I could see her eyes – fierce emeralds. She had the kind of eyes that predisposed you to supporting her every endeavor. And not just beautiful, but hot, too, with her breasts straining against her tight tank top, her curved legs swinging back and forth beneath the swing, flip-flops dangling from her electric-blue-painted toes. It was right then, between when I asked about the labyrinth and when she answered me, that I realized the *importance* of curves, of the thousand places where girls' bodies ease from one place to another, from arc of the foot to ankle to calf, from calf to hip to waist to breast to neck to ski-slope nose to forehead to shoulder to the concave arch of the back to the butt to the etc. I'd *noticed* curves before, of course, but I had never quite apprehended their significance.

Her mouth close enough to me that I could feel her breath warmer than the air, she said, "That's the mystery, isn't it? Is the labyrinth living or dying? Which is he trying to escape – the world or the end of it?" I waited for her to keep talking, but after a while it became obvious she wanted an answer.

"Uh, I don't know," I said finally. "Have you really read all those books in your room?"

5 **get ahold of sth.**: *etwas in die Finger bekommen* 13 **emerald**: *Smaragd*
14 **predispose sb. to sth.**: influence sb. so that they are likely to think or behave in a particular way 14 **endeavour**: attempt to do sth., esp. sth. new or difficult
15 **strain** (v): (here) push hard against sth. 21 **calf**: lower (back) part of the leg
23 **butt** (infml): part of the body that you sit on

She laughed. "Oh God no. I've maybe read a third of 'em. But I'm *going to* read them all. I call it my Life's Library. Every summer since I was little, I've gone to garage sales and bought all the books that looked interesting. So I always have something to read. But there is so much to do: cigarettes to smoke, sex to have, swings to swing on. I'll have more time for reading when I'm old and boring."

She told me that I reminded her of the Colonel when he came to Culver Creek. They were freshmen together, she said, both scholarship kids with, as she put it, "a shared interest in booze and mischief." The phrase *booze and mischief* left me worrying I'd stumbled into what my mother referred to as "the wrong crowd," but for the wrong crowd, they both seemed awfully smart. As she lit a new cigarette off the butt of her previous one, she told me that the Colonel was smart but hadn't done much living when he got to the Creek.

"I got rid of that problem quickly." She smiled. "By November, I'd gotten him his first girlfriend, a perfectly nice non–Weekday Warrior named Janice. He dumped her after a month because she was too rich for his poverty-soaked blood, but whatever. We pulled our first prank that year – we filled Classroom 4 with a thin layer of marbles. We've progressed some since then, of course." She laughed. So Chip became the Colonel – the military-style planner of their pranks, and Alaska was ever Alaska, the larger-than-life creative force behind them.

"You're smart like him," she said. "Quieter, though. And cuter, but I didn't even just say that, because I love my boyfriend."

"Yeah, you're not bad either," I said, overwhelmed by her compliment. "But I didn't just say that, because I love my girlfriend. Oh, wait. Right. I don't have one."

She laughed. "Yeah, don't worry, Pudge. If there's one thing I can get you, it's a girlfriend. Let's make a deal: You figure out what the labyrinth is and how to get out of it, and I'll get you laid."

"Deal." We shook on it.

*

9 **booze** (infml): alcoholic drink 9 **mischief**: bad behaviour 13 **butt**: end (of a cigarette that has been smoked) 31 **get laid** (sl): have sex

Later, I walked toward the dorm circle beside Alaska. The cicadas hummed their one-note song, just as they had at home in Florida. She turned to me as we made our way through the darkness and said, "When you're walking at night, do you ever get creeped out and even though it's silly and embarrassing you just want to run home?" It seemed too secret and personal to admit to a virtual stranger, but I told her, "Yeah, totally."

For a moment, she was quiet. Then she grabbed my hand, whispered, "Run run run run run," and took off, pulling me behind her.

one hundred twenty-seven days before

EARLY THE NEXT AFTERNOON, I blinked sweat from my eyes as I taped a van Gogh poster to the back of the door. The Colonel sat on the couch judging whether the poster was level and fielding my endless questions about Alaska. *What's her story?* "She's from Vine Station. You could drive past it without noticing – and from what I understand, you ought to. Her boyfriend's at Vanderbilt on scholarship. Plays bass in some band. Don't know much about her family." *So she really likes him?* "I guess. She hasn't cheated on him, which is a first." And so on. All morning, I'd been unable to care about anything else, not the van Gogh poster and not video games and not even my class schedule, which the Eagle had brought by that morning. He introduced himself, too:

"Welcome to Culver Creek, Mr. Halter. You're given a large measure of freedom here. If you abuse it, you'll regret it. You seem like a nice young man. I'd hate to have to bid you farewell."

And then he stared at me in a manner that was either serious or seriously malicious. "Alaska calls that the Look of Doom," the Colonel told me after the Eagle left. "The next time you see that, you're busted."

4 **get creeped out** (infml): be frightened 11 **van Gogh**: Dutch painter (1853–1890) 12 **level**: *gerade* 12 **field sth.**: (here) receive and deal with questions or comments 15 **Vanderbilt**: Vanderbilt University 23 **abuse sth.**: make bad use of sth. 26 **malicious**: showing a desire to harm others

"Okay, Pudge," the Colonel said as I stepped away from the poster. Not entirely level, but close enough. "Enough with the Alaska already. By my count, there are ninety-two girls at this school, and every last one of them is less crazy than Alaska, who, I might add, *already has a boyfriend*. I'm going to lunch. It's bufriedo day." He walked out, leaving the door open. Feeling like an overinfatuated idiot, I got up to close the door. The Colonel, already halfway across the dorm circle, turned around. "Christ. Are you coming or what?"

You can say a lot of bad things about Alabama, but you can't say that Alabamans as a people are unduly afraid of deep fryers. In that first week at the Creek, the cafeteria served fried chicken, chicken-fried steak, and fried okra, which marked my first foray into the delicacy that is the fried vegetable. I half expected them to fry the iceberg lettuce. But nothing matched the bufriedo, a dish created by Maureen, the amazingly (and understandably) obese Culver Creek cook. A deep-fried bean burrito, the bufriedo proved beyond the shadow of a doubt that frying always improves a food. Sitting with the Colonel and five guys I didn't know at a circular table in the cafeteria that afternoon, I sank my teeth into the crunchy shell of my first bufriedo and experienced a culinary orgasm. My mom cooked okay, but I immediately wanted to bring Maureen home with me over Thanksgiving.

The Colonel introduced me (as "Pudge") to the guys at the wobbly wooden table, but I only registered the name Takumi, whom Alaska had mentioned yesterday. A thin Japanese guy only a few inches taller than the Colonel, Takumi talked with his mouth full as I chewed slowly, savoring the bean-y crunch.

"God," Takumi said to me, "there's nothing like watching a man eat his first bufriedo."

I didn't say much – partly because no one asked me any questions and partly because I just wanted to eat as much as I could. But Takumi felt no such modesty – he could, and did, eat and chew and swallow while talking.

6 **overinfatuated**: having feelings of love that are too strong 12 **foray into sth.**: short journey to find sth. 15 **obese**: extremely fat 20 **culinary**: connected with food or cooking 32 **modesty**: *Bescheidenheit*

The lunch discussion centered on the girl who was supposed to have been Alaska's roommate, Marya, and her boyfriend, Paul, who had been a Weekday Warrior. They'd gotten kicked out in the last week of the previous school year, I learned, for what the Colonel called "the Trifecta" – they were caught committing three of Culver Creek's expellable offenses at once. Lying naked in bed together ("genital contact" being offense #1), already drunk (#2), they were smoking a joint (#3) when the Eagle burst in on them. Rumors had it that someone had ratted them out, and Takumi seemed intent on finding out who – intent enough, anyway, to shout about it with his mouth jam-packed with bufriedo.

"Paul was an asshole," the Colonel said. "I wouldn't have ratted on them, but anyone who shacks up with a Jaguar-driving Weekday Warrior like Paul deserves what she gets."

"Dude," Takumi responded, "yaw guhfwend," and then he swallowed a bite of food, "is a Weekday Warrior."

"True." The Colonel laughed. "Much to my chagrin, that is an incontestable fact. But she is not as big an asshole as Paul."

"Not quite." Takumi smirked. The Colonel laughed again, and I wondered why he wouldn't stand up for his girlfriend. I wouldn't have cared if my girlfriend was a Jaguar-driving Cyclops with a beard – I'd have been grateful just to have someone to make out with.

That evening, when the Colonel dropped by Room 43 to pick up the cigarettes (he seemed to have forgotten that they were, technically, *mine*), I didn't really care when he didn't invite me out with him. In public school, I'd known plenty of people who made it a habit to hate this kind of person or that kind – the geeks hated the preps, etc. – and it always seemed like a big waste of time to me.

6 **expellable:** for which you will be made to leave school 6 **offense**: crime, illegal act 13 **shack up with sb.** (sl): *(hier) mit jdm. Sex haben* 15 **dude** (sl): man
15 **yaw guhfwend**: (here) your girlfriend 17 **chagrin:** disappointment
18 **incontestable**: that is true and cannot be disagreed with 21 **Cyclops**: (in Greek mythology) a giant with only one eye in the middle of his forehead 22 **make out with sb.** (infml): kiss and touch sb. in a sexual way 27 **prep** (AE): (here) rich students

The Colonel didn't tell me where he'd spent the afternoon, or where he was going to spend the evening, but he closed the door behind him when he left, so I guessed I wasn't welcome.

Just as well: I spent the night surfing the Web (no porn, I swear) and reading *The Final Days*, a book about Richard Nixon and Watergate. For dinner, I microwaved a refrigerated bufriedo the Colonel had snuck out of the cafeteria. It reminded me of nights in Florida – except with better food and no air-conditioning. Lying in bed and reading felt pleasantly familiar.

I decided to heed what I'm sure would have been my mother's advice and get a good night's sleep before my first day of classes. French II started at 8:10, and figuring it couldn't take more than eight minutes to put on some clothes and walk to the classrooms, I set my alarm for 8:02. I took a shower, and then lay in bed waiting for sleep to save me from the heat. Around 11:00, I realized that the tiny fan clipped to my bunk might make more of a difference if I took off my shirt, and I finally fell asleep on top of the sheets wearing just boxers.

A decision I found myself regretting some hours later when I awoke to two sweaty, meaty hands shaking the holy hell out of me. I woke up completely and instantly, sitting up straight in bed, terrified, and I couldn't understand the voices for some reason, couldn't understand why there were any voices at all, and what the hell time was it anyway? And finally my head cleared enough to hear, "C'mon, kid. Don't make us kick your ass. Just get up," and then from the top bunk, I heard, "Christ, Pudge. Just *get up*." So I got up, and saw for the first time three shadowy figures. Two of them grabbed me, one with a hand on each of my upper arms, and walked me out of the room. On the way out, the Colonel mumbled, "Have a good time. Go easy on him, Kevin."

They led me, almost at a jog, behind my dorm building, and then across the soccer field. The ground was grassy but gravelly, too, and

5 **Richard Nixon**: US President (1913–1994) 6 **Watergate**: American political scandal during the presidency of Nixon 10 **heed sth.**: take notice of sth.
32 **gravelly**: full of small stones

I wondered why no one had shown the common courtesy to tell me to put on shoes, and why was I out there in my underwear, chicken legs exposed to the world? A thousand humiliations crossed my mind: *There's the new junior, Miles Halter, handcuffed to the soccer goal wearing only his boxers*. I imagined them taking me into the woods, where we now seemed headed, and beating the shit out of me so that I looked great for my first day of school. And the whole time, I just stared at my feet, because I didn't want to look at them and I didn't want to fall, so I watched my steps, trying to avoid the bigger rocks. I felt the fight-or-flight reflex swell up in me over and over again, but I knew that neither fight nor flight had ever worked for me before. They took me a roundabout way to the fake beach, and then I knew what would happen – a good, old-fashioned dunking in the lake – and I calmed down. I could handle that.

When we reached the beach, they told me to put my arms at my sides, and the beefiest guy grabbed two rolls of duct tape from the sand. With my arms flat against my sides like a soldier at attention, they mummified me from my shoulder to my wrists. Then they threw me down on the ground; the sand from the fake beach cushioned the landing, but I still hit my head. Two of them pulled my legs together while the other one – Kevin, I'd figured out – put his angular, strong-jawed face up so close to mine that the gel-soaked spikes of hair pointing out from his forehead poked at my face, and told me, "This is for the Colonel. You shouldn't hang out with that asshole." They taped my legs together, from ankles to thighs. I looked like a silver mummy. I said, "Please guys, don't," just before they taped my mouth shut. Then they picked me up and hurled me into the water.

Sinking. Sinking, but instead of feeling panic or anything else, I realized that "Please guys, don't" were terrible last words. But then the great miracle of the human species – our buoyancy – came

3 **humiliation**: act of making sb. feel ashamed 10 **swell up**: become bigger 12 **fake**: not real 13 **dunk:** (here) push sb. underwater for a short time 16 **beefy** (infml): (of a person or their body) big or strong 18 **mummify sb.**: *jdn. mumifizieren* 22 **angular**: very thin 23 **poke**: *(hier) stoßen* 27 **hurl sb./sth.**: throw sb./sth. 31 **buoyancy** [ˈbɔɪənsi]: ability to float on water

through, and as I felt myself floating toward the surface, I twisted and turned as best I could so that the warm night air hit my nose first, and I breathed. I wasn't dead and wasn't going to die.

Well, I thought, *that wasn't so bad*.

But there was still the small matter of getting to shore before the sun rose. First, to determine my position vis-à-vis the shoreline. If I tilted my head too much, I felt my whole body start to roll, and on the long list of unpleasant ways to die, "facedown in soaking-wet white boxers" is pretty high up there. So instead I rolled my eyes and craned my neck back, my eyes almost underwater, until I saw that the shore – not ten feet away – was directly behind my head. I began to swim, an armless silver mermaid, using only my hips to generate motion, until finally my ass scraped against the lake's mucky bottom. I turned then and used my hips and waist to roll three times, until I came ashore near a ratty green towel. They'd left me a towel. How thoughtful.

The water had seeped under the duct tape and loosened the adhesive's grip on my skin, but the tape was wrapped around me three layers deep in places, which necessitated wiggling like a fish out of water. Finally it loosened enough for me to slip my left hand up and out against my chest and rip the tape off.

I wrapped myself in the sandy towel. I didn't want to go back to my room and see Chip, because I had no idea what Kevin had meant – maybe if I went back to the room, they'd be waiting for me and they'd get me for real; maybe I needed to show them, "Okay. Got your message. He's just my roommate, not my friend." And anyway, I didn't feel terribly friendly toward the Colonel. *Have a good time*, he'd said. *Yeah*, I thought. *I had a ball*.

So I went to Alaska's room. I didn't know what time it was, but I could see a faint light underneath her door. I knocked softly.

10 **crane** (v): stretch (your neck) 12 **mermaid**: creature with a woman's head and body, and a fish's tail 13 **scrape against sth.**: rub against sth. (esp. a hard surface) 13 **mucky**: dirty 15 **ratty** (AE infml): shabby 18 **adhesive** (n): substance that sticks things together 19 **necessitate sth.**: make sth necessary 19 **wiggle**: *sich winden*

"Yeah," she said, and I came in, wet and sandy and wearing only a towel and soaking boxers. This was not, obviously, how you want the world's hottest girl to see you, but I figured she could explain to me what had just happened.

She put down a book and got out of bed with a sheet wrapped around her shoulders. For a moment, she looked concerned. She looked like the girl I met yesterday, the girl who said I was cute and bubbled over with energy and silliness and intelligence. And then she laughed.

"Guess you went for a swim, huh?" And she said it with such casual malice that I felt that everyone had known, and I wondered why the whole damn school agreed in advance to possibly drown Miles Halter. But Alaska *liked* the Colonel, and in the confusion of the moment, I just looked at her blankly, unsure even of what to ask.

"Give me a break," she said. "Come on. You know what? There are people with real problems. I've got real problems. Mommy ain't here, so buck up, big guy."

I left without saying a word to her and went to my room, slamming the door behind me, waking the Colonel, and stomping into the bathroom. I got in the shower to wash the algae and the lake off me, but the ridiculous faucet of a showerhead failed spectacularly, and how could Alaska and Kevin and those other guys already dislike me? After I finished the shower, I dried off and went into the room to find some clothes.

"So," he said. "What took you so long? Get lost on your way home?"

"They said it was because of you," I said, and my voice betrayed a hint of annoyance. "They said I shouldn't hang out with you."

"What? No, it happens to everybody," the Colonel said. "It happened to me. They throw you in the lake. You swim out. You walk home."

11 **malice**: feeling of evil intention towards sb. 14 **blank**: (here) showing no feeling 18 **buck up**: (here) pull yourself together 20 **stomp**: walk with heavy steps 28 **betray sth.**: show sth.

"I couldn't just swim out," I said softly, pulling on a pair of jean shorts beneath my towel. "They duct-taped me. I couldn't even move, really."

"Wait. Wait," he said, and hopped out of his bunk, staring at me through the darkness. "They *taped* you? How?" And I showed him: I stood like a mummy, with my feet together and my hands at my sides, and showed him how they'd wrapped me up. And then I plopped down onto the couch.

"Christ! You could have drowned! They're just supposed to throw you in the water in your underwear and run!" he shouted. "What the hell were they thinking? Who was it? Kevin Richman and who else? Do you remember their faces?"

"Yeah, I think."

"Why the hell would they do that?" he wondered.

"Did you do something to them?" I asked.

"No, but I'm sure as shit gonna do something to 'em now. We'll get them."

"It wasn't a big deal. I got out fine."

"You could have *died*." And I could have, I suppose. But I didn't.

"Well, maybe I should just go to the Eagle tomorrow and tell him," I said.

"Absolutely not," he answered. He walked over to his crumpled shorts lying on the floor and pulled out a pack of cigarettes. He lit two and handed one to me. I smoked the whole goddamned thing. "You're not," he continued, "because that's not how shit gets dealt with here. And besides, you really don't want to get a reputation for ratting. But we will deal with those bastards, Pudge. I promise you. They will regret messing with one of my friends."

And if the Colonel thought that calling me his friend would make me stand by him, well, he was right. "Alaska was kind of mean to me tonight," I said. I leaned over, opened an empty desk drawer, and used it as a makeshift ashtray.

"Like I said, she's moody."

28 **mess with sb.**: do sth. to harm sb. 33 **moody**: having moods that change quickly and often

I went to bed wearing a T-shirt, shorts, and socks. No matter how miserably hot it got, I resolved, I would sleep in my clothes every night at the Creek, feeling – probably for the first time in my life – the fear and excitement of living in a place where you never know what's going to happen or when.

one hundred twenty-six days before

"WELL, NOW IT'S WAR," the Colonel shouted the next morning. I rolled over and looked at the clock: 7:52. My first Culver Creek class, French, started in eighteen minutes. I blinked a couple times and looked up at the Colonel, who was standing between the couch and the COFFEE TABLE, holding his well-worn, once-white tennis shoes by the laces. For a long time, he stared at me, and I stared at him. And then, almost in slow motion, a grin crept across the Colonel's face.

"I've got to hand it to them," he said finally. "That was pretty clever."

"What?" I asked.

"Last night – before they woke you up, I guess – they pissed in my shoes."

"Are you sure?" I said, trying not to laugh.

"Do you care to smell?" he asked, holding the shoes toward me. "Because I went ahead and smelled them, and yes, I am sure. If there's one thing I know, it's when I've just stepped in another man's piss. It's like my mom always says: 'Ya think you's a-walkin' on water, but turns out you just got piss in your shoes.' Point those guys out to me if you see them today," he added, "because we need to figure out why they're so, uh, pissed at me. And then we need to go ahead and start thinking about how we're going to ruin their miserable little lives."

When I received the Culver Creek Handbook over the summer and noticed happily that the "Dress Code" section contained only two

2 **resolve**: make a firm decision 11 **(shoe)lace**: *Schnürsenkel*

words, *casual modesty*, it never occurred to me that girls would show up for class half asleep in cotton pajama shorts, T-shirts, and flip-flops. Modest, I guess, and casual.

And there was something about girls wearing pajamas (even if modest), which might have made French at 8:10 in the morning bearable, if I'd had any idea what Madame O'Malley was talking about. *Comment dis-tu* "Oh my God, I don't know nearly enough French to pass French II" *en français?* My French I class back in Florida did not prepare me for Madame O'Malley, who skipped the "how was your summer" pleasantries and dove directly into something called the *passé composé*, which is apparently a verb tense. Alaska sat directly across from me in the circle of desks, but she didn't look at me once the entire class, even though I could notice little but her. Maybe she could be mean ... but the way she talked that first night about getting out of the labyrinth – so smart. And the way her mouth curled up on the right side all the time, like she was preparing to smirk, like she'd mastered the right half of the *Mona Lisa's* inimitable smile ...

From my room, the student population seemed manageable, but it overwhelmed me in the classroom area, which was a single, long building just beyond the dorm circle. The building was split into fourteen rooms facing out toward the lake. Kids crammed the narrow sidewalks in front of the classrooms, and even though finding my classes wasn't hard (even with my poor sense of direction, I could get from French in Room 3 to precalc in Room 12), I felt unsettled all day. I didn't know anyone and couldn't even figure out whom I should be trying to know, and the classes were *hard*, even on the first day. My dad had told me I'd have to study, and now I believed him. The teachers were serious and smart and a lot of them went by "Dr.," and so when the time came for my last class before lunch, World Religions, I felt tremendous relief. A vestige from when Culver Creek

1 **casual**: not formal 1 **occur to sb.**: come to sb.'s mind 6 **bearable**: *erträglich* 9 **skip sth.**: (here) not do sth. that one should usually do 10 **pleasantry**: friendly remark 18 **inimitable** [- '- - - -]: too good or individual for anyone else to copy 22 **cram**: move into a small space with the result that it is full 31 **vestige** ['vestɪdʒ]: *Überrest, Spur*

was a Christian boys' school, I figured the World Religions class, required of every junior and senior, might be an easy A.

It was my only class all day where the desks weren't arranged either in a square or a circle, so, not wanting to seem eager, I sat down in the third row at 11:03. I was seven minutes early, partly because I liked to be punctual, and partly because I didn't have anyone to chat with out in the halls. Shortly thereafter, the Colonel came in with Takumi, and they sat down on opposite sides of me.

"I heard about last night," Takumi said. "Alaska's pissed."

"That's weird, since she was such a bitch last night," I blurted out.

Takumi just shook his head. "Yeah, well, she didn't know the whole story. And people are moody, dude. You gotta get used to living with people. You could have worse friends than –"

The Colonel cut him off. "Enough with the psychobabble, MC Dr. Phil. Let's talk counterinsurgency." People were starting to file into class, so the Colonel leaned in toward me and whispered, "If any of 'em are in this class, let me know, okay? Just, here, just put X's where they're sitting," and he ripped a sheet of paper out of his notebook and drew a square for each desk. As people filed in, I saw one of them – the tall one with immaculately spiky hair – Kevin. Kevin stared down the Colonel as he walked past, but in trying to stare, he forgot to watch his step and bumped his thigh against a desk. The Colonel laughed. One of the other guys, the one who was either a little fat or worked out too much, came in behind Kevin, sporting pleated khaki pants and a short-sleeve black polo shirt. As they sat down, I crossed through the appropriate squares on the Colonel's diagram and handed it to him. Just then, the Old Man shuffled in.

He breathed slowly and with great labor through his wide-open mouth. He took tiny steps toward the lectern, his heels not moving

9 **pissed** (AE sl): very angry or annoyed 15 **psychobabble** (infml): *Psychologengequassel* 16 **counterinsurgency**: action taken against a group of people who are trying to take control of a country by force 21 **immaculate**: perfect
21 **spiky**: (of hair) sticking straight up from the head 26 **pleated**: *mit Bügelfalte*
31 **lectern**: stand for holding a book, etc. when you are giving a talk, etc.

much past his toes. The Colonel nudged me and pointed casually to his notebook, which read, *The Old Man only has one lung*, and I did not doubt it. His audible, almost desperate breaths reminded me of my grandfather when he was dying of lung cancer. Barrel-chested and ancient, the Old Man, it seemed to me, might die before he ever reached the podium.

"My name," he said, "is Dr. Hyde. I have a first name, of course. So far as you are concerned, it is Doctor. Your parents pay a great deal of money so that you can attend school here, and I expect that you will offer them some return on their investment by reading what I tell you to read when I tell you to read it and consistently attending this class. And when you are here, you will listen to what I say." Clearly not an easy A.

"This year, we'll be studying three religious traditions: Islam, Christianity, and Buddhism. We'll tackle three more traditions next year. And in my classes, I will talk most of the time, and you will listen most of the time. Because you may be smart, but I've been smart longer. I'm sure some of you do not like lecture classes, but as you have probably noted, I'm not as young as I used to be. I would love to spend my remaining breath chatting with you about the finer points of Islamic history, but our time together is short. I must talk, and you must listen, for we are engaged here in the most important pursuit in history: the search for meaning. What is the nature of being a person? What is the best way to go about being a person? How did we come to be, and what will become of us when we are no longer? In short: What are the rules of this game, and how might we best play it?"

The nature of the labyrinth, I scribbled into my spiral notebook, *and the way out of it*. This teacher rocked. I hated discussion classes. I hated talking, and I hated listening to everyone else stumble on their words and try to phrase things in the vaguest possible way so they wouldn't sound dumb, and I hated how it was all just a game of trying to figure out what the teacher wanted to hear and then saying

1 **nudge sb.**: push sb. gently, esp. with your elbow 3 **audible**: that can be heard 4 **barrel-chested**: *mit gewölbter Brust* 23 **pursuit** [pər'suːt]: (here) act of looking for or trying to find sth. 29 **rock** (AE infml): be very good

it. I'm in *class*, so *teach me*. And teach me he did: In those fifty minutes, the Old Man made me take religion seriously. I'd never been religious, but he told us that religion is important whether or not *we* believed in one, in the same way that historical events are important whether or not you personally lived through them. And then he assigned us fifty pages of reading for the next day – from a book called *Religious Studies*.

That afternoon, I had two classes and two free periods. We had nine fifty-minute class periods each day, which means that most everyone had three "study periods" (except for the Colonel, who had an extra independent-study math class on account of being an Extra Special Genius). The Colonel and I had biology together, where I pointed out the other guy who'd duct-taped me the night before. In the top corner of his notebook, the Colonel wrote, *Longwell Chase. Senior W-day Warrior. Friends w/Sara. Weird.* It took me a minute to remember who Sara was: the Colonel's girlfriend.

I spent my free periods in my room trying to read about religion. I learned that *myth* doesn't mean a lie; it means a traditional story that tells you something about people and their worldview and what they hold sacred. Interesting. I also learned that after the events of the previous night, I was far too tired to care about myths or anything else, so I slept on top of the covers for most of the afternoon, until I awoke to Alaska singing, "WAKE UP, LITTLE PUHHHHHDGIE!" directly into my left ear canal. I held the religion book close up against my chest like a small paperback security blanket.

"That was terrible," I said. "What do I need to do to ensure that never happens to me again?"

"Nothing you can do!" she said excitedly. "I'm unpredictable. God, don't you hate Dr. Hyde? Don't you? He's so condescending."

I sat up and said, "I think he's a genius," partly because I thought it was true and partly because I just felt like disagreeing with her.

She sat down on the bed. "Do you always sleep in your clothes?"

"Yup."

9 **most** (AE infml): almost 15 **W-day**: (here) weekday 15 **w/**: (here) with
20 **sacred**: considered to be holy 28 **unpredictable**: *unberechenbar*
29 **condescending** [- - '- -]: looking down on other people

"Funny," she said. "You weren't wearing much last night." I just glared at her.

"C'mon, Pudge. I'm teasing. You have to be tough here. I didn't know how bad it was – and I'm sorry, and they'll regret it – but you have to be tough." And then she left. That was all she had to say on the subject. *She's cute*, I thought, *but you don't need to like a girl who treats you like you're ten: You've already got a mom.*

one hundred twenty-two days before

AFTER MY LAST CLASS of my first week at Culver Creek, I entered Room 43 to an unlikely sight: the diminutive and shirtless Colonel, hunched over an ironing board, attacking a pink buttondown shirt. Sweat trickled down his forehead and chest as he ironed with great enthusiasm, his right arm pushing the iron across the length of the shirt with such vigor that his breathing nearly duplicated Dr. Hyde's.

"I have a date," he explained. "This is an emergency." He paused to catch his breath. "Do you know" – breath – "how to iron?"

I walked over to the pink shirt. It was wrinkled like an old woman who'd spent her youth sunbathing. If only the Colonel didn't ball up his every belonging and stuff it into random dresser drawers. "I think you just turn it on and press it against the shirt, right?" I said. "I don't know. I didn't even know we *had* an iron."

"We don't. It's Takumi's. But Takumi doesn't know how to iron, either. And when I asked Alaska, she started yelling, 'You're not going to impose the patriarchal paradigm on *me*.' Oh, God, I need to smoke. I need to smoke, but I can't reek when I see Sara's parents. Okay, screw it. We're going to smoke in the bathroom with the shower on. The shower has steam. Steam gets rid of wrinkles, right?

9 **diminutive** (adj): (here) very small 10 **hunch** (v): *sich krümmen* 13 **duplicate sth.**: (here) be almost the same as sth. 17 **wrinkled**: *zerknittert* 19 **random**: *wahllos, willkürlich* 24 **impose sth. on sb.**: (here) make sb. accept the same opinions as your own 24 **patriarchal**: ruled or controlled by men 24 **paradigm** ['perədaɪm]: typical example or pattern of sth. 25 **reek**: smell strongly of sth unpleasant 26 **screw it** (sl) = I don't care

"By the way," he said as I followed him into the bathroom, "if you want to smoke inside during the day, just turn on the shower. The smoke follows the steam up the vents."

Though this made no scientific sense, it seemed to work. The shower's shortage of water pressure and low showerhead made it all but useless for showering, but it worked great as a smoke screen.

Sadly, it made a poor iron. The Colonel tried ironing the shirt once more ("I'm just gonna push really hard and see if that helps") and finally put it on wrinkled. He matched the shirt with a blue tie decorated with horizontal lines of little pink flamingos.

"The one thing my lousy father taught me," the Colonel said as his hands nimbly threaded the tie into a perfect knot, "was how to tie a tie. Which is odd, since I can't imagine when he ever had to wear one."

Just then, Sara knocked on the door. I'd seen her once or twice before, but the Colonel never introduced me to her and didn't have a chance to that night.

"Oh. My God. Can't you at least press your shirt?" she asked, even though the Colonel was standing in front of the ironing board. "We're going out with my *parents*." Sara looked awfully nice in her blue summer dress. Her long, pale blond hair was pulled up into a twist, with a strand of hair falling down each side of her face. She looked like a movie star – a bitchy one.

"Look, I did my best. We don't all have maids to do our ironing."

"Chip, that chip on your shoulder makes you look even shorter."

"Christ, can't we get out the door without fighting?"

"I'm just saying. It's *the opera*. It's a big deal to my parents. Whatever. Let's go." I felt like leaving, but it seemed stupid to hide in the bathroom, and Sara was standing in the doorway, one hand cocked on her hip and the other fiddling with her car keys as if to say, *Let's go*.

3 **vent** (n): opening that allows air to pass out of a room 11 **lousy**: *fies*
12 **nimble**: able to move quickly and easily 23 **bitchy** (infml): saying unpleasant and unkind things about other people 25 **(have) a chip on your shoulder** (infml): (be) sensitive about sth. that happened in the past, esp. in your childhood
30 **cock** (v): raise a part of your body 30 **fiddle with sth.**: keep touching or moving sth. with your hands

"I could wear a tuxedo and your parents would still hate me!" he shouted.

"That's not my fault! You antagonize them!" She held up the car keys in front of him. "Look, we're going now or we're not going."

"Fuck it. I'm not going anywhere with you," the Colonel said.

"Fine. Have a great night." Sara slammed the door so hard that a sizable biography of Leo Tolstoy (last words: "The truth is ... I care a great deal ... what they ... ") fell off my bookshelf and landed with a thud on our checkered floor like an echo of the slamming door.

"AHHHHH!!!!!!!!!!!" he screamed.

"So that's Sara," I said.

"Yes."

"She seems nice."

The Colonel laughed, knelt down next to the minifridge, and pulled out a gallon of milk. He opened it, took a swig, winced, half coughed, and sat down on the couch with the milk between his legs.

"Is it sour or something?"

"Oh, I should have mentioned that earlier. This isn't milk. It's five parts milk and one part vodka. I call it ambrosia. Drink of the gods. You can barely smell the vodka in the milk, so the Eagle can't catch me unless he actually takes a sip. The downside is that it tastes like sour milk and rubbing alcohol, but it's Friday night, Pudge, and my girlfriend is a bitch. Want some?"

"I think I'll pass." Aside from a few sips of champagne on New Year's under the watchful eye of my parents, I'd never really drunk any alcohol, and "ambrosia" didn't seem like the drink with which to start. Outside, I heard the pay phone ring. Given the fact that 190 boarders shared five pay phones, I was amazed at how infrequently it rang. We weren't supposed to have cell phones, but I'd noticed that some of the Weekday Warriors carried them surreptitiously. And

1 **tuxedo** [tʌk'siːdoʊ]: *Smoking* 3 **antagonize sb.** [- '- - -]: do sth. to make sb. angry with you 9 **checkered**: having a pattern of squares of different colors 15 **swig**: quick drink of sth, esp. alcohol 15 **wince**: make an expression with your face showing pain 22 **downside**: disadvantage 29 **infrequent**: not often 31 **surreptitious**: done secretly

most non-Warriors called their parents, as I did, on a regular basis, so parents only called when their kids forgot.

"Are you going to get that?" the Colonel asked me. I didn't feel like being bossed around by him, but I also didn't feel like fighting. Through a buggy twilight, I walked to the pay phone, which was drilled into the wall between Rooms 44 and 45. On both sides of the phone, dozens of phone numbers and esoteric notes were written in pen and marker (*205.555.1584; Tommy to airport 4:20; 773.573.6521; JG–Kuffs?*). Calling the pay phone required a great deal of patience. I picked up on about the ninth ring.

"Can you get Chip for me?" Sara asked. It sounded like she was on a cell phone.

"Yeah, hold on."

I turned, and he was already behind me, as if he knew it would be her. I handed him the receiver and walked back to the room.

A minute later, three words made their way to our room through the thick, still air of Alabama at almost-night. "Screw you too!" the Colonel shouted.

Back in the room, he sat down with his ambrosia and told me, "She says I ratted out Paul and Marya. That's what the Warriors are saying. That I ratted them out. *Me*. That's why the piss in the shoes. That's why the nearly killing you. 'Cause you live with me, and they say I'm a rat."

I tried to remember who Paul and Marya were. The names were familiar, but I had heard so many names in the last week, and I couldn't match "Paul" and "Marya" with faces. And then I remembered why: I'd never seen them. They got kicked out the year before, having committed the Trifecta.

"How long have you been dating her?" I asked.

"Nine months. We never got along. I mean, I didn't even briefly like her. Like, my mom and my dad – my dad would get pissed, and then he would beat the shit out of my mom. And then my dad would

4 **boss sb. around**: tell sb. what to do in an unfriendly way 5 **buggy**: (here) with many insects, mosquitos 7 **esoteric**: *(hier) nur für Eingeweihte verständlich*
28 **Trifecta**: cf. p. 27 32 **beat the shit out of sb.** (sl): attack sb. violently so that you injure them

be all nice, and they'd have like a honeymoon period. But with Sara, there's never a honeymoon period. God, how could she think I was a rat? I know, I know: Why don't we break up?" He ran a hand through his hair, clutching a fistful of it atop his head, and said, "I guess I stay with her because she stays with me. And that's not an easy thing to do. I'm a bad boyfriend. She's a bad girlfriend. We deserve each other."

"But –"

"I can't believe they think that," he said as he walked to the bookshelf and pulled down the almanac. He took a long pull off his ambrosia. "Goddamn Weekday Warriors. It was probably one of them that ratted out Paul and Marya and then blamed me to cover their tracks. Anyway, it's a good night for staying in. Staying in with Pudge and ambrosia."

"I still –" I said, wanting to say that I didn't understand how you could kiss someone who believed you were a rat if being a rat was the worst thing in the world, but the Colonel cut me off.

"Not another word about it. You know what the capital of Sierra Leone is?"

"No."

"Me neither," he said, "but I intend to find out." And with that, he stuck his nose in the almanac, and the conversation was over.

one hundred ten days before

KEEPING UP WITH MY CLASSES proved easier than I'd expected. My general predisposition to spending a lot of time inside reading gave me a distinct advantage over the average Culver Creek student. By the third week of classes, plenty of kids had been sunburned to a bufriedo-like golden brown from days spent chatting outside in the shadeless dorm circle during free periods. But I was barely pink: I studied.

And I listened in class, too, but on that Wednesday morning, when Dr. Hyde started talking about how Buddhists believe that all

7 **deserve sb./sth.**: *jdn./etwas verdienen* 10 **almanac**: *Jahrbuch* 17 **cut sb. off**: stop sb. from talking 24 **predisposition**: *Neigung*

things are interconnected, I found myself staring out the window. I was looking at the wooded, slow-sloping hill beyond the lake. And from Hyde's classroom, things did seem connected: The trees seemed to clothe the hill, and just as I would never think to notice a particular cotton thread in the magnificently tight orange tank top Alaska wore that day, I couldn't see the trees for the forest – everything so intricately woven together that it made no sense to think of one tree as independent from that hill. And then I heard my name, and I knew I was in trouble.

"Mr. Halter," the Old Man said. "Here I am, straining my lungs for your edification. And yet *something* out there seems to have caught your fancy in a way that I've been unable to do. Pray tell: What have you discovered out there?"

Now I felt my own breath shorten, the whole class watching me, thanking God they *weren't* me. Dr. Hyde had already done this three times, kicking kids out of class for not paying attention or writing notes to one another.

"Um, I was just looking outside at the, uh, at the hill and thinking about, um, the trees and the forest, like you were saying earlier, about the way –"

The Old Man, who obviously did not tolerate vocalized rambling, cut me off. "I'm going to ask you to leave class, Mr. Halter, so that you can go out there and discover the relationship between the um-trees and the uh-forest. And tomorrow, when you're ready to take this class seriously, I will welcome you back."

I sat still, my pen resting in my hand, my notebook open, my face flushed and my jaw jutting out into an underbite, an old trick I had to keep from looking sad or scared. Two rows behind me, I heard a chair move and turned around to see Alaska standing up, slinging her backpack over one arm.

1 **interconnect**: be connected to (similar things) 4 **clothe sth.**: (here): cover sth. 5 **tank top** (AE): T-shirt without sleeves 11 **edification**: improvement of sb.'s mind or character 12 **fancy** (n): (here) imagination 21 **vocalize sth.**: express sth. 21 **ramble**: talk about sth. in a confused way 27 **flush**: become red 27 **jut out**: stick out

"I'm sorry, but that's bullshit. You can't just throw him out of class. You drone on and on for an hour every day, and we're not allowed to glance out the *window?*"

The Old Man stared back at Alaska like a bull at a matador, then raised a hand to his sagging face and slowly rubbed the white stubble on his cheek. "For fifty minutes a day, five days a week, you abide by my rules. Or you fail. The choice is yours. Both of you leave."

I stuffed my notebook into my backpack and walked out, humiliated. As the door shut behind me, I felt a tap on my left shoulder. I turned, but there was no one there. Then I turned the other way, and Alaska was smiling at me, the skin between her eyes and temple crinkled into a starburst. "The oldest trick in the book," she said, "but everybody falls for it."

I tried a smile, but I couldn't stop thinking about Dr. Hyde. It was worse than the Duct Tape Incident, because I always knew that the Kevin Richmans of the world didn't like me. But my teachers had always been card-carrying members of the Miles Halter Fan Club.

"I told you he was an asshole," she said.

"I still think he's a genius. He's right. I wasn't listening."

"Right, but he didn't need to be a jerk about it. Like he needs to prove his power by humiliating you?! Anyway," she said, "the only real geniuses are artists: Yeats, Picasso, García Márquez: *geniuses*. Dr. Hyde: bitter old man."

And then she announced we were going to look for four-leaf clovers until class ended and we could go smoke with the Colonel and Takumi, "both of whom," she added, "are big-time assholes for not marching out of class right behind us."

When Alaska Young is sitting with her legs crossed in a brittle, periodically green clover patch leaning forward in search of four-leaf clovers, the pale skin of her sizable cleavage clearly visible, it is a plain fact of human physiology that it becomes impossible to join in

2 **drone on**: talk for a long time in a boring way 5 **sag**: *zusammenfallen*
5 **stubble**: hairs that grow when a man does not shave 8–9 **humiliate sb.**: make sb. feel ashamed or stupid 11 **temple**: *(hier) Schläfe* 12 **starburst**: *Strahlenkranz*
13 **fall for sth.**: be tricked into believing sth. that is not true 25 **clover**: *Kleeblatt*
28 **brittle**: that feels hard and unpleasant 30 **cleavage**: space between a woman's breasts 31 **physiology**: scientific study of the normal functions of living things

her clover search. I'd gotten in enough trouble already for looking where I wasn't supposed to, but still …

After perhaps two minutes of combing through a clover patch with her long, dirty fingernails, Alaska grabbed a clover with three full-size petals and an undersize, runt of a fourth, then looked up at me, barely giving me time to avert my eyes.

"Even though you were *clearly* not doing your part in the clover search, perv," she said wryly, "I really would give you this clover. Except luck is for suckers." She pinched the runt petal between the nails of her thumb and finger and plucked it. "There," she said to the clover as she dropped it onto the ground. "Now you're not a genetic freak anymore."

"Uh, thanks," I said. The bell rang, and Takumi and the Colonel were first out the door. Alaska stared at them.

"What?" asked the Colonel. But she just rolled her eyes and started walking. We followed in silence through the dorm circle and then across the soccer field. We ducked into the woods, following the faint path around the lake until we came to a dirt road. The Colonel ran up to Alaska, and they started fighting about something quietly enough that I couldn't hear the words so much as the mutual annoyance, and I finally asked Takumi where we were headed.

"This road dead-ends into the barn," he said. "So maybe there. But probably the smoking hole. You'll see."

From here, the woods were a totally different creature than from Dr. Hyde's classroom. The ground was thick with fallen branches, decaying pine needles, and brambly green bushes; the path wound past pine trees sprouting tall and thin, their stubbly needles providing a lace of shade from another sunburned day. And the smaller oak and maple trees, which from Dr. Hyde's classroom had been invisible beneath the more majestic pines, showed hints of an as-yet-

5 **runt**: *Kümmerling* 6 **avert your eyes**: turn your eyes away from sth. 8 **perv** (infml): pervert 8 **wry** [raɪ]: *(hier) sarkastisch* 9 **sucker** (infml): stupid person who easily believes sth. 20 **mutual**: shared by two or more people 25 **branch**: *Ast, Zweig* 26 **brambly**: (here) having thorns 27 **sprout**: start to grow 28 **oak**: *Eiche* 29 **maple tree**: *Ahorn*

thermally-unforeseeable fall: Their still-green leaves were beginning to droop.

We came to a rickety wooden bridge – just thick plywood laid over a concrete foundation – over Culver Creek, the winding rivulet that doubled back over and over again through the outskirts of campus. On the far side of the bridge, there was a tiny path leading down a steep slope. Not even a path so much as a series of hints – a broken branch here, a patch of stomped-down grass there – that people had come this way before. As we walked down single file, Alaska, the Colonel, and Takumi each held back a thick maple branch for one another, passing it along until I, last in line, let it snap back into place behind me. And there, beneath the bridge, an oasis. A slab of concrete, three feet wide and ten feet long, with blue plastic chairs stolen long ago from some classroom. Cooled by the creek and the shade of the bridge, I felt unhot for the first time in weeks.

The Colonel dispensed the cigarettes. Takumi passed; the rest of us lit up.

"He has no right to condescend to us is all I'm saying," Alaska said, continuing her conversation with the Colonel. "Pudge is done with staring out the window, and I'm done with going on tirades about it, but he's a terrible teacher, and you won't convince me otherwise."

"Fine," the Colonel said. "Just don't make another scene. Christ, you nearly killed the poor old bastard."

"Seriously, you'll never win by crossing Hyde," Takumi said. "He'll eat you alive, shit you out, and then piss on his dump. Which by the way is what we should be doing to whoever ratted on Marya. Has anyone heard anything?"

"It must have been some Weekday Warrior," Alaska said. "But apparently they think it was the Colonel. So who knows. Maybe the Eagle just got lucky. She was stupid; she got caught; she got expelled;

1 **thermal**: (here) connected with heat 3 **rickety**: not stable 3 **plywood**: *Sperrholz* 4 **wind** [waɪnd]: have many bends and twists 4 **rivulet**: small river 9 **(in) single file**: one after the other 13 **slab**: thick flat piece of stone 13 **concrete**: *Beton* 16 **dispense sth.**: give sth. out to people 20 **tirade**: long angry speech criticizing sb./sth. 25 **cross sb.**: fight with sb. 26 **dump** (sl): *Stuhl*

it's over. That's what happens when you're stupid and you get caught." Alaska made an O with her lips, moving her mouth like a goldfish eating, trying unsuccessfully to blow smoke rings.

"Wow," Takumi said, "if I ever get kicked out, remind me to even the score myself, since I sure can't count on you."

"Don't be ridiculous," she responded, not angry so much as dismissive. "I don't understand why you're so obsessed with figuring out everything that happens here, like we have to unravel every mystery. God, it's over. Takumi, you gotta stop stealing other people's problems and get some of your own." Takumi started up again, but Alaska raised her hand as if to swat the conversation away.

I said nothing – I hadn't known Marya, and anyway, "listening quietly" was my general social strategy.

"Anyway," Alaska said to me. "I thought the way he treated you was just awful. I wanted to cry. I just wanted to kiss you and make it better."

"Shame you didn't," I deadpanned, and they laughed.

"You're adorable," she said, and I felt the intensity of her eyes on me and looked away nervously. "Too bad I love my boyfriend." I stared at the knotted roots of the trees on the creek bank, trying hard not to look like I'd just been called adorable.

Takumi couldn't believe it either, and he walked over to me, tussling my hair with his hand, and started rapping to Alaska. "Yeah, Pudge is adorable/but you want incorrigible/so Jake is more endurable /'cause he's so – damn. Damn. I almost had four rhymes on *adorable*. But all I could think of was *unfloorable*, which isn't even a word."

Alaska laughed. "That made me not be mad at you anymore. God, rapping is sexy. Pudge, did you even know that you're in the presence of the sickest emcee in Alabama?"

"Um, no."

6–7 **dismissive**: *abweisend* 11 **swat sth.**: hit sth., esp. an insect 18 **adorable**: very attractive and easy to love 20 **creek**: river 23 **tussle sth.**: *etwas durchwühlen* 24 **incorrigible** [- '- - - -]: having bad habits which cannot be changed or improved 25 **endurable**: *erträglich* 30 **emcee**: rapper who uses rhyming verses

"Drop a beat, Colonel Catastrophe," Takumi said, and I laughed at the idea that a guy as short and dorky as the Colonel could have a rap name. The Colonel cupped his hands around his mouth and started making some absurd noises that I suppose were intended to be beats. *Puh-chi. Puh-puhpuh-chi.* Takumi laughed.

"Right here, by the river, you want me to kick it? / If your smoke was a Popsicle, I'd surely lick it / My rhymin' is old school, sort of like the ancient Romans / The Colonel's beats is sad like Arthur Miller's Willy Loman / Sometimes I'm accused of being a showman / ICanRhymeFast and I can rhyme slow, man."

He paused, took a breath, and then finished.

"Like Emily Dickinson, I ain't afraid of slant rhyme / And that's the end of this verse; emcee's out on a high."

I didn't know slant rhyme from regular rhyme, but I was suitably impressed. We gave Takumi a soft round of applause. Alaska finished her cigarette and flicked it into the river.

"Why do you smoke so damn fast?" I asked.

She looked at me and smiled widely, and such a wide smile on her narrow face might have looked goofy were it not for the unimpeachably elegant green in her eyes. She smiled with all the delight of a kid on Christmas morning and said, "Y'all smoke to enjoy it. I smoke to die."

one hundred nine days before

DINNER IN THE CAFETERIA the next night was meat loaf, one of the rare dishes that didn't arrive deep-fried, and, perhaps as a result, meat loaf was Maureen's greatest failure – a stringy, gravy-soaked concoction that did not much resemble a loaf and did not much taste like meat. Although I'd never ridden in it, Alaska apparently had a car, and she offered to drive the Colonel and me to McDonald's,

2 **dorky**: not cool or impressive 7 **Popsicle** (brand name): *Eis am Stiel* 12 **slant rhyme**: rhyme in which either the vowels of the final stressed syllables are similar but not identical 13 **be out on a high**: (here) finish on a good note 16 **flick sth.**: *etwas wegschnipsen* 19 **goofy** (infml): silly, stupid 20 **unimpeachable**: that you cannot doubt or question 26 **concoction**: strange unusual mixture

but the Colonel didn't have any money, and I didn't have much either, what with constantly paying for his extravagant cigarette habit.

So instead the Colonel and I reheated two-day-old bufriedos – unlike, say, french fries, a microwaved bufriedo lost nothing of its taste or its satisfying crunch – after which the Colonel insisted on attending the Creek's first basketball game of the season.

"Basketball in the fall?" I asked the Colonel. "I don't know much about sports, but isn't that when you play football?"

"The schools in our league are too small to have football teams, so we play basketball in the fall. Although, man, the Culver Creek football team would be a thing of beauty. Your scrawny ass could probably start at lineman. Anyway, the basketball games are great."

I hated sports. I hated sports, and I hated people who played them, and I hated people who watched them, and I hated people who didn't hate people who watched or played them. In third grade – the very last year that one could play T-ball – my mother wanted me to make friends, so she forced me onto the Orlando Pirates. I made friends all right – with a bunch of kindergartners, which didn't really bolster my social standing with my peers. Primarily because I towered over the rest of the players, I nearly made it onto the T-ball all-star team that year. The kid who beat me, Clay Wurtzel, had one arm. I was an unusually tall third grader with two arms, and I got beat out by kindergartner Clay Wurtzel. And it wasn't some pity-the-one-armed-kid thing, either. Clay Wurtzel could flat-out *hit*, whereas I sometimes struck out even with the ball sitting on the tee. One of the things that appealed to me most about Culver Creek was that my dad assured me there was no PE requirement.

"There is only one time when I put aside my passionate hatred for the Weekday Warriors and their country-club bullshit," the Colonel told me. "And that's when they pump up the air-conditioning in the

6 **crunch** (n): *Knusprigkeit* 12 **scrawny**: very thin in a way that is not attractive 13 **lineman**: player in the front line of an American football team 17 **T-ball**: game similar to baseball for young children 20 **bolster sth.**: improve sth. 25 **flat-out** (AE infml): definite 28 **PE** : physical education, sport taught at school

gym for a little old-fashioned Culver Creek basketball. You can't miss the first game of the year."

As we walked toward the airplane hangar of a gym, which I had seen but never even thought to approach, the Colonel explained to me the most important thing about our basketball team: They were not very good. The "star" of the team, the Colonel said, was a senior named Hank Walsten, who played power forward despite being five-foot-eight. Hank's primary claim to campus fame, I already knew, was that he always had weed, and the Colonel told me that for four years, Hank started every game without ever once playing sober.

"He loves weed like Alaska loves sex," the Colonel said. "This is a man who once constructed a bong using only the barrel of an air rifle, a ripe pear, and an eight-by-ten glossy photograph of Anna Kournikova. Not the brightest gem in the jewelry shop, but you've got to admire his single-minded dedication to drug abuse."

From Hank, the Colonel told me, it went downhill until you reached Wilson Carbod, the starting center, who was almost six feet tall. "We're so bad," the Colonel said, "we don't even have a mascot. I call us the Culver Creek Nothings."

"So they just suck?" I asked. I didn't quite understand the point of watching your terrible team get walloped, though the air-conditioning was reason enough for me.

"Oh, they suck," the Colonel replied. "But we always beat the shit out of the deaf-and-blind school." Apparently, basketball wasn't a big priority at the Alabama School for the Deaf and Blind, and so we usually came out of the season with a single victory.

When we arrived, the gym was packed with most every Culver Creek student – I noticed, for instance, the Creek's three goth girls reapplying their eyeliner as they sat on the top row of the gym's bleachers. I'd never attended a school basketball game back home,

1 **gym**: room or for doing physical exercise 7 **power forward**: player in basketball 9 **weed** (infml): cannabis 12 **bong**: long pipe for smoking cannabis and other drugs 14 **gem**: *Edelstein* 15 **dedication**: hard work and effort that sb. puts into an activity 17 **starting centre**: player in basketball 20 **suck** (AE sl): be no good 21 **wallop sb.** (here): defeat sb. completely in a match 28 **goth**: person who listens to goth music and wears black clothes 30 **bleachers**: *Tribüne*

but I doubted the crowds there were quite so inclusive. Even so, I was surprised when none other than Kevin Richman sat down on the bleacher directly in front of me while the opposing school's cheerleading team (their unfortunate school colors were mud-brown and dehydrated-piss-yellow) tried to fire up the small visitors' section in the crowd. Kevin turned around and stared at the Colonel.

Like most of the other guy Warriors, Kevin dressed preppy, looking like a lawyer-who-enjoys-golfing waiting to happen. And his hair, a blond mop, short on the sides and spiky on top, was always soaked through with so much gel that it looked perennially wet. I didn't hate him like the Colonel did, of course, because the Colonel hated him on principle, and principled hate is a hell of a lot stronger than "Boy, I wish you hadn't mummified me and thrown me into the lake" hate. Still, I tried to stare at him intimidatingly as he looked at the Colonel, but it was hard to forget that this guy had seen my skinny ass in nothing but boxers a couple weeks ago.

"You ratted out Paul and Marya. We got you back. Truce?" Kevin asked.

"I didn't rat them out. Pudge here *certainly* didn't rat them out, but you brought him in on your fun. Truce? Hmm, let me take a poll real quick." The cheerleaders sat down, holding their pompoms close to their chest as if praying. "Hey, Pudge," the Colonel said. "What do you think of a truce?"

"It reminds me of when the Germans demanded that the U.S. surrender at the Battle of the Bulge," I said. "I guess I'd say to this truce offer what General McAuliffe said to that one: Nuts."

"Why would you try to kill this guy, Kevin? He's a genius. Nuts to your truce."

5 **dehydrated**: *vertrocknet* 5 **fire sb. up**: make sb. excited about sth. 7 **preppy**: young person who goes or went to an expensive private school and who dresses and acts in a way that is thought to be typical of such a school 10 **perennial**: lasting for a very long time 14 **intimidating** (adj): frightening in a way which makes a person feel less confident 17 **truce**: agreement between enemies to stop fighting
25 **Battle of the Bulge**: strong but unsuccessful attack by German forces against the Allies in southern Belgium in 1944 26 **General McAuliffe**: US general who fought in World War II

"Come on, dude. I know you ratted them out, and we had to defend our friend, and now it's over. Let's end it." He seemed very sincere, perhaps due to the Colonel's reputation for pranking.

"I'll make you a deal. You pick one dead American president. If Pudge doesn't know that guy's last words, truce. If he does, you spend the rest of your life lamenting the day you pissed in my shoes."

"That's retarded."

"All right, no truce," the Colonel shot back.

"Fine. Millard Fillmore," Kevin said. The Colonel looked at me hurriedly, his eyes saying, *Was that guy a president?* I just smiled.

"When Fillmore was dying, he was super hungry. But his doctor was trying to starve his fever or whatever. Fillmore wouldn't shut up about wanting to eat, though, so finally the doctor gave him a tiny teaspoon of soup. And all sarcastic, Fillmore said, 'The nourishment is palatable,' and then died. No truce."

Kevin rolled his eyes and walked away, and it occurred to me that I could have made up any last words for Millard Fillmore and Kevin probably would have believed me if I'd used that same tone of voice, the Colonel's confidence rubbing off on me.

"That was your first badass moment!" The Colonel laughed. "Now, it's true that I gave you an easy target. But still. Well done."

Unfortunately for the Culver Creek Nothings, we weren't playing the deaf-and-blind school. We were playing some Christian school from downtown Birmingham, a team stocked with huge, gargantuan apemen with thick beards and a strong distaste for turning the other cheek.

At the end of the first quarter: 20–4.

And that's when the fun started. The Colonel led all of the cheers.

"Cornbread!" he screamed.

7 **retarded** (derog): less developed mentally than is normal for a particular age
9 **Millard Fillmore**: US president (1850–1853) 15 **palatable**: having a pleasant or acceptable taste 19 **rub off on sb.**: *auf jdn. abfärben* 24 **gargantuan**: enormous
25–26 **turn the other cheek**: *(im Christentum) die andere Wange hinhalten*

"CHICKEN!" the crowd responded.

"Rice!"

"PEAS!"

And then, all together: "WE GOT HIGHER SATs."

"Hip Hip Hip Hooray!" the Colonel cried.

"YOU'LL BE WORKIN' FOR US SOMEDAY!"

The opposing team's cheerleaders tried to answer our cheers with "The roof, the roof, the roof is on fire! Hell is in your future if you give in to desire," but we could always do them one better.

"Buy!"

"SELL!"

"Trade!"

"BARTER!"

"YOU'RE MUCH BIGGER, BUT WE ARE SMARTER!"

When the visitors shoot a free throw on most every court in the country, the fans make a lot of noise, screaming and stomping their feet. It doesn't work, because players learn to tune out white noise. At Culver Creek, we had a much better strategy. At first, everyone yelled and screamed like in a normal game. But then everyone said, *"Shh!"* and there was absolute silence. Just as our hated opponent stopped dribbling and prepared for his shot, the Colonel stood up and screamed something. Like:

"For the love of God, please shave your back hair!" Or:

"I need to be saved. Can you minister to me after your shot?!"

Toward the end of the third quarter, the Christian-school coach called a time-out and complained to the ref about the Colonel, pointing at him angrily. We were down 56–13. The Colonel stood up. "What?! You have a problem with me!?"

The coach screamed, "You're bothering my players!"

"THAT'S THE POINT, SHERLOCK!" the Colonel screamed back. The ref came over and kicked him out of the gym. I followed him.

9 **do them one better**: *etwas übertrumpfen* 13 **barter**: exchange goods without using money 24 **minister to sb.**: care for sb., esp. by giving religious help 26 **ref = referee**: *Schiedsrichter/in* 30 **Sherlock**: reference to the fictional detective Sherlock Holmes

"I've gotten thrown out of thirty-seven straight games," he said.

"Damn."

"Yeah. Once or twice, I've had to go really crazy. I ran onto the court with eleven seconds left once and stole the ball from the other team. It wasn't pretty. But, you know. I have a streak to maintain."

The Colonel ran ahead of me, gleeful at his ejection, and I jogged after him, trailing in his wake. I wanted to be one of those people who have streaks to maintain, who scorch the ground with their intensity. But for now, at least I knew such people, and they needed me, just like comets need tails.

one hundred eight days before

THE NEXT DAY, Dr. Hyde asked me to stay after class. Standing before him, I realized for the first time how hunched his shoulders were, and he seemed suddenly sad and kind of old. "You like this class, don't you?" he asked.

"Yessir."

"You've got a lifetime to mull over the Buddhist understanding of interconnectedness." He spoke every sentence as if he'd written it down, memorized it, and was now reciting it. "But while you were looking out the window, you missed the chance to explore the equally interesting Buddhist belief in being present for every facet of your daily life, of being truly present. Be present in this class. And then, when it's over, be present out there," he said, nodding toward the lake and beyond.

"Yessir."

one hundred one days before

ON THE FIRST MORNING of October, I knew something was wrong as soon as I woke up enough to turn off the alarm clock. The bed didn't smell right. And I didn't feel right. It took me a groggy minute before

5 **streak**: (here) series of successes or failures 6 **gleeful**: happy 6 **ejection**: act of forcing sb. to leave a place 7 **wake** (n): *Bugwelle* 8 **scorch sth.**: burn and slightly damage the surface of sth.

I realized: I felt *cold*. Well, at the very least, the small fan clipped to my bunk seemed suddenly unnecessary. "It's cold!" I shouted.

"Oh God, what time is it?" I heard above me.

"Eight-oh-four," I said.

The Colonel, who didn't have an alarm clock but almost always woke up to take a shower before mine went off, swung his short legs over the side of the bed, jumped down, and dashed to his dresser. "I suppose I missed my window of opportunity to shower," he said as he put on a green CULVER CREEK BASKETBALL T-shirt and a pair of shorts. "Oh well. There's always tomorrow. And it's not cold. It's probably eighty."

Grateful to have slept fully dressed, I just put on shoes, and the Colonel and I jogged to the classrooms. I slid into my seat with twenty seconds to spare. Halfway through class, Madame O'Malley turned around to write something in French on the blackboard, and Alaska passed me a note.

Nice bedhead. Study at McDonald's for lunch?

Our first significant precalc test was only two days away, so Alaska grabbed the six precalc kids she did not consider Weekday Warriors and piled us into her tiny blue two-door. By happy coincidence, a cute sophomore named Lara ended up sitting on my lap. Lara'd been born in Russia or someplace, and she spoke with a slight accent. Since we were only four layers of clothes from doing it, I took the opportunity to introduce myself.

"I know who you are." She smiled. "You're Alaska's freend from FlowReeda."

"Yup. Get ready for a lot of dumb questions, 'cause I suck at precalc," I said.

She started to answer, but then she was thrown back against me as Alaska shot out of the parking lot.

"Kids, meet Blue Citrus. So named because she is a lemon," Alaska said. "Blue Citrus, meet the kids. If you can find them, you

17 **bedhead**: (here) untidy hair 18 **precalc** = **precalculus**: form of algebra
20 **pile sb. into sth.**: make sb. get into sth. 31 **lemon** (AE infml): person considered to be useless

might want to fasten your seat belts. Pudge, you might want to serve as a seat belt for Lara." What the car lacked in speed, Alaska made up for by refusing to move her foot from the accelerator, damn the consequences. Before we even got off campus, Lara was lurching helplessly whenever Alaska took hard turns, so I took Alaska's advice and wrapped my arms around Lara's waist.

"Thanks," she said, almost inaudibly.

After a fast if reckless three miles to McDonald's, we ordered seven large french fries to share and then went outside and sat on the lawn. We sat in a circle around the trays of fries, and Alaska taught class, smoking while she ate.

Like any good teacher, she tolerated little dissension. She smoked and talked and ate for an hour without stopping, and I scribbled in my notebook as the muddy waters of tangents and cosines began to clarify. But not everyone was so fortunate.

As Alaska zipped through something obvious about linear equations, stoner/baller Hank Walsten said, "Wait, wait. I don't get it."

"That's because you have eight functioning brain cells."

"Studies show that marijuana is better for your health than those cigarettes," Hank said.

Alaska swallowed a mouthful of french fries, took a drag on her cigarette, and blew smoke at Hank. "I may die young," she said. "But at least I'll die smart. Now, back to tangents."

one hundred days before

"NOT TO ASK the obvious question, but why *Alaska?*" I asked. I'd just gotten my precalc test back, and I was awash with admiration for Alaska, since her tutoring had paved my way to a B-plus. She and I sat alone in the TV lounge watching MTV on a drearily cloudy Saturday. Furnished with couches left behind by previous generations of Culver Creek students, the TV room had the musty air of dust

4 **lurch**: make a sudden, unsteady movement forward or sideways 7 **inaudible**: that cannot be heard 12 **dissension** (fml): disagreement between people
14 **cosine** ['koʊsaɪn]: *Kosinus* 16–17 **linear equation**: *lineare Gleichung*
17 **stoner** (infml): *Kiffer/in* 17 **baller** (infml): person who plays basketball
29 **musty**: smelling unpleasant because of a lack of fresh air

and mildew – and, perhaps for that reason, was almost perennially unoccupied. Alaska took a sip of Mountain Dew and grabbed my hand in hers.

"Always comes up eventually. All right, so my mom was something of a hippie when I was a kid. You know, wore oversize sweaters she knitted herself, smoked a lot of pot, et cetera. And my dad was a real Republican type, and so when I was born, my mom wanted to name me Harmony Springs Young, and my dad wanted to name me Mary Frances Young." As she talked, she bobbed her head back and forth to the MTV music, even though the song was the kind of manufactured pop ballad she professed to hate.

"So instead of naming me Harmony *or* Mary, they agreed to let me decide. So when I was little, they called me Mary. I mean, they called me sweetie or whatever, but like on school forms and stuff, they wrote *Mary Young*. And then on my seventh birthday, my present was that I got to pick my name. Cool, huh? So I spent the whole day looking at my dad's globe for a really cool name. And so my first choice was Chad, like the country in Africa. But then my dad said that was a boy's name, so I picked Alaska."

I wish my parents had let me pick my name. But they went ahead and picked the only name firstborn male Halters have had for a century. "But why Alaska?" I asked her.

She smiled with the right side of her mouth. "Well, later, I found out what it means. It's from an Aleut word, *Alyeska*. It means 'that which the sea breaks against,' and I love that. But at the time, I just saw Alaska up there. And it was big, just like I wanted to be. And it was damn far away from Vine Station, Alabama, just like I wanted to be."

I laughed. "And now you're all grown up and fairly far away from home," I said, smiling. "So congratulations." She stopped the head bobbing and let go of my (unfortunately sweaty) hand.

1 **mildew**: *Schimmel (an den Wänden)* 2 **Mountain Dew** (brand name): type of soft drink 7 **Republican**: member or supporter of the Republican Party 11 **profess**: declare 24 **Aleut** (ə'lu:t): native inhabitant of Alaska

"Getting out isn't that easy," she said seriously, her eyes on mine like I knew the way out and wouldn't tell her. And then she seemed to switch conversational horses in midstream. "Like after college, know what I want to do? Teach disabled kids. I'm a good teacher, right? Shit, if I can teach you precalc, I can teach anybody. Like maybe kids with autism."

She talked softly and thoughtfully, like she was telling me a secret, and I leaned in toward her, suddenly overwhelmed with the feeling that we must kiss, that we ought to kiss right now on the dusty orange couch with its cigarette burns and its decades of collected dust. And I would have: I would have kept leaning toward her until it became necessary to tilt my face so as to miss her ski-slope nose, and I would have felt the shock of her so-soft lips. I would have. But then she snapped out of it.

"No," she said, and I couldn't tell at first whether she was reading my kiss-obsessed mind or responding to herself out loud. She turned away from me, and softly, maybe to herself, said, "Jesus, I'm not going to be one of those people who sits around talking about what they're gonna do. I'm just going to do it. Imagining the future is a kind of nostalgia."

"Huh?" I asked.

"You spend your whole life stuck in the labyrinth, thinking about how you'll escape it one day, and how awesome it will be, and imagining that future keeps you going, but you never do it. You just use the future to escape the present."

I guess that made sense. I had imagined that life at the Creek would be a bit more exciting than it was – in reality, there'd been more homework than adventure – but if I hadn't imagined it, I would never have gotten to the Creek at all.

She turned back to the TV, a commercial for a car now, and made a joke about Blue Citrus needing its own car commercial. Mimicking the deep-voiced passion of commercial voice-overs, she said, "It's

6 **autism**: mental condition in which a person is unable to communicate well or form relationships with others 12 **tilt sth.**: *etwas neigen, etwas schräg stellen*
12 **slope**: *Abhang* 32 **voice-over**: words said in a film by a person who is not seen on the screen

small, it's slow, and it's shitty, but it runs. Sometimes. Blue Citrus: See Your Local Used-Car Dealer." But I wanted to talk more about her and Vine Station and the future.

"Sometimes I don't get you," I said.

She didn't even glance at me. She just smiled toward the television and said, "You never get me. That's the whole point."

ninety-nine days before

I SPENT MOST of the next day lying in bed, immersed in the miserably uninteresting fictional world of *Ethan Frome*, while the Colonel sat at his desk, unraveling the secrets of differential equations or something. Although we tried to ration our smoke breaks amid the shower's steam, we ran out of cigarettes before dark, necessitating a trip to Alaska's room. She lay on the floor, holding a book over her head.

"Let's go smoke," he said.

"You're out of cigarettes, aren't you?" she asked without looking up.

"Well. Yes."

"Got five bucks?" she asked.

"Nope."

"Pudge?" she asked.

"Yeah, all right." I fished a five out of my pocket, and Alaska handed me a pack of twenty Marlboro Lights. I knew I'd smoke maybe five of them, but so long as I subsidized the Colonel's smoking, he couldn't really attack me for being another rich kid, a Weekday Warrior who just didn't happen to live in Birmingham.

We grabbed Takumi and walked down to the lake, hiding behind a few trees, laughing. The Colonel blew smoke rings, and Takumi called them "pretentious," while Alaska followed the smoke rings with her fingers, stabbing at them like a kid trying to pop bubbles.

7 **immersed in sth.**: completely involved in sth. 8 **Ethan Frome**: novel by Edith Wharton published in 1911 17 **buck** (infml): dollar 18 **nope** (infml): no 22 **subsidize sb.**: give sb. money to help pay for sth. 27 **pretentious**: trying to appear important or clever or skillful to impress other people

And then we heard a branch break. It might have been a deer, but the Colonel busted out anyway. A voice directly behind us said, "Don't run, Chipper," and the Colonel stopped, turned around, and returned to us sheepishly.

The Eagle walked toward us slowly, his lips pursed in disgust. He wore a white shirt and a black tie, like always. He gave each of us in turn the Look of Doom.

"Y'all smell like a North Carolina tobacco field in a wildfire," he said.

We stood silent. I felt disproportionately terrible, like I had just been caught fleeing the scene of a murder. Would he call my parents?

"I'll see you in Jury tomorrow at five," he announced, and then walked away. Alaska crouched down, picked up the cigarette she had thrown away, and started smoking again. The Eagle wheeled around, his sixth sense detecting Insubordination To Authority Figures. Alaska dropped the cigarette and stepped on it. The Eagle shook his head, and even though he must have been crazy mad, I swear to God he smiled.

"He loves me," Alaska told me as we walked back to the dorm circle. "He loves all y'all, too. He just loves the school more. That's the thing. He thinks busting us is good for the school and good for us. It's the eternal struggle, Pudge. The Good versus the Naughty."

"You're awfully philosophical for a girl that just got busted," I told her.

"Sometimes you lose a battle. But mischief always wins the war."

ninety-eight days before

ONE OF THE UNIQUE THINGS about Culver Creek was the Jury. Every semester, the faculty elected twelve students, three from each class, to serve on the Jury. The Jury meted out punishment for nonexpellable

1 **deer**: *Reh* 10 **disproportionate**: too large or too small when compared with sth. else 14 **crouch down**: *niederkauern* 16 **insubordination**: refusal to obey orders 23 **eternal**: without an end 29 **mete sth. out** (fml): give sb. a punishment

offenses, for everything from staying out past curfew to smoking. Usually, it was smoking or being in a girl's room after seven. So you went to the Jury, you made your case, and they punished you. The Eagle served as the judge, and he had the right to overturn the Jury's verdict (just like in the real American court system), but he almost never did.

I made my way to Classroom 4 right after my last class – forty minutes early, just to be safe. I sat in the hall with my back against the wall and read my American history textbook (kind of remedial reading for me, to be honest) until Alaska showed up and sat down next to me. She was chewing on her bottom lip, and I asked whether she was nervous.

"Well, yeah. Listen, just sit tight and don't talk," she told me. "*You* don't need to be nervous. But this is the seventh time I've been caught smoking. I just don't want – whatever. I don't want to upset my dad."

"Does your mom smoke or something?" I asked.

"Not anymore," Alaska said. "It's fine. You'll be fine."

I didn't start to worry until it got to be 4:50 and the Colonel and Takumi were still unaccounted for. The members of the Jury filed in one by one, walking past us without any eye contact, which made me feel worse. I counted all twelve by 4:56, plus the Eagle.

At 4:58, the Colonel and Takumi rounded the corner toward the classrooms.

I never saw anything like it. Takumi wore a starched white shirt with a red tie with a black paisley print; the Colonel wore his wrinkled pink button-down and flamingo tie. They walked in step, heads up and shoulders back, like some kind of action-movie heroes.

I heard Alaska sigh. "The Colonel's doing his Napoleon walk."

"It's all good," the Colonel told me. "Just don't say anything."

1 **curfew**: time after which nobody is allowed outside 4 **overturn sth.**: *etwas aufheben* 5 **verdict**: *Urteil* 9 **remedial** [ri'mi:diəl]: (here) below his knowledge level 20 **unaccounted for**: *vermisst* 25 **starch sth.**: make sth. (esp. clothes and sheets) stiff 26 **paisley**: type of flowery pattern

We walked in – two of us wearing ties, and two of us wearing ratty T-shirts – and the Eagle banged an honest-to-God gavel against the podium in front of him. The Jury sat in a line behind a rectangular table. At the front of the room, by the blackboard, were four chairs. We sat down, and the Colonel explained exactly what happened.

"Alaska and I were smoking down by the lake. We usually go off campus, but we forgot. We're sorry. It won't happen again."

I didn't know what was going on. But I knew my job: sit tight and shut up. One of the kids looked at Takumi and asked, "What about you and Halter?"

"We were keeping them company," Takumi said calmly.

The kid turned to the Eagle then and asked, "Did you see anyone smoking?"

"I only saw Alaska, but Chip ran away, which struck me as cowardly, as does Miles and Takumi's aw-shucks routine," the Eagle said, giving me the Look of Doom. I didn't want to look guilty, but I couldn't hold his stare, so I just looked down at my hands.

The Colonel gritted his teeth, like it pained him to lie. "It is the truth, sir."

The Eagle asked if any of us wanted to say anything, and then asked if there were any more questions, and then sent us outside.

"What the hell was that?" I asked Takumi when we got outside.

"Just sit tight, Pudge."

Why have Alaska confess when she'd already been in trouble so many times? Why the Colonel, who literally couldn't afford to get in serious trouble? Why not me? I'd never been busted for anything. I had the least to lose. After a couple minutes, the Eagle came out and motioned for us to come back inside.

"Alaska and Chip," a member of the Jury said, "you get ten work hours – doing dishes in the cafeteria – and you're both officially one problem away from a phone call home. Takumi and Miles, there's nothing in the rules about watching someone smoke, but the Jury will remember your story if you break the rules again. Fair?"

2 **gavel**: small hammer 15 **cowardly**: acting like person who does not have the courage to do things 15 **aw-shucks**: (here) attempting to look innocent 18 **grit your teeth**: bite your teeth tightly

"Fair," Alaska said quickly, obviously relieved. On my way out, the Eagle spun me around. "Don't abuse your privileges at this school, young man, or you will regret it." I nodded.

eighty-nine days before

"WE FOUND YOU A GIRLFRIEND," Alaska said to me. Still, no one had explained to me what happened the week before with the Jury. It didn't seem to have affected Alaska, though, who was *1*. in our room after dark with the door closed, and 2. smoking a cigarette as she sat on the mostly foam couch. She had stuffed a towel into the bottom of our door and insisted it was safe, but I worried – about the cigarette and the "girlfriend."

"All I have to do now," she said, "is convince you to like her and convince her to like you."

"Monumental tasks," the Colonel pointed out. He lay on the top bunk, reading for his English class. *Moby-Dick*.

"How can you read and talk at the same time?" I asked.

"Well, I usually can't, but neither the book nor the conversation is particularly intellectually challenging."

"I like that book," Alaska said.

"Yes." The Colonel smiled and leaned over to look at her from his top bunk. "You would. Big white whale is a metaphor for everything. You live for pretentious metaphors."

Alaska was unfazed. "So, Pudge, what's your feeling on the former Soviet bloc?"

"Um. I'm in favor of it?"

She flicked the ashes of her cigarette into my pencil holder. I almost protested, but why bother. "You know that girl in our precalc class," Alaska said, "soft voice, says thees, not this. Know that girl?"

"Yeah. Lara. She sat on my lap on the way to McDonald's."

1 **relieved**: feeling happy because sth. unpleasant has stopped or not happened
14 **Moby-Dick**: novel by Herman Melville published in 1851 22 **unfazed**: not worried or surprised by sth. unexpected that happens 26 **bother** (v): spend time and energy doing sth.

"Right. I know. And she liked you. You thought she was quietly discussing precalc, when she was clearly talking about having hot sex with you. Which is why you need me."

"She has great breasts," the Colonel said without looking up from the whale.

"DO NOT OBJECTIFY WOMEN'S BODIES!" Alaska shouted.

Now he looked up. "Sorry. Perky breasts."

"That's not any better!"

"Sure it is," he said. "*Great* is a judgment on a woman's body. *Perky* is merely an observation. They *are* perky. I mean, Christ."

"You're hopeless," she said. "So she thinks you're cute, Pudge."

"Nice."

"Doesn't mean anything. Problem with you is that if you talk to her you'll 'uh um uh' your way to disaster."

"Don't be so hard on him," the Colonel interrupted, as if he was my mom. "God, I understand whale anatomy. Can we move on now, Herman?"

"So Jake is going to be in Birmingham this weekend, and we're going on a triple date. Well, triple and a half, since Takumi will be there, too. Very low pressure. You won't be able to screw up, because I'll be there the whole time."

"Okay."

"Who's my date?" the Colonel asked.

"Your girlfriend is your date."

"All right," he said, and then deadpanned, "but we don't get along very well."

"So Friday? Do you have plans for Friday?" And then I laughed, because the Colonel and I didn't have plans for this Friday, or for any other Friday for the rest of our lives.

"I didn't think so." She smiled. "Now, we gotta go do dishes in the cafeteria, Chipper. God, the sacrifices I make."

7 **perky:** (here) firm 17 **Herman**: Herman Melville 20 **screw sth. up** (sl): do sth. badly; spoil sth.

eighty-seven days before

OUR TRIPLE-AND-A-HALF DATE started off well enough. I was in Alaska's room – for the sake of getting me a girlfriend, she'd agreed to iron a green button-down shirt for me – when Jake showed up. With blond hair to his shoulders, dark stubble on his cheeks, and the kind of faux-ruggedness that gets you a career as a catalog model, Jake was every bit as good-looking as you'd expect Alaska's boyfriend to be. She jumped onto him and wrapped her legs around him (*God forbid anyone ever does that to me*, I thought. *I'll fall over*). I'd heard Alaska *talk* about kissing, but I'd never seen her kiss until then: As he held her by her waist, she leaned forward, her pouty lips parted, her head just slightly tilted, and enveloped his mouth with such passion that I felt I should look away but couldn't. A good while later, she untangled herself from Jake and introduced me.

"This is Pudge," she said. Jake and I shook hands.

"I've heard a lot about ya." He spoke with a slight Southern accent, one of the few I'd heard outside of McDonald's. "I hope your date works out tonight, 'cause I wouldn't want you stealin' Alaska out from under me."

"God, you're so adorable," Alaska said before I could answer, kissing him again. "I'm sorry." She laughed. "I just can't seem to stop kissing my boyfriend."

I put on my freshly starched green shirt, and the three of us gathered up the Colonel, Sara, Lara, and Takumi and then walked to the gym to watch the Culver Creek Nothings take on Harsden Academy, a private day school in Mountain Brook, Birmingham's richest suburb. The Colonel's hatred for Harsden burned with the fire of a thousand suns. "The only thing I hate more than rich people," he told me as we walked to the gym, "is stupid people. And all the kids at Harsden are rich, and they're all too stupid to get into the Creek."

Since we were supposed to be on a date and all, I thought I'd sit next to Lara at the game, but as I tried to walk past a seated Alaska

5 **faux** [foʊ]: *unecht, gekünstelt* 5 **ruggedness**: quality of having strong, attractive features 13 **untangle sth.**: *etwas entwirren*

on my way to Lara, Alaska shot me a look and patted the empty spot next to her on the bleachers.

"I'm not allowed to sit next to my date?" I asked.

"Pudge, one of us has been a girl her whole life. The other of us has never gotten to second base. If I were you, I'd sit down, look cute, and be your pleasantly aloof self."

"Okay. Whatever you say."

Jake said, "That's pretty much my strategy for pleasing Alaska."

"Aww," she said, "so sweet! Pudge, did I tell you that Jake is recording an album with his band? They're fantastic. They're like Radiohead meets the Flaming Lips. Did I tell you that I came up with their name, Hickman Territory?" And then, realizing she was being silly: "Did I tell you that Jake is hung like a horse and a beautiful, sensual lover?"

"Baby, Jesus." Jake smiled. "Not in front of the kids."

I wanted to hate Jake, of course, but as I watched them together, smiling and fumbling all over each other, I didn't hate him. I wanted to *be* him, sure, but I tried to remember I was ostensibly on a date with someone else.

Harsden Academy's star player was a six-foot-seven Goliath named Travis Eastman that everyone – even his mother, I suspect – called the Beast. The first time the Beast got to the free-throw line, the Colonel could not keep himself from swearing while he taunted:

"You owe everything to your daddy, you stupid redneck bastard."

The Beast turned around and glared, and the Colonel almost got kicked out after the first free throw, but he smiled at the ref and said, "Sorry!"

"I want to stay around for a good part of this one," he said to me.

At the start of the second half, with the Creek down by a surprisingly slim margin of twenty-four points and the Beast at the

5 **second base** (AE sl): *fummeln* 11 **Radiohead**: British rock group 11 **Flaming Lips**: US rock group 13 **be hung like a horse** (sl): have a huge penis
18 **ostensibly**: apparently 24 **taunt**: try to make sb. angry by saying unkind things
25 **redneck** (infml): *Landei* 32 **margin**: amount of points by which sb. wins

foul line, the Colonel looked at Takumi and said, "It's time." Takumi and the Colonel stood up as the crowd went, "*Shhh* …"

"I don't know if this is the best time to tell you this," the Colonel shouted at the Beast, "but Takumi here hooked up with your girlfriend just before the game."

That made everyone laugh – except the Beast, who turned from the free throw line and walked calmly, with the ball, toward us.

"I think we run now," Takumi said.

"I haven't gotten kicked out," the Colonel answered.

"Later," Takumi said.

I don't know whether it was the general anxiety of being on a date (albeit one with my would-be date sitting five people away from me) or the specific anxiety of having the Beast stare in my direction, but for some reason, I took off running after Takumi. I thought we were in the clear as we began to round the corner of the bleachers, but then I saw, out of the corner of my eye, a cylindrical orange object getting bigger and bigger, like a fast-approaching sun.

I thought: *I think that is going to hit me.*

I thought: *I should duck.*

But in the time between when something gets thought and when it gets done, the ball hit me square across the side of the face. I fell, the back of my head slamming against the gym floor. I then stood up immediately, as if unhurt, and left the gym.

Pride had gotten me off the floor of the gym, but as soon as I was outside, I sat down.

"I am concussed," I announced, entirely sure of my self-diagnosis.

"You're fine," Takumi said as he jogged back toward me. "Let's get out of here before we're killed."

"I'm sorry," I said. "But I can't get up. I have suffered a mild concussion."

Lara ran out and sat down next to me.

"Are you okay?"

"I am concussed," I said.

4 **hook up with sb.** (infml): meet sb and spend time with them
12 **albeit** [ɑːlˈbiːɪt]: although 26 **be concussed**: *eine Gehirnerschütterung haben*

Takumi sat down with me and looked me in the eye. "Do you know what happened to you?"

"The Beast got me."

"Do you know where you are?"

"I'm on a triple-and-a-half date."

"You're fine," Takumi said. "Let's go."

And then I leaned forward and threw up onto Lara's pants. I can't say why I didn't lean backward or to the side. I leaned forward and aimed my mouth toward her jeans – a nice, butt-flattering pair of jeans, the kind of pants a girl wears when she wants to look nice but not look like she is trying to look nice – and I threw up all over them.

Mostly peanut butter, but also clearly some corn.

"Oh!" she said, surprised and slightly horrified.

"Oh God," I said. "I'm so sorry."

"I think you might have a concussion," Takumi said, as if the idea had never been suggested.

"I am suffering from the nausea and dizziness typically associated with a mild concussion," I recited. While Takumi went to get the Eagle and Lara changed pants, I lay on the concrete sidewalk. The Eagle came back with the school nurse, who diagnosed me with – get this – a concussion, and then Takumi drove me to the hospital with Lara riding shotgun. Apparently I lay in the back and slowly repeated the words "The. Symptoms. Generally. Associated. With. Concussion."

So I spent my date at the hospital with Lara and Takumi. The doctor told me to go home and sleep a lot, but to make sure and have someone wake me up every four hours or so.

I vaguely remember Lara standing in the doorway, the room dark and the outside dark and everything mild and comfortable but sort of spinny, the world pulsing as if from a heavy bass beat. And I vaguely remember Lara smiling at me from the doorway, the glittering ambiguity of a girl's smile, which seems to promise an answer to the

18 **nausea** ['nɔːziə]: feeling that you have when you want to vomit 18 **dizziness**: *Schwindel* 23 **ride shotgun** (infml): ride in the front passenger seat of a car or truck

question but never gives it. *The* question, the one we've all been asking since girls stopped being gross, the question that is too simple to be uncomplicated: Does she like me or *like* me? And then I fell deeply, endlessly asleep and slept until three in the morning, when the Colonel woke me up.

"She dumped me," he said.

"I am concussed," I responded.

"So I heard. Hence my waking you up. Video game?"

"Okay. But keep it on mute. My head hurts."

"Yeah. Heard you puked on Lara. Very suave."

"Dumped?" I asked, getting up.

"Yeah. Sara told Jake that I had a hard-on for Alaska. Those words. In that order. And I was like, 'Well, I don't have a hard-on for *anything* at this moment. You can check if you'd like,' and Sara thought I was being too glib, I suppose, because then she said she knew for a fact I'd hooked up with Alaska. Which, incidentally, is ridiculous. I. Don't. Cheat," he said, and finally the game finished loading and I half listened as I drove a stock car in circles around a silent track in Talladega. The circles nauseated me, but I kept at it.

"So Alaska went ballistic, basically." He affected Alaska's voice then, making it more shrill and headache-inducing than it actually was. "'No woman should ever lie about another woman! You've violated the sacred covenant between women! How will stabbing one another in the back help women to rise above patriarchal oppression?!' And so on. And then Jake came to Alaska's defense, saying that she would never cheat because she loved him, and then I was like, 'Don't worry about Sara. She just likes bullying people.' And then Sara asked me why I never stood up for her, and somewhere in there I called her a crazy bitch, which didn't go over particularly well. And then the waitress asked us to leave, and so we were

6 **dump sb.**: end a relationship with sb. 10 **suave**: (of a man) confident, elegant and polite 12 **hard-on** (sl): strong feelings; erection 18 **stock car**: an ordinary car that has been made stronger 19 **Talladega**: town in Alabama 20 **go ballistic** (sl): become very angry 23 **covenant**: promise or legal agreement 28 **stand up for sb.**: support or defend sb. 29 **go over** (infml): (here) make a good impression on sb.

standing in the parking lot and she said, 'I've had enough,' and I just stared at her and she said, 'Our relationship is over.' "

He stopped talking then. " 'Our relationship is over?' " I repeated. I felt very spacey and thought it was just best to repeat the last phrase of whatever the Colonel said so he could keep talking.

"Yeah. So that's it. You know what's lame, Pudge? I really care about her. I mean, we were hopeless. Badly matched. But still. I mean, I said I loved her. I lost my virginity to her."

"You lost your virginity to her?"

"Yeah. Yeah. I never told you that? She's the only girl I've slept with. I don't know. Even though we fought, like, ninety-four percent of the time, I'm really sad."

"You're really sad?"

"Sadder than I thought I'd be, anyway. I mean, I knew it was inevitable. We haven't had a pleasant moment this whole year. Ever since I got here, I mean, we were just on each other relentlessly. I should have been nicer to her. I don't know. It's sad."

"It is sad," I repeated.

"I mean, it's stupid to miss someone you didn't even get along with. But, I don't know, it was nice, you know, having someone you could always fight with."

"Fighting," I said, and then, confused, barely able to drive, I added, "is nice."

"Right. I don't know what I'll do now. I mean, it was nice to have her. I'm a mad guy, Pudge. What do I do with that?"

"You can fight with me," I said. I put my controller down and leaned back on our foam couch and was asleep. As I drifted off, I heard the Colonel say, "I can't be mad at you, you harmless skinny bastard."

4 **spacey**: not completely conscious of what is happening around you 6 **lame**: difficult to believe; that sounds stupid 15 **inevitable** [- '- - - -]: *unvermeidbar* 27 **drift off**: fall asleep

eighty-four days before

THREE DAYS LATER, the rain began. My head still hurt, and the sizable knot above my left temple looked, the Colonel thought, like a miniaturized topographical map of Macedonia, which I had not previously known was a place, let alone a country. And as the Colonel and I walked over the parched, half-dead grass that Monday, I said, "I suppose we could use some rain," and the Colonel looked up at the low clouds coming in fast and threatening, and then he said, "Well, use it or not, we're sure as shit going to get some."

And we sure as shit did. Twenty minutes into French class, Madame O'Malley was conjugating the verb *to believe* in the subjunctive. *Que je croie. Que tu croies. Qu'il ou qu'elle croie.* She said it over and over, like it wasn't a verb so much as a Buddhist mantra. *Que je croie; que tu croies; qu'il ou qu'elle croie.* What a funny thing to say over and over again: I would believe; you would believe; he or she would believe. *Believe what?* I thought, and right then, the rain came.

It came all at once and in a furious torrent, like God was mad and wanted to flood us out. Day after day, night after night, it rained. It rained so that I couldn't see across the dorm circle, so that the lake swelled up and lapped against the Adirondack swing, swallowing half of the fake beach. By the third day, I abandoned my umbrella entirely and walked around in a perpetual state of wetness. Everything at the cafeteria tasted like the minor acid of rainwater and everything stank of mildew and showers became ludicrously inappropriate because the whole goddamned world had better water pressure than the showers.

And the rain made hermits of us all. The Colonel spent every not-in-class moment sitting on the couch, reading the almanac and playing video games, and I wasn't sure whether he wanted to talk or whether he just wanted to sit on the white foam and drink his ambrosia in peace.

5 **parched**: very dry 17 **torrent**: large amount of water 21 **abandon sth.**: not use sth. any more 22 **perpetual**: continuous 23 **acid**: *Säure* 24 **ludicrous**: absurdly 27 **hermit**: *Eremit*

After the disaster that was our "date," I felt it best not to speak to Lara under any circumstances, lest I suffer a concussion and/or an attack of puking, even though she'd told me in precalc the next day that it was "no beeg deal."

And I saw Alaska only in class and could never talk to her, because she came to every class late and left the moment the bell rang, before I could even cap my pen and close my notebook. On the fifth evening of the rain, I walked into the cafeteria fully prepared to go back to my room and eat a reheated bufriedo for dinner if Alaska and/or Takumi weren't eating (I knew full well the Colonel was in Room 43, dining on milk 'n' vodka). But I stayed, because I saw Alaska sitting alone, her back to a rain-streaked window. I grabbed a heaping plate of fried okra and sat down next to her.

"God, it's like it'll never end," I said, referring to the rain.

"Indeed," she said. Her wet hair hung from her head and mostly covered her face. I ate some. She ate some.

"How've you been?" I finally asked.

"I'm really not up for answering any questions that start with *how, when, where, why,* or *what*."

"What's wrong?" I asked.

"That's a *what*. I'm not doing *what's* right now. All right, I should go." She pursed her lips and exhaled slowly, like the way the Colonel blew out smoke.

"What –" Then I stopped myself and reworded. "Did I do something?" I asked.

She gathered her tray and stood up before answering. "Of course not, sweetie."

Her "sweetie" felt condescending, not romantic, like a boy enduring his first biblical rainstorm couldn't possibly understand her problems – whatever they were. It took a sincere effort not to roll my eyes at her, though she wouldn't have even noticed as she walked out of the cafeteria with her hair dripping over her face.

2 **lest**: *damit nicht* 22 **purse your lips**: *Lippen schürzen*

seventy-six days before

"I FEEL BETTER," the Colonel told me on the ninth day of the rainstorm as he sat down next to me in religion class. "I had an epiphany. Do you remember that night when she came to the room and was a complete and total bitch?"

"Yeah. The opera. The flamingo tie."

"Right."

"What about it?" I asked.

The Colonel pulled out a spiral notebook, the top half of which was soaking wet, and slowly pulled the pages apart until he found his place. "That was the epiphany. She's a complete and total bitch."

Hyde hobbled in, leaning heavily on a black cane. As he made his way toward his chair, he drily noted, "My trick knee is warning me that we might have some rain. So prepare yourselves." He stood in front of his chair, leaned back cautiously, grabbed it with both hands, and collapsed into the chair with a series of quick, shallow breaths – like a woman in labor.

"Although it isn't due for more than two months, you'll be receiving your paper topic for this semester today. Now, I'm quite sure that you've all read the syllabus for this class with such frequency and seriousness that by now you've committed it to memory." He smirked. "But a reminder: This paper is fifty percent of your grade. I encourage you to take it seriously. Now, about this Jesus fellow."

Hyde talked about the Gospel of Mark, which I hadn't read until the day before, although I was a Christian. I guess. I'd been to church, uh, like four times. Which is more frequently than I'd been to a mosque or a synagogue.

He told us that in the first century, around the time of Jesus, some of the Roman coins had a picture of the Emperor Augustus on them, and that beneath his picture were inscribed the words *Filius Dei*. The Son of God.

"We are speaking," he said, "of a time in which gods had sons. It was not so unusual to be a son of God. The miracle, at least in that

2 **epiphany**: *Erscheinnung (einer Gottheit)* 11 **cane**: walking stick 16 **in labor**: giving birth to a baby 23 **Gospel of Mark**: part of the New Testament
26 **mosque**: building in which Muslims worship

time and in that place, was that *Jesus* – a peasant, a Jew, a nobody in an empire ruled exclusively by somebodies – was the son of *that* God, the all-powerful God of Abraham and Moses. That God's son was not an emperor. Not even a trained rabbi. A peasant and a Jew. A nobody like you. While the Buddha was special because he abandoned his wealth and noble birth to seek enlightenment, Jesus was special because he lacked wealth and noble birth, but inherited the ultimate nobility: King of Kings. Class over. You can pick up a copy of your final exam on the way out. Stay dry." It wasn't until I stood up to leave that I noticed Alaska had skipped class – how could she skip the only class worth attending? I grabbed a copy of the final for her.

The final exam: *What is the most important question human beings must answer? Choose your question wisely, and then examine how Islam, Buddhism, and Christianity attempt to answer it.*

"I hope that poor bastard lives the rest of the school year," the Colonel said as we jogged home through the rain, "because I'm sure starting to enjoy that class. What's your most important question?"

After thirty seconds of running, I was already winded. "What happens … to us … when we die?"

"Christ, Pudge, if you don't stop running, you're going to find out." He slowed to a walk. "My question is: Why do good people get rotten lots in life? Holy shit, is that Alaska?"

She was running at us at full speed, and she was screaming, but I couldn't hear her over the pounding rain until she was so close to us that I could see her spit flying.

"The fuckers flooded my room. They ruined like a hundred of my books! Goddamned pissant Weekday Warrior shit. Colonel, they poked a hole in the gutter and connected a plastic tube from the gutter down through my back window into my room! The whole place is soaking wet. My copy of *The General in His Labyrinth* is absolutely *ruined*."

1 **peasant**: *Kleinbauer/-bäuerin* 6 **enlightenment**: *Erleuchtung* 7 **inherit sth.**: get sth. (e.g. money) from sb when that person dies 19 **winded**: unable to breathe easily 23 **lot** (n): (here) destiny 28 **pissant** (AE sl): loser 29 **tube**: *Rohr*

"That's pretty good," the Colonel said, like an artist admiring another's work.

"Hey!" she shouted.

"Sorry. Don't worry, dude," he said. "God will punish the wicked. And before He does, we will."

sixty-seven days before

SO THIS IS HOW NOAH FELT. You wake up one morning and God has forgiven you and you walk around squinting all day because you've forgotten how sunlight feels warm and rough against your skin like a kiss on the cheek from your dad, and the whole world is brighter and cleaner than ever before, like central Alabama has been put in the washing machine for two weeks and cleaned with extra-superstrength detergent with color brightener, and now the grass is greener and the bufriedos are crunchier.

I stayed by the classrooms that afternoon, lying on my stomach in the newly dry grass and reading for American history – the Civil War, or as it was known around these parts, the War Between the States. To me, it was the war that spawned a thousand good last words. Like General Albert Sidney Johnston, who, when asked if he was injured, answered, "Yes, and I fear seriously." Or Robert E. Lee, who, many years after the war, in a dying delirium, announced, "Strike the tent!"

I was mulling over why the Confederate generals had better last words than the Union ones (Ulysses S. Grant's last word, "Water," was pretty lame) when I noticed a shadow blocking me from the sun. It had been some time since I'd seen a shadow, and it startled me a bit. I looked up.

"I brought you a snack," Takumi said, dropping an oatmeal cream pie onto my book.

4 **wicked** ['wɪkɪd]: evil 7 **squint**: *blinzeln* 12 **detergent**: liquid or powder that helps remove dirt 22–23 **Confederate/Union**: 11 southern states (Confederate states) left the US in 1861 to form a new nation, which led to the civil war. The Union (north) fought against the Confederate states (south).
27 **oatmeal**: *Hafermehl*

“Very nutritious.” I smiled.

“You’ve got your oats. You’ve got your meal. You’ve got your cream. It’s a fuckin’ food pyramid.”

“Hell yeah it is.”

And then I didn’t know what to say. Takumi knew a lot about hiphop; I knew a lot about last words and video games. Finally, I said, “I can’t believe those guys flooded Alaska’s room.”

“Yeah,” Takumi said, not looking at me. “Well, they had their reasons. You have to understand that with like everybody, even the Weekday Warriors, Alaska is famous for pranking. I mean, last year, we put a Volkswagen Beetle in the library. So if they have a reason to try and one-up her, they’ll try. And that’s pretty ingenious, to divert water from the gutter to her room. I mean, I don’t *want* to admire it …”

I laughed. “Yeah. That will be tough to top.” I unwrapped the cream pie and bit into it. Mmm … hundreds of delicious calories per bite.

“She’ll think of something,” he said. “Pudge,” he said. “Hmm. Pudge, you need a cigarette. Let’s go for a walk.”

I felt nervous, as I invariably do when someone says my name twice with a *hmm* in between. But I got up, leaving my books behind, and walked toward the Smoking Hole. But as soon as we got to the edge of the woods, Takumi turned away from the dirt road. “Not sure the Hole is safe,” he said. *Not safe?* I thought. *It’s the safest place to smoke a cigarette in the known universe.* But I just followed him through the thick brush, weaving through pine trees and threatening, chest-high brambly bushes. After a while, he just sat down. I cupped my hand around my lighter to protect the flame from the slight breeze and lit up.

“Alaska ratted out Marya,” he said. “So the Eagle might know about the Smoking Hole, too. I don’t know. I’ve never seen him down that way, but who knows what she told him.”

1 **nutritious**: good for you and your body 12 **one-up sb.** (infml): *jdm. voraus sein*
12 **ingenious**: *genial* 12 **divert sth.**: make sth. change direction
20 **invariably**: *ausnahmslos*

"Wait, how do you know?" I asked, dubious.

"Well, for one thing, I figured it out. And for another, Alaska admitted it. She told me at least part of the truth, that right at the end of school last year, she tried to sneak off campus one night after lights-out to go visit Jake and then got busted. She said she was careful – no headlights or anything – but the Eagle caught her, and she had a bottle of wine in her car, so she was fucked. And the Eagle took her into his house and gave her the same offer he gives to everyone when they get fatally busted. 'Either tell me everything you know or go to your room and pack up your stuff.' So Alaska broke and told him that Marya and Paul were drunk and in her room right then. And then she told him God knows what else. And so the Eagle let her go, because he needs rats to do his job. She was smart, really, to rat on one of her friends, because no one ever thinks to blame the friends. That's why the Colonel is so sure it was Kevin and his boys. I didn't believe it could be Alaska, either, until I figured out that she was the only person on campus who could've known what Marya was doing. I suspected Paul's roommate, Longwell – one of the guys who pulled the armless-mermaid bit on you. Turns out he was at home that night. His aunt had died. I checked the obit in the paper. Hollis Burnis Chase – hell of a name for a woman."

"So the Colonel doesn't know?" I asked, stunned. I put out my cigarette, even though I wasn't quite finished, because I felt spooked. I'd never suspected Alaska could be disloyal. Moody, yes. But not a rat.

"No, and he can't know, because he'll go crazy and get her expelled. The Colonel takes all this honor and loyalty shit pretty seriously, if you haven't noticed."

"I've noticed."

Takumi shook his head, his hands pushing aside leaves to dig into the still-wet dirt beneath. "I just don't get why she'd be so afraid of getting expelled. I'd hate to get expelled, but you have to take your lumps. I don't get it."

20 **obit = obituary**: *Todesanzeige* 23 **spooked**: frightened 32–33 **take your lumps**: accept bad things that happen to you without complaining

"Well, she obviously doesn't like home."

"True. She only goes home over Christmas and the summer, when Jake is there. But whatever. I don't like home, either. But I'd never give the Eagle the satisfaction." Takumi picked up a twig and dug it into the soft red dirt. "Listen, Pudge. I don't know what kind of prank Alaska and the Colonel are going to come up with to end this, but I'm sure we'll both be involved. I'm telling you all this so you can know what you're getting into, because if you get caught, you had better take it."

I thought of Florida, of my "school friends," and realized for the first time how much I would miss the Creek if I ever had to leave it. I stared down at Takumi's twig sticking erect out of the mud and said, "I swear to God I won't rat."

I finally understood that day at the Jury: Alaska wanted to show us that we could trust her. Survival at Culver Creek meant loyalty, and she had ignored that. But then she'd shown me the way. She and the Colonel had taken the fall for me to show me how it was done, so I would know what to do when the time came.

fifty-eight days before

ABOUT A WEEK LATER I woke up at 6:30 – 6:30 on a Saturday! – to the sweet melody of Decapitation: automatic gunfire blasted out above the menacing, bass-heavy background music of the video game. I rolled over and saw Alaska pulling the controller up and to the right, as if that would help her escape certain death. I had the same bad habit.

"Can you at least mute it?"

"*Pudge,*" she said, faux-condescending, "the sound is an integral part of the artistic experience of this video game. Muting Decapitation would be like reading only every other word of *Jane Eyre*. The

4 **twig**: *kleiner Zweig* 17 **take the fall for sb.** take the blame instead of sb. else 20 **decapitation**: *Enthauptung (hier: Name eines Videospiels)* 21 **menace** (v): threaten 25 **mute sth.**: make the sound of sth quieter 28 **Jane Eyre**: novel by Charlotte Brontë published in 1847

Colonel woke up about half an hour ago. He seemed a little annoyed, so I told him to go sleep in my room."

"Maybe I'll join him," I said groggily.

Rather than answering my question, she remarked, "So I heard Takumi told you. Yeah, I ratted out Marya, and I'm sorry, and I'll never do it again. In other news, are you staying here for Thanksgiving? Because I am."

I rolled back toward the wall and pulled the comforter over my head. I didn't know whether to trust Alaska, and I'd certainly had enough of her unpredictability – cold one day, sweet the next; irresistibly flirty one moment, resistibly obnoxious the next. I preferred the Colonel: At least when he was cranky, he had a *reason*.

In a testament to the power of fatigue, I managed to fall asleep quickly, convinced that the shrieking of dying monsters and Alaska's delighted squeals upon killing them were nothing more than a pleasant sound track by which to dream. I woke up half an hour later, when she sat down on my bed, her butt against my hip. *Her underwear, her jeans, the comforter, my corduroys, and my boxers between us*, I thought. Five layers, and yet I felt it, the nervous warmth of touching – a pale reflection of the fireworks of one mouth on another, but a reflection nonetheless. And in the almostness of the moment, I cared at least enough. I wasn't sure whether I liked her, and I doubted whether I could trust her, but I cared at least enough to try to find out. Her on my bed, wide green eyes staring down at me. The enduring mystery of her sly, almost smirking, smile. Five layers between us.

She continued as if I hadn't been asleep. "Jake has to study. So he doesn't want me in Nashville. Says he can't pay attention to musicology while staring at me. I said I would wear a burka, but he wasn't convinced, so I'm staying here."

"I'm sorry," I said.

10–11 **irresistible** [- - '- - -]: so attractive that you feel you must have it
11 **obnoxious** [ɑːb'nɑːkkʃəs]: offensive 12 **cranky** (AE): bad-tempered 15 **squeal** (n): long high cry or sound 18 **corduroys**: *Kordsamthosen* 25 **sly** (here): knowing
29 **burka**: long loose piece of clothing that covers the whole body, including the head and face, worn in public by some Muslim women

"Oh, don't be. I'll have loads to do. There's a prank to plan. But I was thinking you should stay here, too. In fact, I have composed a list."

"A list?"

She reached into her pocket and pulled out a heavily folded piece of notebook paper and began to read.

"*Why Pudge Should Stay at the Creek for Thanksgiving: A List*, by Alaska Young.

"*One*. Because he is a very conscientious student, Pudge has been deprived of many wonderful Culver Creek experiences, including but not limited to *A*. drinking wine with me in the woods, and *B*. getting up early on a Saturday to eat breakfast at McInedible and then driving through the greater Birmingham area smoking cigarettes and talking about how pathetically boring the greater Birmingham area is, and also *C*. going out late at night and lying in the dewy soccer field and reading a Kurt Vonnegut book by moonlight.

"*Two*. Although she certainly does not excel at endeavors such as teaching the French language, Madame O'Malley makes a mean stuffing, and she invites all the students who stay on campus to Thanksgiving dinner. Which is usually just me and the South Korean exchange student, but whatever. Pudge would be welcome.

"*Three*. I don't really have a *Three*, but *One* and *Two* were awfully good."

One and *Two* appealed to me, certainly, but mostly I liked the idea of just her and just me on campus. "I'll talk to my parents. Once they wake up," I said. She coaxed me onto the couch, and we played Decapitation together until she abruptly dropped the controller.

"I'm not flirting. I'm just tired," she said, kicking off her flipflops. She pulled her feet onto the foam couch, tucking them behind a cushion, and scooted up to put her head in my lap. My corduroys. My boxers. Two layers. I could feel the warmth of her cheek on my thigh.

9 **conscientious** [ˌkɑːnʃiənʃes]: taking care to do things carefully and correctly
10 **deprive sb of sth.**: prevent sb. from having or doing sth. 12 **inedible**: that cannot be eaten 14 **pathetic**: *(hier) erbärmlich* 15 **dewy**: *mit Tau benetzt*
16 **Kurt Vonnegut**: US author (1922–2007) 19 **stuffing**: *Füllung (für Geflügel)*
26 **coax sb.**: gently persuade sb. to do sth. 30 **scoot up:** (here) move yourself forwards

There are times when it is appropriate, even preferable, to get an erection when someone's face is in close proximity to your penis.

This was not one of those times.

So I stopped thinking about the layers and the warmth, muted the TV, and focused on Decapitation.

At 8:30, I turned off the game and scooted out from underneath Alaska. She turned onto her back, still asleep, the lines of my corduroy pants imprinted on her cheek.

I usually only called my parents on Sunday afternoons, so when my mom heard my voice, she instantly overreacted. "What's wrong, Miles? Are you okay?"

"I'm fine, Mom. I think – if it's okay with you, I think I might stay here for Thanksgiving. A lot of my friends are staying" – lie – "and I have a lot of work to do" – double lie. "I had no idea how hard the classes would be, Mom" – truth.

"Oh, sweetie. We miss you so much. And there's a big Thanksgiving turkey waiting for you. And all the cranberry sauce you can eat."

I hated cranberry sauce, but for some reason my mom persisted in her lifelong belief that it was my very favorite food, even though every single Thanksgiving I politely declined to include it on my plate.

"I know, Mom. I miss you guys, too. But I really want to do well here" – truth – "and plus it's really nice to have, like, *friends*" – truth.

I knew that playing the friend card would sell her on the idea, and it did. So I got her blessing to stay on campus after promising to hang out with them for every minute of Christmas break (as if I had other plans).

I spent the morning at the computer, flipping back and forth between my religion and English papers. There were only two weeks of classes before exams – the coming one and the one after Thanksgiving – and so far, the best personal answer I had to "What happens to people after they die?" was "Well, something. Maybe."

2 **proximity** (fml): state of being near sb./sth. in distance 24 **sell sb. on sth.** (AE infml): *jdn. für etwas begeistern*

The Colonel came in at noon, his thick übermath book cradled in his arms.

"I just saw Sara," he said.

"How'd that work out for ya?"

"Bad. She said she still loved me. God, 'I love you' really is the gateway drug of breaking up. Saying 'I love you' while walking across the dorm circle inevitably leads to saying 'I love you' while you're doing it. So I just bolted." I laughed. He pulled out a notebook and sat down at his desk.

"Yeah. Ha-ha. So Alaska said you're staying here."

"Yeah. I feel a little guilty about ditching my parents, though."

"Yeah, well. If you're staying here in hopes of making out with Alaska, I sure wish you wouldn't. If you unmoor her from the rock that is Jake, God have mercy on us all. That would be some drama, indeed. And as a rule, I like to avoid drama."

"It's not because I want to make out with her."

"Hold on." He grabbed a pencil and scrawled excitedly at the paper as if he'd just made a mathematical breakthrough and then looked back up at me. "I just did some calculations, and I've been able to determine that you're full of shit."

And he was right. How could I abandon my parents, who were nice enough to pay for my education at Culver Creek, my parents who had always loved me, just because I maybe liked some girl with a boyfriend? How could I leave them alone with a giant turkey and mounds of inedible cranberry sauce? So during third period, I called my mom at work. I wanted her to say it was okay, I guess, for me to stay at the Creek for Thanksgiving, but I didn't quite expect her to excitedly tell me that she and Dad had bought plane tickets to England immediately after I called and were planning to spend Thanksgiving in a castle on their second honeymoon.

1 **übermath**: (hier) advanced mathematics   1 **cradle sb./sth.**: hold sb./sth. gently in your arms or hands   6 **gateway drug**: *Einstiegsdroge*   8 **bolt**: run away
11 **ditch sb.** (infml): get rid of sb.   13 **unmoor sb./sth.**: *jdn./etwas losbinden*

"Oh, that – that's awesome," I said, and then quickly got off the phone because I did not want her to hear me cry. I guess Alaska heard me slam down the phone from her room, because she opened the door as I turned away, but said nothing. I walked across the dorm circle, and then straight through the soccer field, bushwhacking through the woods, until I ended up on the banks of Culver Creek just down from the bridge. I sat with my butt on a rock and my feet in the dark dirt of the creek bed and tossed pebbles into the clear, shallow water, and they landed with an empty *plop*, barely audible over the rumbling of the creek as it danced its way south. The light filtered through the leaves and pine needles above as if through lace, the ground spotted in shadow.

I thought of the one thing about home that I missed, my dad's study with its built-in, floor-to-ceiling shelves sagging with thick biographies, and the black leather chair that kept me just uncomfortable enough to keep from feeling sleepy as I read. It was stupid, to feel as upset as I did. *I* ditched *them*, but it felt the other way around. Still, I felt unmistakably homesick.

I looked up toward the bridge and saw Alaska sitting on one of the blue chairs at the Smoking Hole, and though I'd thought I wanted to be alone, I found myself saying, "Hey." Then, when she did not turn to me, I screamed, "Alaska!" She walked over.

"I was looking for you," she said, joining me on the rock.

"Hey."

"I'm really sorry, Pudge," she said, and put her arms around me, resting her head against my shoulder. It occurred to me that she didn't even know what had happened, but she still sounded sincere.

"What am I going to do?"

"You'll spend Thanksgiving with me, silly. Here."

"So why don't you go home for vacations?" I asked her.

"I'm just scared of ghosts, Pudge. And home is full of them."

5 **bushwhack**: cut your way through bushes and plants in wild country
9 **shallow**: not deep 9 **audible**: that can be heard 10 **rumble**: make a long deep sound 11 **lace**: *Spitze* 14 **sag**: hang or bend down in the middle because of weight or pressure 27 **sincere**: *ehrlich*

fifty-two days before

AFTER EVERYONE LEFT; after the Colonel's mom showed up in a beat-up hatchback and he threw his giant duffel bag into the backseat; and after he said, "I'm not much for saying good-bye. I'll see you in a week. Don't do anything I wouldn't do"; and after a green limousine arrived for Lara, whose father was the only doctor in some small town in southern Alabama; and after I joined Alaska on a harrowing, we-don't-need-no-stinking-brakes drive to the airport to drop off Takumi; and after the campus settled into an eerie quiet, with no doors slamming and no music playing and no one laughing and no one screaming; after all that:

We made our way down to the soccer field, and she took me to the edge of the field where the woods start, the same steps I'd walked on my way to being thrown into the lake. Beneath the full moon she cast a shadow, and you could see the curve from her waist to her hips in the shadow, and after a while she stopped and said, "Dig."

And I said, "Dig?" and she said, "Dig," and we went on like that for a bit, and then I got on my knees and dug through the soft black dirt at the edge of the woods, and before I could get very far, my fingers scratched glass, and I dug around the glass until I pulled out a bottle of pink wine – Strawberry Hill, it was called, I suppose because if it had not tasted like vinegar with a dash of maple syrup, it might have tasted like strawberries.

"I have a fake ID," she said, "but it sucks. So every time I go to the liquor store, I try to buy ten bottles of this, and some vodka for the Colonel. And so when it finally works, I'm covered for a semester. And then I give the Colonel his vodka, and he puts it wherever he puts it, and I take mine and bury it."

"Because you're a pirate," I said.

"Aye, matey. Precisely. Although wine consumption has risen a bit this semester, so we'll need to take a trip tomorrow. This is the last bottle." She unscrewed the cap – no corks here – sipped, and handed it to me. "Don't worry about the Eagle tonight," she said. "He's just

2 **hatchback**: car with a sloping door at the back that opens upwards
6 **harrowing** (adj): very frightening 8 **eerie** ['ɪri]: strange, mysterious
21 **vinegar**: *Essig* 23 **ID**: identification

happy most everyone's gone. He's probably masturbating for the first time in a month."

I worried about it for a moment as I held the bottle by the neck, but I wanted to trust her, and so I did. I took a minor sip, and as soon as I swallowed, I felt my body rejecting the stinging syrup of it. It washed back up my esophagus, but I swallowed hard, and there, yes, I did it. I was drinking on campus.

So we lay in the tall grass between the soccer field and the woods, passing the bottle back and forth and tilting our heads up to sip the wince-inducing wine. As promised in the list, she brought a Kurt Vonnegut book, *Cat's Cradle*, and she read aloud to me, her soft voice mingling with the frogs' croaking and the grasshoppers landing softly around us. I did not hear her words so much as the cadence of her voice. She'd obviously read the book many times before, and so she read flawlessly and confidently, and I could hear her smile in the reading of it, and the sound of that smile made me think that maybe I would like novels better if Alaska Young read them to me. After a while, she put down the book, and I felt warm but not drunk with the bottle resting between us – my chest touching the bottle and her chest touching the bottle but us not touching each other, and then she placed her hand on my leg.

Her hand just above my knee, the palm flat and soft against my jeans and her index finger making slow, lazy circles that crept toward the inside of my thigh, and with one layer between us, God I wanted her. And lying there, amid the tall, still grass and beneath the star-drunk sky, listening to the just-this-side-of-inaudible sound of her rhythmic breathing and the noisy silence of the bullfrogs, the grasshoppers, the distant cars rushing endlessly on I-65, I thought it might be a fine time to say the Three Little Words. And I steeled myself to say them as I stared up at that starriest night, convinced myself that she felt it, too, that her hand so alive and vivid against

5 **stinging**: causing a sharp pain 6 **esophagus** [iː'sɑːfəgəs]: the tube through which food passes from the mouth to the stomach 10 **wince** (n): *Zusammenzucken*
10 **induce**: (here) cause 13 **cadence** ['keɪdəns]: (of a voice) rise and fall
15 **flawless**: perfect 23 **index finger**: *Zeigefinger* 28 **I-65 = Interstate 65**: number of the highway 29–30 **steel yourself**: prepare yourself to deal with sth. unpleasant

my leg was more than playful, and fuck Lara and fuck Jake because I do, Alaska Young, I do love you and what else matters but that and my lips parted to speak and before I could even begin to breathe out the words, she said, "It's not life or death, the labyrinth."

"Um, okay. So what is it?"

"Suffering," she said. "Doing wrong and having wrong things happen to you. That's the problem. Bolívar was talking about the pain, not about the living or dying. How do you get out of the labyrinth of suffering?"

"What's wrong?" I asked. And I felt the absence of her hand on me.

"Nothing's wrong. But there's always suffering, Pudge. Homework or malaria or having a boyfriend who lives far away when there's a good-looking boy lying next to you. Suffering is universal. It's the one thing Buddhists, Christians, and Muslims are all worried about."

I turned to her. "Oh, so maybe Dr. Hyde's class isn't total bullshit." And both of us lying on our sides, she smiled, our noses almost touching, my unblinking eyes on hers, her face blushing from the wine, and I opened my mouth again but this time not to speak, and she reached up and put a finger to my lips and said, "Shh. Shh. Don't ruin it."

fifty-one days before

THE NEXT MORNING, I didn't hear the knocking, if there was any.

I just heard, "UP! Do you know what time it is?!"

I looked at the clock and groggily muttered, "It's seven thirty-six."

"No, Pudge. It's party time! We've only got seven days left before everyone comes back. Oh God, I can't even tell you how nice it is to have you here. Last Thanksgiving, I spent the whole time constructing one massive candle using the wax from all my little candles. God, it was boring. I counted the ceiling tiles. Sixty-seven down, eighty-four across. Talk about suffering! Absolute torture."

"I'm really tired. I –" I said, and then she cut me off.

30 **ceiling**: top inside surface of a room 30 **tile**: *Fliese*

"Poor Pudge. Oh, poor poor Pudge. Do you want me to climb into bed with you and cuddle?"

"Well, if you're offering –"

"NO! UP! NOW!"

She took me behind a wing of Weekday Warrior rooms – 50 to 59 – and stopped in front of a window, placed her palms flat against it, and pushed up until the window was half open, then crawled inside. I followed.

"What do you see, Pudge?"

I saw a dorm room – the same cinder-block walls, the same dimensions, even the same layout as my own. Their couch was nicer, and they had an actual coffee table instead of COFFEE TABLE. They had two posters on the wall. One featured a huge stack of hundred-dollar bills with the caption THE FIRST MILLION IS THE HARDEST. On the opposite wall, a poster of a red Ferrari. "Uh, I see a dorm room."

"You're not looking, Pudge. When I go into your room, I see a couple of guys who love video games. When I look at my room, I see a girl who loves books." She walked over to the couch and picked up a plastic soda bottle. "Look at this," she said, and I saw that it was half filled with a brackish, brown liquid. Dip spit. "So they dip. And they obviously aren't hygienic about it. So are they going to care if we pee on their toothbrushes? They won't care enough, that's for sure. Look. Tell me what these guys love."

"They love money," I said, pointing to the poster. She threw up her hands, exasperated.

"They *all* love money, Pudge. Okay, go into the bathroom. Tell me what you see there."

The game was annoying me a little, but I went into the bathroom as she sat down on that inviting couch. Inside the shower, I found a dozen bottles of shampoo and conditioner. In the medicine cabinet, I found a cylindrical bottle of something called Rewind. I opened it – the bluish gel smelled like flowers and rubbing alcohol, like a

2 **cuddle**: hold sb./sth. close in your arms to show love or affection 5 **wing**: *Flügel (eines Gebäudes)* 20 **brackish**: dirty 20 **dip spit**: saliva caused by chewing tobacco, which is then spat into a container (**dip**: chew) 25 **exasperated**: extremely annoyed

fancy hair salon. (Under the sink, I also found a tub of Vaseline so big that it could have only had one possible use, which I didn't care to dwell on.) I came back into the room and excitedly said, "They love their hair."

"*Precisely!*" she shouted. "Look on the top bunk." Perilously positioned on the thin wooden headboard of the bed, a bottle of STAWET gel. "Kevin doesn't just *wake up* with that spiky bedhead look, Pudge. He *works* for it. He loves that hair. They leave their hair products here, Pudge, because they have *duplicates* at home. All those boys do. And you know why?"

"Because they're compensating for their tiny little penises?" I asked.

"Ha ha. No. That's why they're macho assholes. They love their hair because they aren't smart enough to love something more interesting. So we hit them where it hurts: the scalp."

"Ohh-kaay," I said, unsure of how, exactly, to prank someone's scalp.

She stood up and walked to the window and bent over to shimmy out. "Don't look at my ass," she said, and so I looked at her ass, spreading out wide from her thin waist. She effortlessly somersaulted out the half-opened window. I took the feetfirst approach, and once I got my feet on the ground, I limboed my upper body out the window.

"Well," she said. "That looked awkward. Let's go to the Smoking Hole."

She shuffled her feet to kick up dry orange dirt on the road to the bridge, seeming not to walk so much as cross-country ski. As we followed the almost-trail down from the bridge to the Hole, she turned around and looked back at me, stopping. "I wonder how one

1 **sink** (n): *Waschbecken* 3 **dwell on sth.**: think or talk a lot about sth. 5 **bunk**: one of two beds that are fixed together, one above the other 5 **perilous** ['- - -]: very dangerous 18 **shimmy** (v): use your hips and shoulders to move
20 **somersault** ['sʌmərsɑːlt] : turn over completely in the air 22 **limbo**: lean backwards and move the lower part of your body first

would go about acquiring industrial-strength blue dye," she said, and then held a tree branch back for me.

forty-nine days before

TWO DAYS LATER – Monday, the first real day of vacation – I spent the morning working on my religion final and went to Alaska's room in the afternoon. She was reading in bed.

"Auden," she announced. "What were his last words?"

"Don't know. Never heard of him."

"Never *heard* of him? You poor, illiterate boy. Here, read this line." I walked over and looked down at her index finger. "You shall love your crooked neighbour / With your crooked heart," I read aloud. "Yeah. That's pretty good," I said.

"Pretty good? Sure, and bufriedos are pretty good. Sex is pretty fun. The sun is pretty hot. Jesus, it says so much about love and brokenness – it's perfect."

"Mm-hmm." I nodded unenthusiastically.

"You're hopeless. Wanna go porn hunting?"

"Huh?"

"We can't love our neighbors till we know how crooked their hearts are. Don't you like porn?" she asked, smiling.

"Um," I answered. The truth was that I hadn't seen much porn, but the idea of looking at porn with Alaska had a certain appeal.

We started with the 50s wing of dorms and made our way backward around the hexagon – she pushed open the back windows while I looked out and made sure no one was walking by.

I'd never been in most people's rooms. After three months, I knew most people, but I regularly talked to very few – just the Colonel and Alaska and Takumi, really. But in a few hours, I got to know my classmates quite well.

Wilson Carbod, the center for the Culver Creek Nothings, had hemorrhoids, or at least he kept hemorrhoidal cream secreted away

1 **acquire sth.**: obtain sth., get hold of sth. 1 **industrial strength**: very strong or powerful 1 **dye**: substance that changes the color of sth. 6 **W. H. Auden** (1907–1973): British author 8 **illiterate**: unable to read or write

in the bottom drawer of his desk. Chandra Kilers, a cute girl who loved math a little too much, and who Alaska believed was the Colonel's future girlfriend, collected Cabbage Patch Kids. I don't mean that she collected Cabbage Patch Kids when she was, like, five. She collected them now – dozens of them – black, white, Latino, and Asian, boys and girls, babies dressed like farmhands and budding businessmen. A senior Weekday Warrior named Holly Moser sketched nude self-portraits in charcoal pencil, portraying her rotund form in all its girth.

I was stunned by how many people had booze. Even the Weekday Warriors, who got to go home every weekend, had beer and liquor stashed everywhere from toilet tanks to the bottoms of dirtyclothes hampers.

"God, I could have ratted out anyone," Alaska said softly as she unearthed a forty-ounce bottle of Magnum malt liquor from Longwell Chase's closet. I wondered, then, why she had chosen Paul and Marya.

Alaska found everyone's secrets so fast that I suspected she'd done this before, but she couldn't possibly have had advance knowledge of the secrets of Ruth and Margot Blowker, ninth-grade twin sisters who were new and seemed to socialize even less than I did. After crawling into their room, Alaska looked around for a moment, then walked to the bookshelf. She stared at it, then pulled out the King James Bible, and there – a purple bottle of Maui Wowie wine cooler.

"How clever," she said as she twisted off the cap. She drank it down in two long sips, and then proclaimed, "Maui WOWIE!"

"They'll know you were here!" I shouted.

Her eyes widened. "Oh no, you're right, Pudge!" she said. "Maybe they'll go to the Eagle and tell him that someone stole their wine cooler!" She laughed and leaned out the window, throwing the empty bottle into the grass.

3 **Cabbage Patch Kids**: *eine Art Stoffpuppe* 6 **farmhand**: person who works for a farmer 7 **budding** (adj): beginning to develop or become successful 9 **rotund** (fml): having a fat round body 9 **girth**: *Körperumfang* 13 **hamper**: large basket that you keep your dirty clothes in 23–24 **King James Bible**: 17th century English translation of the Bible 24 **Maui Wowie**: brand name 24 **wine cooler**: drink made from wind and fruit juice

And we found plenty of porn magazines haphazardly stuffed in between mattresses and box springs. It turns out that Hank Walsten did like something other than basketball and pot: he liked *Juggs*. But we didn't find a *movie* until Room 32, occupied by a couple of guys from Mississippi named Joe and Marcus. They were in our religion class and sometimes sat with the Colonel and me at lunch, but I didn't know them well.

Alaska read the sticker on the top of the video. "*The Bitches of Madison County*. Well. Ain't that just delightful."

We ran with it to the TV room, closed the blinds, locked the door, and watched the movie. It opened with a woman standing on a bridge with her legs spread while a guy knelt in front of her, giving her oral sex. No time for dialogue, I suppose. By the time they started doing it, Alaska commenced with her righteous indignation. "They just don't make sex look fun for women. The girl is just an object. Look! Look at that!"

I was already looking, needless to say. A woman crouched on her hands and knees while a guy knelt behind her. She kept saying "Give it to me" and moaning, and though her eyes, brown and blank, betrayed her lack of interest, I couldn't help but take mental notes. *Hands on her shoulders*, I noted. *Fast, but not too fast or it's going to be over, fast. Keep your grunting to a minimum.*

As if reading my mind, she said, "God, Pudge. Never do it that hard. That would *hurt*. That looks like torture. And all she can do is just sit there and take it? This is not a *man* and a *woman*. It's a penis and a vagina. What's erotic about that? Where's the kissing?"

"Given their position, I don't think they can kiss right now," I noted.

"That's my point. Just by virtue of how they're doing it, it's objectification. He can't even see her face! This is what can happen to women, Pudge. That woman is someone's daughter. This is what you make us do for money."

2 **box spring**: *Matrazenfeder* 3 **juggs** (sl): female breasts 10 **blind** (n): covering for a window 14 **righteous** ['raɪtʃəs]: morally right and good 19 **moan**: make a long deep sound 22 **grunting** (n): short low sound 28 **by virtue of sth.** (fml): because of sth. 28–29 **objectification** (fml): act of treating people as if they are objects

"Well, not *me*," I said defensively. "I mean, not technically. I don't, like, produce porn movies."

"Look me in the eye and tell me this doesn't turn you on, Pudge."

I couldn't. She laughed. It was fine, she said. Healthy. And then she got up, stopped the tape, lay down on her stomach across the couch, and mumbled something.

"What did you say?" I asked, walking to her, putting my hand on the small of her back.

"Shhhh," she said. "I'm sleeping."

Just like that. From a hundred miles an hour to asleep in a nanosecond. I wanted so badly to lie down next to her on the couch, to wrap my arms around her and sleep. Not fuck, like in those movies. Not even have sex. Just sleep together, in the most innocent sense of the phrase. But I lacked the courage and she had a boyfriend and I was gawky and she was gorgeous and I was hopelessly boring and she was endlessly fascinating. So I walked back to my room and collapsed on the bottom bunk, thinking that if people were rain, I was drizzle and she was a hurricane.

forty-seven days before

ON WEDNESDAY MORNING, I woke up with a stuffy nose to an entirely new Alabama, a crisp and cold one. As I walked to Alaska's room that morning, the frosty grass of the dorm circle crunched beneath my shoes. You don't run into frost much in Florida – and I jumped up and down like I was stomping on bubble wrap. *Crunch. Crunch. Crunch.*

Alaska was holding a burning green candle in her hand upside down, dripping the wax onto a larger, homemade volcano that looked a bit like a Technicolor middle-school-science-project volcano.

"Don't burn yourself," I said as the flame crept up toward her hand.

"Night falls fast. Today is in the past," she said without looking up.

"Wait, I've read that before. What is that?" I asked.

18 **drizzle**: light rain 23 **bubble wrap**: *Bläschenpapier* 27 **Technicolor**: (here) having bright colors

With her free hand, she grabbed a book and tossed it toward me. It landed at my feet. "Poem," she said. "Edna St. Vincent Millay. You've read that? I'm stunned."

"Oh, I read her biography! Didn't have her last words in it, though. I was a little bitter. All I remember is that she had a lot of sex."

"I know. She's my hero," Alaska said without a trace of irony. I laughed, but she didn't notice. "Does it seem at all odd to you that you enjoy biographies of great writers a lot more than you enjoy their actual writing?"

"Nope!" I announced. "Just because they were interesting people doesn't mean I care to hear their musings on nighttime."

"It's about depression, dumb-ass."

"Oooooh, really? Well, jeez, then it's *brilliant*," I answered.

She sighed. "All right. The snow may be falling in the winter of my discontent, but at least I've got sarcastic company. Sit down, will ya?"

I sat down next to her with my legs crossed and our knees touching. She pulled a clear plastic crate filled with dozens of candles out from underneath her bed. She looked at it for a moment, then handed me a white one and a lighter.

We spent all morning burning candles – well, and occasionally lighting cigarettes off the burning candles after we stuffed a towel into the crack at the bottom of her door. Over the course of two hours, we added a full foot to the summit of her polychrome candle volcano.

"Mount St. Helens on acid," she said.

At 12:30, after two hours of me begging for a ride to McDonald's, Alaska decided it was time for lunch. As we began to walk to the student parking lot, I saw a strange car. A small green car. A hatchback. *I've seen that car*, I thought. *Where have I seen the car?* And then the Colonel jumped out and ran to meet us.

2 **Edna St. Vincent Millay**: American poet and playwright (1892–1950)
7 **trace**: *Spur* 8 **odd**: strange 12 **musings** (n, usu. pl): thoughts, ideas
19 **crate**: container for transporting goods 25 **polychrome**: with many colors
27 **acid** (infml): LSD

Rather than, like, I don't know, "hello" or something, the Colonel began, "I have been instructed to invite you to Thanksgiving dinner at Chez Martín."

Alaska whispered into my ear, and then I laughed and said, "I have been instructed to accept your invitation." So we walked over to the Eagle's house, told him we were going to eat turkey trailer-park style, and sped away in the hatchback.

The Colonel explained it to us on the two-hour car ride south. I was crammed into the backseat because Alaska had called shotgun. She usually drove, but when she didn't, she was shotgun-calling queen of the world. The Colonel's mother heard that we were on campus and couldn't bear the thought of leaving us familyless for Thanksgiving. The Colonel didn't seem too keen on the whole idea – "I'm going to have to sleep in a tent," he said, and I laughed.

Except it turns out he did have to sleep in a tent, a nice four-person green outfit shaped like half an egg, but still a tent. The Colonel's mom lived in a trailer, as in the kind of thing you might see attached to a large pickup truck, except this particular one was old and falling apart on its cinder blocks, and probably couldn't have been hooked up to a truck without disintegrating. It wasn't even a particularly big trailer. I could just barely stand up to my full height without scraping the ceiling. Now I understood why the Colonel was short – he couldn't afford to be any taller. The place was really one long room, with a full-size bed in the front, a kitchenette, and a living area in the back with a TV and a small bathroom – so small that in order to take a shower, you pretty much had to sit on the toilet.

"It ain't much," the Colonel's mom ("That's Dolores, not Miss Martin") told us. "But y'alls a-gonna have a turkey the size o' the kitchen." She laughed. The Colonel ushered us out of the trailer immediately after our brief tour, and we walked through the neighborhood, a series of trailers and mobile homes on dirt roads.

6 **trailer**: mobile home 20 **disintegrate**: fall apart 28 **y'alls** (dialect): you
28 **a-gonna** (dialect): are going to 29 **usher sb**: show sb. where they should go

"Well, now you get why I hate rich people." And I did. I couldn't fathom how the Colonel grew up in such a small place. The entire trailer was smaller than our dorm room. I didn't know what to say to him, how to make him feel less embarrassed.

"I'm sorry if it makes you uncomfortable," he said. "I know it's probably foreign."

"Not to me," Alaska piped up.

"Well, you don't live in a trailer," he told her.

"Poor is poor."

"I suppose," the Colonel said.

Alaska decided to go help Dolores with dinner. She said that it was sexist to leave the cooking to the women, but better to have good sexist food than crappy boy-prepared food. So the Colonel and I sat on the pull-out couch in the living room, playing video games and talking about school.

"I finished my religion paper. But I have to type it up on your computer when we get back. I think I'm ready for finals, which is good, since we have an ank-pray to an-play."

"Your mom doesn't know pig Latin?" I smirked.

"Not if I talk fast. Christ, be quiet."

The food – fried okra, steamed corn on the cob, and pot roast that was so tender it fell right off the plastic fork – convinced me that Dolores was an even better cook than Maureen. Culver Creek's okra had less grease, more crunch. Dolores was also the funniest mom I'd ever met. When Alaska asked her what she did for work, she smiled and said, "I'm a culnary engineeyer. That's a short-order cook at the Waffle House to y'all."

"Best Waffle House in Alabama." The Colonel smiled, and then I realized, he wasn't embarrassed of his mom at all. He was just scared that we would act like condescending boarding-school snobs. I'd always found the Colonel's I-hate-the-rich routine a little overwrought

2 **fathom**: understand 7 **pipe up** (infml): say sth. suddenly 13 **crappy** (sl): of very bad quality 17 **finals** (pl): final exams 18 **ank-pray**: prank 18 **anplay**: plan 19 **pig Latin**: secret language 26 **culnary** (dialect) = **culinary**: connected with food and cooking 26 **short-order cook**: cook at fast-food restaurant 31 **overwrought** [ˌoʊvəˈrɑːt] (here): overdone

until I saw him with his mom. He was the same Colonel, but in a totally different context. It made me hope that one day, I could meet Alaska's family, too.

Dolores insisted that Alaska and I share the bed, and she slept on the pull-out while the Colonel was out in his tent. I worried he would get cold, but frankly I wasn't about to give up my bed with Alaska. We had separate blankets, and there were never fewer than three layers between us, but the possibilities kept me up half the night.

forty-six days before

BEST THANKSGIVING FOOD I'd ever had. No crappy cranberry sauce. Just huge slabs of moist white meat, corn, green beans cooked in enough bacon fat to make them taste like they weren't good for you, biscuits with gravy, pumpkin pie for dessert, and a glass of red wine for each of us. "I believe," Dolores said, "that yer s'posed to drink white with turkey, but – now I don't know 'bout y'all – but I don't s'pose I give a shit."

We laughed and drank our wine, and then after the meal, we each listed our gratitudes. My family always did that before the meal, and we all just rushed through it to get to the food. So the four of us sat around the table and shared our blessings. I was thankful for the fine food and the fine company, for having a home on Thanksgiving. "A trailer, at least," Dolores joked.

"Okay, my turn," Alaska said. "I'm grateful for having just had my best Thanksgiving in a decade."

Then the Colonel said, "I'm just grateful for you, Mom," and Dolores laughed and said, "That dog won't hunt, boy."

I didn't exactly know what that phrase meant, but apparently it meant, "That was inadequate," because then the Colonel expanded his list to acknowledge that he was grateful to be "the smartest human being in this trailer park," and Dolores laughed and said, "Good enough."

10 **slab**: thick, flat slice or piece of sth. 12 **pumpkin**: *Kürbis* 17 **gratitudes**: things for which people are thankful

And Dolores? She was grateful that her phone was back on, that her boy was home, that Alaska helped her cook and that I had kept the Colonel out of her hair, that her job was steady and her coworkers were nice, that she had a place to sleep and a boy who loved her.

I sat in the back of the hatchback on the drive home – and that is how I thought of it: home – and fell asleep to the highway's monotonous lullaby.

forty-four days before

"COOSA LIQUORS' entire business model is built around selling cigarettes to minors and alcohol to adults." Alaska looked at me with disconcerting frequency when she drove, particularly since we were winding through a narrow, hilly highway south of school, headed to the aforementioned Coosa Liquors. It was Saturday, our last day of real vacation. "Which is great, if all you need is cigarettes. But we need booze. And they card for booze. And my ID blows. But I'll flirt my way through." She made a sudden and unsignaled left turn, pulling onto a road that dropped precipitously down a hill with fields on either side, and she gripped the steering wheel tight as we accelerated, and she waited until the last possible moment to brake, just before we reached the bottom of the hill. There stood a plywood gas station that no longer sold gas with a faded sign bolted to the roof: COOSA LIQUORS: WE CATER TO YOUR SPIRITUAL NEEDS.

Alaska went in alone and walked out the door five minutes later weighed down by two paper bags filled with contraband: three cartons of cigarettes, five bottles of wine, and a fifth of vodka for the Colonel. On the way home, Alaska said, "You like knock-knock jokes?"

"Knock-knock jokes?" I asked. "You mean like, 'Knock knock …'"

2–3 **keep sb. out of sb. else's hair**: occupy sb. so that they don't bother sb. else 7 **lullaby**: soft gentle song sung to make a child go to sleep 10 **disconcerting** (adj): that makes sb. feel anxious or confused 12 **aforementioned**: mentioned before 14 **card** (v, sl): ask for ID cards 14 **blow**: (here) be not convincing 16 **precipitous**: *jäh, steil* 23 **contraband**: illegal goods

"Who's there?" replied Alaska.

"Who."

"Who Who?"

"What are you, an owl?" I finished. Lame.

"That was brilliant," said Alaska. "I have one. You start."

"Okay. Knock knock."

"Who's there?" said Alaska.

I looked at her blankly. About a minute later, I got it, and laughed.

"My mom told me that joke when I was six. It's still funny."

So I could not have been more surprised when she showed up sobbing at Room 43 just as I was putting the finishing touches on my final paper for English. She sat down on the couch, her every exhalation a mix of whimper and scream.

"I'm sorry," she said, heaving. Snot was dribbling down her chin.

"What's wrong?" I asked. She picked up a Kleenex from the COFFEE TABLE and wiped at her face.

"I don't …" she started, and then a sob came like a tsunami, her cry so loud and childlike that it scared me, and I got up, sat down next her, and put my arm around her. She turned away, pushing her head into the foam of the couch. "I don't understand why I screw everything up," she said.

"What, like with Marya? Maybe you were just scared."

"Scared isn't a good excuse!" she shouted into the couch. "Scared is the excuse everyone has always used!" I didn't know who "everyone" was, or when "always" was, and as much as I wanted to understand her ambiguities, the slyness was growing annoying.

"Why are you upset about this *now*?"

"It's not just that. It's everything. But I told the Colonel in the car." She sniffled but seemed done with the sobs. "While you were sleeping in the back. And he said he'd never let me out of his sight

4 **lame** (here): not very funny 12 **sob**: cry 14 **exhalation**: breathing out of air 14 **whimper**: low weak cry 27 **ambiguity** [ˌæmbɪˈgjuːəti]: (here) things that are difficult to understand 27 **slyness**: behavior that is intended to trick people

during pranks. That he couldn't trust me on my own. And I don't blame him. I don't even trust me."

"It took guts to tell him," I said.

"I have guts, just not when it counts. Will you – um," and she sat up straight and then moved toward me, and I raised my arm as she collapsed into my skinny chest and cried. I felt bad for her, but she'd done it to herself. She didn't *have* to rat.

"I don't want to upset you, but maybe you just need to tell us all why you told on Marya. Were you scared of going home or something?"

She pulled away from me and gave me a Look of Doom that would have made the Eagle proud, and I felt like she hated me or hated my question or both, and then she looked away, out the window, toward the soccer field, and said, "There's no home."

"Well, you *have* a family," I backpedaled. She'd talked to me about her mom just that morning. How could the girl who told that joke three hours before become a sobbing mess?

Still staring at me, she said, "I try not to be scared, you know. But I still ruin everything. I still fuck up."

"Okay," I told her. "It's okay." I didn't even know what she was talking about anymore. One vague notion after another.

"Don't you know who you love, Pudge? You love the girl who makes you laugh and shows you porn and drinks wine with you. You don't love the crazy, sullen bitch."

And there was something to that, truth be told.

christmas

WE ALL WENT HOME for Christmas break – even purportedly homeless Alaska.

I got a nice watch and a new wallet – "grown-up gifts," my dad called them. But mostly I just studied for those two weeks. Christmas vacation wasn't really a vacation, on account of how it was our last chance to study for exams, which started the day after we got back.

15 **backpedal**: change an earlier statement or opinion 24 **sullen**: bad-tempered
26 **purportedly**: *angeblich*

I focused on precalc and biology, the two classes that most deeply threatened my goal of a 3.4 GPA. I wish I could say I was in it for the thrill of learning, but mostly I was in it for the thrill of getting into a worthwhile college.

So, yeah, I spent a lot of my time at home studying math and memorizing French vocab, just like I had before Culver Creek. Really, being at home for two weeks was just like my entire life before Culver Creek, except my parents were more emotional. They talked very little about their trip to London. I think they felt guilty. That's a funny thing about parents. Even though I pretty much stayed at the Creek over Thanksgiving because I wanted to, my parents still felt guilty. It's nice to have people who will feel guilty for you, although I could have lived without my mom crying during every single family dinner. She would say, "I'm a bad mother," and my dad and I would immediately reply, "No, you're not."

Even my dad, who is affectionate but not, like, *sentimental*, randomly, while we were watching *The Simpsons*, said he missed me. I said I missed him, too, and I did. Sort of. They're such nice people. We went to movies and played card games, and I told them the stories I could tell without horrifying them, and they listened. My dad, who sold real estate for a living but read more books than anyone I knew, talked with me about the books I was reading for English class, and my mom insisted that I sit with her in the kitchen and learn how to make simple dishes – macaroni, scrambled eggs – now that I was "living on my own." Never mind that I didn't have, or want, a kitchen. Never mind that I didn't like eggs *or* macaroni and cheese. By New Year's Day, I could make them anyway.

When I left, they both cried, my mom explaining that it was just empty-nest syndrome, that they were just so proud of me, that they loved me so much. That put a lump in my throat, and I didn't care about Thanksgiving anymore. I had a family.

2 **GPA = grade point average**: *Notendurchschnitt* 17 **randomly**: (here) for no real reason 21 **real estate**: land or buildings 30 **lump in your throat**: *Kloß im Hals*

eight days before

ALASKA WALKED IN on the first day back from Christmas break and sat beside the Colonel on the couch. The Colonel was hard at work, breaking a land-speed record on the PlayStation.

She didn't say she missed us, or that she was glad to see us. She just looked at the couch and said, "You really need a new couch."

"Please don't address me when I'm racing," the Colonel said. "God. Does Jeff Gordon have to put up with this shit?"

"I've got an idea," she said. "It's great. What we need is a pre-prank that coincides with an attack on Kevin and his minions," she said.

I was sitting on the bed, reading the textbook in preparation for my American history exam the next day.

"A pre-prank?" I asked.

"A prank designed to lull the administration into a false sense of security," the Colonel answered, annoyed by the distraction. "After the pre-prank, the Eagle will think the junior class has done its prank and won't be waiting for it when it actually comes." Every year, the junior and senior classes pulled off a prank at some point in the year – usually something lame, like Roman candles in the dorm circle at five in the morning on a Sunday.

"Is there always a pre-prank?" I asked.

"No, you idiot," the Colonel said. "If there was always a pre-prank, then the Eagle would *expect* two pranks. The last time a pre-prank was used – hmm. Oh, right: 1987. When the pre-prank was cutting off electricity to campus, and then the actual prank was putting five hundred live crickets in the heating ducts of the classrooms. Sometimes you can still hear the chirping."

"Your rote memorization is, like, so impressive," I said.

"You guys are like an old married couple." Alaska smiled. "In a creepy way."

9 **minion**: *Günstling* 14 **lull sb. into sth.**: make sb. feel confident, so they don't expect anything unpleasant 18 **pull sth. off** (infml): succeed in doing sth. difficult 19 **Roman candles**: firework 26 **cricket**: *Grille* 26 **duct**: *Röhre, Leitung* 28 **rote**: *auswending* 30 **creepy**: strange and unpleasant

"You don't know the half of it," the Colonel said. "You should see this kid try to crawl into bed with me at night."

"Hey!"

"Let's get on subject!" Alaska said. "Pre-prank. This weekend, since there's a new moon. We're staying at the barn. You, me, the Colonel, Takumi, and, as a special gift to you, Pudge, Lara Buterskaya."

"The Lara Buterskaya I puked on?"

"She's just shy. She still likes you." Alaska laughed. "Puking made you look – vulnerable."

"Very perky boobs," the Colonel said. "Are you bringing Takumi for me?"

"You need to be single for a while."

"True enough," the Colonel said.

"Just spend a few more months playing video games," she said. "That hand-eye coordination will come in handy when you get to third base."

"Gosh, I haven't heard the base system in so long, I think I've forgotten third base," the Colonel responded. "I would roll my eyes at you, but I can't afford to look away from the screen."

"French, Feel, Finger, Fuck. It's like you skipped third grade," Alaska said.

"I *did* skip third grade," the Colonel answered.

"So," I said, "what's our pre-prank?"

"The Colonel and I will work that out. No need to get you into trouble – yet."

"Oh. Okay. Um, I'm gonna go for a cigarette, then."

I left. It wasn't the first time Alaska had left me out of the loop, certainly, but after we'd been together so much over Thanksgiving, it seemed ridiculous to plan the prank with the Colonel but without me. Whose T-shirts were wet with her tears? Mine. Who'd listened to her read Vonnegut? Me. Who'd been the butt of the world's worst

5 **barn**: *Scheune* 10 **vulnerable**: easily hurt, sensitive 21 **French** (infm): (here) give a deep kiss 28 **out of the loop** (infml): not part of a group of people that is dealing with sth important 32 **be the butt of sth.** (infml): be the person that other people often joke about

knock-knock joke? Me. I walked to the Sunny Konvenience Kiosk across from school and smoked. This never happened to me in Florida, this oh-so-high-school angst about who likes whom more, and I hated myself for letting it happen now. *You don't* have *to care about her*, I told myself. *Screw her*.

four days before

THE COLONEL WOULDN'T TELL ME a word about the preprank, except that it was to be called Barn Night, and that when I packed, I should pack for two days.

Monday, Tuesday, and Wednesday were torture. The Colonel was always with Alaska, and I was never invited. So I spent an inordinate amount of time studying for finals, which helped my GPA considerably. And I finally finished my religion paper.

My answer to the question was straightforward enough, really. Most Christians and Muslims believe in a heaven and a hell, though there's a lot of disagreement within both religions over what, exactly, will get you into one afterlife or the other. Buddhists are more complicated – because of the Buddha's doctrine of *anatta*, which basically says that people don't have eternal souls. Instead, they have a bundle of energy, and that bundle of energy is transitory, migrating from one body to another, reincarnating endlessly until it eventually reaches enlightenment.

I never liked writing concluding paragraphs to papers – where you just repeat what you've already said with phrases like *In summation*, and *To conclude*. I didn't do that – instead I talked about why I thought it was an important question. People, I thought, wanted security. They couldn't bear the idea of death being a big black nothing, couldn't bear the thought of their loved ones not existing, and couldn't even *imagine* themselves not existing. I finally decided that people believed in an afterlife because they couldn't bear not to.

10 **inordinate** (fml): far more than is expected 19 **transitory**: not lasting forever
20 **reincarnate**: be born again in another body

three days before

ON FRIDAY, after a surprisingly successful precalc exam that brought my first set of Culver Creek finals to a close, I packed clothes ("Think New York trendy," the Colonel advised. "Think black. Think sensible. Comfortable, but warm.") and my sleeping bag into a backpack, and we picked up Takumi in his room and walked to the Eagle's house. The Eagle was wearing his only outfit, and I wondered whether he just had thirty identical white buttondown shirts and thirty identical black ties in his closet. I pictured him waking up in the morning, staring at his closet, and thinking, *Hmm … hmm … how about a white shirt and a black tie?* Talk about a guy who could use a wife.

"I'm taking Miles and Takumi home for the weekend to New Hope," the Colonel told him.

"Miles liked his taste of New Hope that much?" the Eagle asked me.

"Yee haw! There's a gonna be a hoedown at the trailer park!" the Colonel said. He could actually have a Southern accent when he wanted to, although like most everyone at Culver Creek, he didn't usually speak with one.

"Hold on one moment while I call your mom," the Eagle said to the Colonel.

Takumi looked at me with poorly disguised panic, and I felt lunch – fried chicken – rising in my stomach. But the Colonel just smiled. "Sure thing."

"Chip and Miles and Takumi will be at your house this weekend? … Yes, ma'am. … Ha! … Okay. Bye now." The Eagle looked up at the Colonel. "Your mom is a wonderful woman." The Eagle smiled.

"You're tellin' me." The Colonel grinned. "See you on Sunday."

As we walked toward the gym parking lot, the Colonel said, "I called her yesterday and asked her to cover for me, and she didn't even ask why. She just said, 'I sure trust you, son,' and hot damn she does."

15 **hoedown** (AE): party with singing and dancing 27 **you're telling me**: I completely agree with you 29 **cover for sb.**: *jdn. decken* 30 **hot damn**: term of exaggeration

Once out of sight of the Eagle's house, we took a sharp right into the woods.

We walked on the dirt road over the bridge and back to the school's barn, a dilapidated leak-prone structure that looked more like a long-abandoned log cabin than a barn. They still stored hay there, although I don't know what for. It wasn't like we had an equestrian program or anything. The Colonel, Takumi, and I got there first, setting up our sleeping bags on the softest bales of hay. It was 6:30.

Alaska came shortly after, having told the Eagle she was spending the weekend with Jake. The Eagle didn't check that story, because Alaska spent at least one weekend there every month, and he knew that her parents never cared. Lara showed up half an hour later. She'd told the Eagle that she was driving to Atlanta to see an old friend from Romania. The Eagle called Lara's parents to make sure that they knew she was spending a weekend off campus, and they didn't mind.

"They trust me." She smiled.

"You don't sound like you have an accent sometimes," I said, which was pretty stupid, but a darn sight better than throwing up on her.

"Eet's only soft i's."

"No soft i's in Russian?" I asked.

"Romanian," she corrected me. Turns out Romanian is a language. Who knew? My cultural sensitivity quotient was going to have to drastically increase if I was going to share a sleeping bag with Lara anytime soon.

Everybody was sitting on sleeping bags, Alaska smoking with flagrant disregard for the overwhelming flammability of the structure, when the Colonel pulled out a single piece of computer paper and read from it.

4 **dilapidated**: old and in a bad condition 4 **leak**: *lecken* 4 **prone**: be likely to do sth. unpleasant 5 **log cabin**: small house built of wood 7 **equestrian**: connected with riding horses 8 **bale**: *Ballen* 20 **darn** (sl): used to emphasize sth.
29 **flagrant** ['fleɪgrənt]: *schamlos* 29 **flammability**: state of being able to catch fire quickly

"The point of this evening's festivities is to prove once and for all that we are to pranking what the Weekday Warriors are to sucking. But we'll also have the opportunity to make life unpleasant for the Eagle, which is always a welcome pleasure. And so," he said, pausing as if for a drumroll, "we fight tonight a battle on three fronts:

"Front One: The pre-prank: We will, as it were, light a fire under the Eagle's ass.

"Front Two: Operation Baldy: Wherein Lara flies solo in a retaliatory mission so elegant and cruel that it could only have been the brainchild of, well, me."

"Hey!" Alaska interrupted. "It was *my* idea."

"Okay, fine. It was Alaska's idea." He laughed. "And finally, Front Three: The Progress Reports: We're going to hack into the faculty computer network and use their grading database to send out letters to Kevin et al.'s families saying that they are failing some of their classes."

"We are definitely going to get expelled," I said.

"I hope you didn't bring the Asian kid along thinking he's a computer genius. Because I am not," Takumi said.

"We're not going to get expelled and I'm the computer genius. The rest of you are muscle and distraction. We won't get expelled even if we get caught because there are no expellable offenses here – well, except for the five bottles of Strawberry Hill in Alaska's backpack, and that will be well hidden. We're just, you know, wreaking a little havoc."

The plan was laid out, and it left no room for error. The Colonel relied so heavily on perfect synchronicity that if one of us messed up even slightly, the endeavor would collapse entirely.

He had printed up individual itineraries for each of us, including times exact to the second. Our watches synchronized, our clothes black, our backpacks on, our breath visible in the cold, our minds

5 **drumroll**: *Trommelwirbel* 8 **baldy** (infml)(n): person who has no hair
8–9 **retaliatory**: taking revenge 10 **brainchild**: idea of one person
15 **et al** (Latin): and other people 25 **wreak havoc**: create great confusion
27 **synchronicity**: fact of two or more things happening at exactly the same time
28 **endeavor** [ɪn'devər]: *Bemühung* 29 **itinerary** [ai'tɪnəreri]: time plan

längerfristig in Leder-Brieftaschen (enthalten Gerbmittel) aufbewahren und eine längere Einwirkung von Sonnen- und Neonlicht vermeiden.

Ermächtigung zum Lastschrifteinzug
Ich ermächtige hiermit das umseitig genannte Unternehmen, den umseitig ausgewiesenen Rechnungsbetrag von meinem durch Konto-Nummer und Bankleitzahl bezeichneten Konto durch Lastschrift einzuziehen.

Ermächtigung zur Adressenweitergabe
Ich weise mein Kreditinstitut an, das durch die umseitig angegebene Bankleitzahl bezeichnet ist, bei Nichteinlösung oder bei Widerspruch gegen die Lastschrift dem Unternehmen oder einem von ihm beauftragten Dritten auf Aufforderung meinen Namen und meine Adresse mitzuteilen. In diesem Falle behält sich das Unternehmen vor, zu meinen Lasten seinen Anspruch gegen mich geltend zu machen. Verzug tritt gemäß § 286 III BGB bei Rücklastschriften ohne Mahnung ein.

Unterschrift (Betrag siehe Vorderseite)

Haltbarkeit des Kassenbons
Dieser Kassenbon ist im Thermo-Druck-Verfahren erstellt und verblasst im Laufe der Zeit. Um diesen Prozess nicht zu beschleunigen, bitte den Kassenbon nicht in Klarsichthüllen (enthalten Weichmacher) oder längerfristig in Leder-Brieftaschen (enthalten Gerbmittel) aufbewahren und eine längere Einwirkung von Sonnen- und Neonlicht vermeiden.

Ermächtigung zum Lastschrifteinzug
Ich ermächtige hiermit das umseitig genannte Unternehmen, den umseitig ausgewiesenen Rechnungsbetrag von meinem durch Konto-Nummer und Bankleitzahl bezeichneten Konto durch Lastschrift einzuziehen.

Ermächtigung zur Adressenweitergabe
Ich weise mein Kreditinstitut an, das durch die umseitig angegebene Bankleitzahl bezeichnet ist, bei Nichteinlösung oder bei Widerspruch gegen die Lastschrift dem Unternehmen oder einem von ihm beauftragten Dritten auf Aufforderung meinen Namen und meine Adresse mitzuteilen. In diesem Falle behält sich das Unternehmen vor, zu meinen Lasten seinen Anspruch gegen mich geltend zu machen. Verzug tritt gemäß § 286 III BGB bei Rücklastschriften ohne Mahnung ein.

Unterschrift (Betrag siehe Vorderseite)

Kennen Sie unseren Onlineshop?

Bei uns können Sie aus
über 7 Millionen Artikeln

filled with the minute details of the plan, our hearts racing, we walked out of the barn together once it was completely dark, around seven. The five of us walking confidently in a row, I'd never felt cooler. The Great Perhaps was upon us, and we were invincible. The plan may have had faults, but we did not.

After five minutes, we split up to go to our destinations. I stuck with Takumi. We were the distraction.

"We're the fucking Marines," he said.

"First to fight. First to die," I agreed nervously.

"Hell yes."

He stopped and opened his bag.

"Not here, dude," I said. "We have to go to the Eagle's."

"I know. I know. Just – hold on." He pulled out a thick headband. It was brown, with a plush fox head on the front. He put it on his head.

I laughed. "What the hell is that?"

"It's my fox hat."

"Your fox hat?"

"Yeah, Pudge. My *fox hat*."

"Why are you wearing your *fox hat?*" I asked.

"Because no one can catch the motherfucking fox."

Two minutes later, we were crouched behind the trees fifty feet from the Eagle's back door. My heart thumped like a techno drumbeat.

"Thirty seconds," Takumi whispered, and I felt the same spooked nervousness that I had felt that first night with Alaska when she grabbed my hand and whispered *run run run run run*. But I stayed put.

I thought: *We are not close enough.*

I thought: *He will not hear it.*

I thought: *He will hear it and be out so fast that we will have no chance.*

I thought: *Twenty seconds*. I was breathing hard and fast.

1 **minute** (adj) [maɪˈnuːt]: very detailed, careful 4 **invincible**: too strong to be defeated or beaten 14 **plush**: *Plüsch*

"Hey, Pudge," Takumi whispered, "you can do this, dude. It's just running."

"Right." *Just running. My knees are good. My lungs are fair. It's just running.*

"Five," he said. "Four. Three. Two. One. Light it. Light it. Light it."

It lit with a sizzle that reminded me of every July Fourth with my family. We stood still for a nanosecond, staring at the fuse, making sure it was lit. *And now*, I thought. *Now. Run run run run run*. But my body didn't move until I heard Takumi shout-whisper, "Go go go fucking go."

And we went.

Three seconds later, a huge burst of pops. It sounded, to me, like the automatic gunfire in Decapitation, except louder. We were twenty steps away already, and I thought my eardrums would burst.

I thought: *Well, he will certainly hear it.*

We ran past the soccer field and into the woods, running uphill and with only the vaguest sense of direction. In the dark, fallen branches and moss-covered rocks appeared at the last possible second, and I slipped and fell repeatedly and worried that the Eagle would catch up, but I just kept getting up and running beside Takumi, away from the classrooms and the dorm circle. We ran like we had golden shoes. I ran like a cheetah – well, like a cheetah that smoked too much. And then, after precisely one minute of running, Takumi stopped and ripped open his backpack.

My turn to count down. Staring at my watch. Terrified. By now, he was surely out. He was surely running. I wondered if he was fast. He was old, but he'd be mad.

"Five four three two one," and the sizzle. We didn't pause that time, just ran, still west. Breath heaving. I wondered if I could do this for thirty minutes. The firecrackers exploded.

The pops ended, and a voice cried out, "STOP RIGHT NOW!" But we did not stop. Stopping was not in the plan.

7 **sizzle**: make the sound of food frying in hot oil 23 **golden shoes**: very fast shoes
23 **cheetah**: *Gepard* 30 **heave**: breathe heavily

"I'm the motherfucking fox," Takumi whispered, both to himself and to me. "No one can catch the fox."

A minute later, I was on the ground. Takumi counted down. The fuse lit. We ran.

But it was a dud. We had prepared for one dud, bringing an extra string of firecrackers. Another, though, would cost the Colonel and Alaska a minute. Takumi crouched down on the ground, lit the fuse, and ran. The popping started. The fireworks *bangbangbanged* in sync with my heartbeat.

When the firecrackers finished, I heard, "STOP OR I'LL CALL THE POLICE!" And though the voice was distant, I could feel his Look of Doom bearing down on me.

"The pigs can't stop the fox; I'm too quick," Takumi said to himself. "I can rhyme while I run; I'm that slick."

The Colonel warned us about the police threat, told us not to worry. The Eagle didn't like to bring the police to campus. Bad publicity. So we ran. Over and under and through all manner of trees and bushes and branches. We fell. We got up. We ran. If he couldn't follow us with the firecrackers, he could sure as hell follow the sound of our whispered *shits* as we tripped over dead logs and fell into briar bushes.

One minute. I knelt down, lit the fuse, ran. *Bang*.

Then we turned north, thinking we'd gotten past the lake. This was key to the plan. The farther we got while still staying on campus, the farther the Eagle would follow us. The farther he followed us, the farther he would be from the classrooms, where the Colonel and Alaska were working their magic. And then we planned to loop back near the classrooms and swing east along the creek until we came to the bridge over our Smoking Hole, where we would rejoin the road and walk back to the barn, triumphant.

But here's the thing: We made a slight error in navigation. We weren't past the lake; instead we were staring at a field and then the lake. Too close to the classrooms to run anywhere but along the

5 **dud**: thing that is useless 8 **in sync**: working at exactly the same speed as sb./sth. else 14 **slick**: (here) skillful 21 **briar bush** (AE): wild bush with thorns

lakefront, I looked over at Takumi, who was running with me stride for stride, and he just said, "Drop one now."

So I dropped down, lit the fuse, and we ran. We were running through a clearing now, and if the Eagle was behind us, he could see us. We got to the south corner of the lake and started running along the shore. The lake wasn't all that big – maybe a quarter mile long, so we didn't have far to go when I saw it.

The swan.

Swimming toward us like a swan possessed. Wings flapping furiously as it came, and then it was on the shore in front of us, making a noise that sounded like nothing else in this world, like all the worst parts of a dying rabbit plus all the worst parts of a crying baby, and there was no other way, so we just ran. I hit the swan at a full run and felt it bite into my ass. And then I was running with a noticeable limp, because my ass was on fire, and I thought to myself, *What the hell is in swan saliva that burns so badly?*

The twenty-third string was a dud, costing us one minute. At that point, I wanted a minute. I was dying. The burning sensation in my left buttock had dulled to an intense aching, magnified each time I landed on my left leg, so I was running like an injured gazelle trying to evade a pride of lions. Our speed, needless to say, had slowed considerably. We hadn't heard the Eagle since we got across the lake, but I didn't think he had turned around. He was trying to lull us into complacency, but it would not work. Tonight, we were invincible.

Exhausted, we stopped with three strings left and hoped we'd given the Colonel enough time. We ran for a few more minutes, until we found the bank of the creek. It was so dark and so still that the tiny stream of water seemed to roar, but I could still hear our hard, fast breaths as we collapsed on wet clay and pebbles beside the creek. Only when we stopped did I look at Takumi. His face and arms were scratched, the fox head now directly over his left ear. Looking at my own arms, I noticed blood dripping from the deeper cuts. There

1 **stride** (n): one long step 15 **limp**: *Hinken* 16 **saliva** [sə'laɪvə]: liquid in your mouth 19 **buttock**: either of the two round soft parts you sit on 19 **dull** (v): become weaker 21 **pride** (n): group of lions 24 **complacency** [kəm'pleɪsənsi]: feeling of satisfaction with yourself 27 **bank**: the side of the creek 29 **clay**: *Lehm*

were, I remembered now, some wicked briar patches, but I was feeling no pain.

Takumi picked thorns out of his leg. "The fox is fucking tired," he said, and laughed.

"The swan bit my ass," I told him.

"I saw." He smiled. "Is it bleeding?" I reached my hand into my pants to check. No blood, so I smoked to celebrate.

"Mission accomplished," I said.

"Pudge, my friend, we are indefuckingstructible."

We couldn't figure out where we were, because the creek doubles back so many times through the campus, so we followed the creek for about ten minutes, figuring we walked half as fast as we ran, and then turned left.

"Left, you think?" Takumi asked.

"I'm pretty lost," I said.

"The fox is pointing left. So left." And, sure enough, the fox took us right back to the barn.

"You're okay!" Lara said as we walked up. "I was worried. I saw the Eagle run out of hees house. He was wearing pajamas. He sure looked mad."

I said, "Well, if he was mad then, I wouldn't want to see him now."

"What took you so long?" she asked me.

"We took the long way home," Takumi said. "Plus Pudge is walking like an old lady with hemorrhoids 'cause the swan bit him on the ass. Where's Alaska and the Colonel?"

"I don't know," Lara said, and then we heard footsteps in the distance, mutters and cracking branches. In a flash, Takumi grabbed our sleeping bags and backpacks and hid them behind bales of hay. The three of us ran through the back of the barn and into the waisthigh grass, and lay down. *He tracked us back to the barn*, I thought. *We fucked everything up*.

8 **accomplish sth.**: succeed in doing or completing sth. 28 **in a flash**: very quickly and suddenly

But then I heard the Colonel's voice, distinct and very annoyed, saying, "Because it narrows the list of possible suspects by twenty-three! Why couldn't you just follow the plan? Christ, where is everybody?"

We walked back to the barn, a bit sheepish from having overreacted. The Colonel sat down on a bale of hay, his elbows on his knees, his head bowed, his palms against his forehead. Thinking.

"Well, we haven't been caught yet, anyway. Okay, first," he said without looking up, "tell me everything else went all right. Lara?"

She started talking. "Yes. Good."

"Can I have some more detail, please?"

"I deed like your paper said. I stayed behind the Eagle's house until I saw heem run after Miles and Takumi, and then I ran behind the dorms. And then I went through the weendow eento Keveen's room. Then I put the stuff een the gel and the conditioner, and then I deed the same thing een Jeff and Longwell's room."

"The stuff?" I asked.

"Undiluted industrial-strength blue number-five hair dye," Alaska said. "Which I bought with your cigarette money. Apply it to wet hair, and it won't wash out for months."

"We dyed their hair blue?"

"Well, technically," the Colonel said, still speaking into his lap, "they're going to dye their own hair blue. But we have certainly made it easier for them. I know you and Takumi did all right, because we're here and you're here, so you did your job. And the good news is that the three assholes who had the gall to prank us have progress reports coming saying that they are failing three classes."

"Uh-oh. What's the bad news?" Lara asked.

"Oh, c'mon," Alaska said. "The *other* good news is that while the Colonel was worried he'd heard something and ran into the woods, I saw to it that twenty other Weekday Warriors *also* have progress reports coming. I printed out reports for all of them, stuffed them into metered school envelopes, and then put them in the mailbox." She turned to the Colonel. "You were sure gone a long time," she said. "The wittle Colonel: so scared of getting expelled."

17 **undiluted**: *unverdünnt* 25 **have the gall to do sth.**: do sth. that shows you are not worried and do not care about the consequences 34 **wittle**: (here) little

The Colonel stood up, towering over the rest of us as we sat. "That is not good news! That was not in the plan! That means there are twenty-three people who the Eagle can eliminate as suspects. Twenty-three people who might figure out it was us and rat!"

"If that happens," Alaska said very seriously, "I'll take the fall."

"Right." The Colonel sighed. "Like you took the fall for Paul and Marya. You'll say that while you were traipsing through the woods lighting firecrackers you were simultaneously hacking into the faculty network and printing out false progress reports on school stationery? Because I'm sure that will fly with the Eagle!"

"Relax, dude," Takumi said. "First off, we're not gonna get caught. Second off, if we do, I'll take the fall with Alaska. You've got more to lose than any of us." The Colonel just nodded. It was an undeniable fact: The Colonel would have no chance at a scholarship to a good school if he got expelled from the Creek.

Knowing that nothing cheered up the Colonel like acknowledging his brilliance, I asked, "So how'd you hack the network?"

"I climbed in the window of Dr. Hyde's office, booted up his computer, and I typed in his password," he said, smiling.

"You guessed it?"

"No. On Tuesday I went into his office and asked him to print me a copy of the recommended reading list. And then I watched him type the password: *J3ckylnhyd3*."

"Well, shit," Takumi said. "I could have done that."

"Sure, but then you wouldn't have gotten to wear that sexy hat," the Colonel said, laughing. Takumi took the headband off and put it in his bag.

"Kevin is going to be pissed about his hair," I said.

"Yeah, well, I'm really pissed about my waterlogged library. Kevin is a blowup doll," Alaska said. "Prick us, we bleed. Prick him, he pops."

3 **suspect** ['- -] (n): person who is suspected of a crime 7 **traipse**: walk somewhere slowly when you are tired and unwilling 13 **undeniable**: true or certain 30 **prick** (v): make a very small hole in sth with a sharp point (reference to a quote from Shakespeare's *The Merchant of Venice*, "If you prick us, do we not bleed?") 31 **pop**: *(auf)platzen*

"It's true," said Takumi. "The guy is a dick. He kind of tried to kill you, after all."

"Yeah, I guess," I acknowledged.

"There are a lot of people here like that," Alaska went on, still fuming. "You know? Fucking blowup-doll rich kids."

But even though Kevin had sort of tried to kill me and all, he really didn't seem worth hating. Hating the cool kids takes an awful lot of energy, and I'd given up on it a long time ago. For me, the prank was just a response to a previous prank, just a golden opportunity to, as the Colonel said, wreak a little havoc. But to Alaska, it seemed to be something else, something more.

I wanted to ask her about it, but she lay back down behind the piles of hay, invisible again. Alaska was done talking, and when she was done talking, that was it. We didn't coax her out for two hours, until the Colonel unscrewed a bottle of wine. We passed around the bottle till I could feel it in my stomach, sour and warm.

I wanted to like booze more than I actually did (which is more or less the precise opposite of how I felt about Alaska). But that night, the booze felt great, as the warmth of the wine in my stomach spread through my body. I didn't like feeling stupid or out of control, but I liked the way it made everything (laughing, crying, peeing in front of your friends) easier. Why did we drink? For me, it was just fun, particularly since we were risking expulsion. The nice thing about the constant threat of expulsion at Culver Creek is that it lends excitement to every moment of illicit pleasure. The bad thing, of course, is that there is always the possibility of actual expulsion.

two days before

I WOKE UP EARLY the next morning, my lips dry and my breath visible in the crisp air. Takumi had brought a camp stove in his backpack, and the Colonel was huddled over it, heating instant coffee. The sun shone bright but could not combat the cold, and I sat with the Colonel and sipped the coffee ("The thing about instant coffee is that

1 **dick** (sl): idiot 5 **fume**: be very angry about sth. 25 **illicit**: illegal
29 **be huddled**: *sich kauern*

it smells pretty good but tastes like stomach bile," the Colonel said), and then one by one, Takumi and Lara and Alaska woke up, and we spent the day hiding out, but loudly. Hiding out loud.

At the barn that afternoon, Takumi decided we needed to have a freestyle contest.

"You start, Pudge," Takumi said. "Colonel Catastrophe, you're our beat box."

"Dude, I can't rap," I pled.

"That's okay. The Colonel can't drop beats, either. Just try and rhyme a little and then send it over to me."

With his hand cupped over his mouth, the Colonel started to make absurd noises that sounded more like farting than bass beats, and I, uh, rapped.

"Um, we're sittin' in the barn and the sun's goin' down / when I was a kid at Burger King I wore a crown / dude, I can't rhyme for shit / so I'll let my boy Takumi rip it."

Takumi took over without pausing. "Damn, Pudge, I'm not sure I'm quite ready / but like *Nightmare on Elm Street*'s Freddy / I've always got the goods to rip shit up / last night I drank wine it was like hiccup hiccup / the Colonel's beats are sick like malaria / when I rock the mike the ladies suffer hysteria / I represent Japan as well as Birmingham / when I was a kid they called me yellow man / but I ain't ashamed a' my skin color / and neither are the countless bitches that call me lover."

Alaska jumped in.

"Oh shit did you just diss the feminine gender / I'll pummel your ass then stick you in a blender / you think I like Tori and Ani so I can't rhyme / but I got flow like Ghostbusters got slime / objectify women and it's fuckin' on / you'll be dead and gone like ancient Babylon."

Takumi picked it up again.

1 **bile**: *Gallenflüssigkeit* 7 **beat box**: machine that produces drum sounds 8 **plead (pled – pled)**: beg 16 **rip** (sl): speak or do sth. with great force 18 **Nightmare on Elm Street**: horror film series 19 **get the goods**: (here) have the skill 21 **mike**: microphone 26 **diss sb.**: show a lack of respect for sb. by saying insulting things about them 26 **pummel sb./sth.**: beat sb./sth. 27 **blender**: *Mixer*

"If my eye offends me I will pluck it out / I got props for girls like old men got gout / oh shit now my rhyming got all whack / Lara help me out and pick up the slack."

Lara rhymed quietly and nervously – and with even more flagrant disregard for the beat than me. "My name's Lara and I'm from Romania / thees is pretty hard, um, I once visited Albania / I love riding in Alaska's Geo / My two best vowels in English are *EO* / I'm not so good weeth the leetle *i*'s / but they make me sound cosmo-poleeteen, right? / Oh, Takumi, I think I'm done / end thees game weeth some fun."

"I drop bombs like Hiroshima, or better yet Nagasaki / when girls hear me flow they think that I'm Rocky / to represent my homeland I still drink sake / the kids don't get my rhymin' so sometimes they mock me / my build ain't small but I wouldn't call it stocky / then again, unlike Pudge, I'm not super gawky / I'm the fuckin' fox and this is my crew / our freestyle's infused with funk like my gym shoes. And we're out."

The Colonel rapped it up with freestyle beat-boxing, and we gave ourselves a round of applause.

"You ripped it up, Alaska," Takumi says, laughing.

"I do what I can to represent the ladies. Lara had my back."

"Yeah, I deed."

And then Alaska decided that although it wasn't nearly dark yet, it was time for us to get shitfaced.

"Two nights in a row is maybe pushing our luck," Takumi said as Alaska opened the wine.

"Luck is for suckers." She smiled and put the bottle to her lips. We had saltines and a hunk of Cheddar cheese provided by the Colonel for dinner, and sipping the warm pink wine out of the bottle

1 **pluck sth.**: pull sth. out (reference to a quotation from the Bible: "And if thine eye offend thee, pluck it out") 1 **prop**: (here) sexual parts of the body 2 **gout** [gaʊt]: *Gicht* 2 **whack** (adj): (here) incorrect, out of order 3 **pick up the slack**: (here) bring sth. into order again 5 **disregard for sth.**: act of ignoring sth. 7 **Geo**: (brand name) small car 13 **sake** ['sɑːki]: Japanese alcoholic drink made from rice 14 **stocky**: short, with a strong body 15 **gawky**: *schlaksig* 16 **infuse with sth.**: make sb./sth. have a particular quality 24 **shitfaced** (sl): (here) very drunk 28 **saltines**: *Salzstangen* 28 **hunk**: large piece of sth.

with our cheese and saltines made for a fine dinner. And when we ran out of cheese, well, all the more room for Strawberry Hill.

"We have to slow down or I'll puke," I remarked after we finished the first bottle.

"I'm sorry, Pudge. I wasn't aware that someone was holding open your throat and pouring wine down it," the Colonel responded, tossing me a bottle of Mountain Dew.

"It's a little charitable to call this shit wine," Takumi cracked.

And then, as if out of nowhere, Alaska announced, "Best Day/Worst Day!"

"Huh?" I asked.

"We are all going to puke if we just drink. So we'll slow it down with a drinking game. Best Day/Worst Day."

"Never heard of it," the Colonel said.

"'Cause I just made it up." She smiled. She lay on her side across two bales of hay, the afternoon light brightening the green in her eyes, her tan skin the last memory of fall. With her mouth half open, it occurred to me that she must already be drunk as I noticed the far-off look in her eyes. *The thousand-yard stare of intoxication*, I thought, and as I watched her with an idle fascination, it occurred to me that, yeah, I was a little drunk, too.

"Fun! What are the rules?" Lara asked.

"Everybody tells the story of their best day. The best storyteller doesn't have to drink. Then everybody tells the story of their worst day, and the best storyteller doesn't have to drink. Then we keep going, second best day, second worst day, until one of y'all quits."

"How do you know it'll be one of us?" Takumi asked.

"'Cause I'm the best drinker and the best storyteller," she answered. Hard to disagree with that logic. "You start, Pudge. Best day of your life."

"Um. Can I take a minute to think of one?"

"Couldn'ta been that good if you have to think about it," the Colonel said.

6 **pour sth.**: *etwas gießen* 8 **crack** (v; infml): joke 19 **intoxication**: *Rausch*
20 **idle** ['aɪdl]: (here) with no particular purpose; lazy

"Fuck you, dude."

"Touchy."

"Best day of my life was today," I said. "And the story is that I woke up next to a very pretty Hungarian girl and it was cold but not too cold and I had a cup of lukewarm instant coffee and ate Cheerios without milk and then walked through the woods with Alaska and Takumi. We skipped stones across the creek, which sounds dumb but it wasn't. I don't know. Like the way the sun is right now, with the long shadows and that kind of bright, soft light you get when the sun isn't quite setting? That's the light that makes everything better, everything prettier, and today, everything just seemed to be in that light. I mean, I didn't do anything. But just sitting here, even if I'm watching the Colonel whittle, or whatever. Whatever. Great day. Today. Best day of my life."

"You think I'm pretty?" Lara said, and laughed, bashful. I thought, *It'd be good to make eye contact with her now*, but I couldn't. "And I'm *Romaneean!*"

"That story ended up being a hell of a lot better than I thought it would be," Alaska said, "but I've still got you beat."

"Bring it on, baby," I said. A breeze picked up, the tall grass outside the barn tilting away from it, and I pulled my sleeping bag over my shoulders to stay warm.

"Best day of my life was January 9, 1997. I was eight years old, and my mom and I went to the zoo on a class trip. I liked the bears. She liked the monkeys. Best day ever. End of story."

"That's it?!" the Colonel said. "That's the best day of your whole life?!"

"Yup."

"I liked eet," Lara said. "I like the monkeys, too."

"Lame," said the Colonel. I didn't think it was lame so much as more of Alaska's intentional vagueness, another example of her furthering her own mysteriousness. But still, even though I knew it was intentional, I couldn't help but wonder: *What's so fucking great about the zoo?* But before I could ask, Lara spoke.

2 **touchy**: sensitive 5 **Cheerios**: type of cereal 13 **whittle**: *schnitzen* 15 **bashful**: shy and easily embarrassed

"'Kay, my turn," said Lara. "Eet's easy. The day I came here. I knew Engleesh and my parents deedn't, and we came off the airplane and my relatives were here, aunts and uncles I had not ever seen, in the airport, and my parents were so happy. I was twelve, and I had always been the leetle baby, but that was the first day that my parents needed me and treated me like a grown-up. Because they did not know the language, right? They need me to order food and to translate tax and immigration forms and everytheeng else, and that was the day they stopped treating me like a keed. Also, in Romania, we were poor. And here, we're kinda reech." She laughed.

"All right." Takumi smiled, grabbing the bottle of wine. "I lose. Because the best day of my life was the day I lost my virginity. And if you think I'm going to tell you that story, you're gonna have to get me drunker than this."

"Not bad," the Colonel said. "That's not bad. Want to know my best day?"

"That's the game, Chip," Alaska said, clearly annoyed.

"Best day of my life hasn't happened yet. But I know it. I see it every day. The best day of my life is the day I buy my mom a huge fucking house. And not just like out in the woods, but in the middle of Mountain Brook, with all the Weekday Warriors' parents. With all y'all's parents. And I'm not buying it with a mortgage either. I'm buying it with cash money, and I am driving my mom there, and I'm going to open her side of the car door and she'll get out and look at this house – this house is like picket fence and two stories and everything, you know – and I'm going to hand her the keys to her house and I'll say, 'Thanks.' Man, she helped fill out my application to this place. And she let me come here, and that's no easy thing when you come from where we do, to let your son go away to school. So that's the best day of my life."

Takumi tilted the bottle up and swallowed a few times, then handed it to me. I drank, and so did Lara, and then Alaska put her head back and turned the bottle upside down, quickly downing the last quarter of the bottle.

1 **'kay**: okay 22 **mortgage** ['mɔːrgɪdʒ]: money borrowed from the bank to buy a house or apartment 25 **picket fence**: *Lattenzaun* 31 **tilt sth.**: *etwas kippen*

As she unscrewed the next bottle, Alaska smiled at the Colonel. "You won that round. Now what's your worst day?"

"Worst day was when my dad left. He's old – he's like seventy now – and he was old when he married my mom, and he *still* cheated on her. And she caught him, and she got pissed, so he hit her. And then she kicked him out, and he left. I was here, and my mom called, and she didn't tell me the whole story with the cheating and everything and the hitting until later. She just said that he was gone and not coming back. And I haven't seen him since. All that day, I kept waiting for him to call me and explain it, but he never did. He never called at all. I at least thought he would say good-bye or something. That was the worst day."

"Shit, you got me beat again," I said. "My worst day was in seventh grade, when Tommy Hewitt pissed on my gym clothes and then the gym teacher said I had to wear my uniform or I'd fail the class. Seventh-grade gym, right? There are worse things to fail. But it was a big deal then, and I was crying, and trying to explain to the teacher what happened, but it was so embarrassing, and he just yelled and yelled and yelled until I put on these piss-soaked shorts and T-shirt. That was the day I stopped caring what people did. I just never cared anymore, about being a loser or not having friends or any of that. So I guess it was good for me in a way, but that moment was awful. I mean, imagine me playing volleyball or whatever in pee-soaked gym clothes while Tommy Hewitt tells everyone what he did. That was the worst day."

Lara was laughing. "I'm sorry, Miles."

"All good," I said. "Just tell me yours so I can laugh at *your* pain," and I smiled, and we laughed together.

"My worst day was probably the same day as my best. Because I left everytheeng. I mean, eet sounds dumb, but my childhood, too, because most twelve-year-olds do not, you know, have to feegure out W-2 forms."

"What's a W-2 form?" I asked.

"That's my point. Eet's for taxes. So. Same day."

4–5 **cheat on sb.**: have sex with another person who is not your partner

Lara had always needed to talk for her parents, I thought, and so maybe she never learned how to talk for herself. And I wasn't great at talking for myself either. We had something important in common, then, a personality quirk I didn't share with Alaska or anybody else, although almost by definition Lara and I couldn't express it to each other. So maybe it was just the way the not-yet-setting sun shone against her lazy dark curls, but at that moment, I wanted to kiss her, and we did not need to talk in order to kiss, and the puking on her jeans and the months of mutual avoidance melted away.

"Eet's your turn, Takumi."

"Worst day of my life," Takumi said. "June 9, 2000. My grandmother died in Japan. She died in a car accident, and I was supposed to leave to go see her two days later. I was going to spend the whole summer with her and my grandfather, but instead I flew over for her funeral, and the only time I really saw what she looked like, I mean other than in pictures, was at her funeral. She had a Buddhist funeral, and they cremated her, but before they did she was on this, like – well, it's not really Buddhist. I mean, religion is complicated there, so it's a little Buddhist and a little Shinto, but y'all don't care – point being that she was on this, like, funeral pyre or whatever. And that's the only time I ever saw her, was just before they burned her up. That was the worst day."

The Colonel lit a cigarette, threw it to me, and lit one of his own. It was eerie, that he could tell when I wanted a cigarette. We *were* like an old married couple. For a moment, I thought, *It's massively unwise to throw lit cigarettes around a barn full of hay*, but then the moment of caution passed, and I just made a sincere effort not to flick ash onto any hay.

"No clear winner yet," the Colonel said. "The field is wide open. Your turn, buddy."

Alaska lay on her back, her hands locked behind her head. She spoke softly and quickly, but the quiet day was becoming a quieter

4 **quirk**: (here) aspect of sb.'s personality or behavior that is a little strange
9 **melt away**: disappear gradually 17 **cremate sb.**: burn a dead body
20 **pyre**: large pile of wood on which a dead body is placed and burned in a funeral ceremony

night – the bugs gone now with the arrival of winter – and we could hear her clearly.

"The day after my mom took me to the zoo where she liked the monkeys and I liked the bears, it was a Friday. I came home from school. She gave me a hug and told me to go do my homework in my room so I could watch TV later. I went into my room, and she sat down at the kitchen table, I guess, and then she screamed, and I ran out, and she had fallen over. She was lying on the floor, holding her head and jerking. And I freaked out. I should have called 911, but I just started screaming and crying until finally she stopped jerking, and I thought she had fallen asleep and that whatever had hurt didn't hurt anymore. So I just sat there on the floor with her until my dad got home an hour later, and he's screaming, 'Why didn't you call 911?' and trying to give her CPR, but by then she was plenty dead. Aneurysm. Worst day. I win. You drink."

And so we did.

No one talked for a minute, and then Takumi asked, "Your dad blamed you?"

"Well, not after that first moment. But yeah. How could he not?"

"Well, you were a little kid," Takumi argued. I was too surprised and uncomfortable to talk, trying to fit this into what I knew about Alaska's family. Her mom told her the knock-knock joke – when Alaska was six. Her mom used to smoke – but didn't anymore, obviously.

"Yeah. I was a little kid. Little kids can dial 911. They do it all the time. Give me the wine," she said, deadpan and emotionless. She drank without lifting her head from the hay.

"I'm sorry," Takumi said.

"Why didn't you ever tell me?" the Colonel asked, his voice soft.

"It never came up." And then we stopped asking questions. *What the hell do you say?*

In the long quiet that followed, as we passed around the wine and slowly became drunker, I found myself thinking about President

14 **CPR = cardiopulmonary resuscitation**: *Wiederbelebungsversuch* 15 **aneurysm** [ˈænjəˌrɪzəm]: *örtlich begrenzte Erweiterung einer Arterie*

William McKinley, the third American president to be assassinated. He lived for several days after he was shot, and toward the end, his wife started crying and screaming, "I want to go, too! I want to go, too!" And with his last measure of strength, McKinley turned to her and spoke his last words: "We are all going."

It was the central moment of Alaska's life. When she cried and told me that she fucked everything up, I knew what she meant now. And when she said she failed everyone, I knew whom she meant. It was the everything and the everyone of her life, and so I could not help but imagine it: I imagined a scrawny eight-year-old with dirty fingers, looking down at her mother convulsing. So she sat down with her dead-or-maybe-not mother, who I imagine was not breathing by then but wasn't yet cold either. And in the time between dying and death, a little Alaska sat with her mother in silence. And then through the silence and my drunkenness, I caught a glimpse of her as she might have been. She must have come to feel so powerless, I thought, that the one thing she might have done – pick up the phone and call an ambulance – never even occurred to her. There comes a time when we realize that our parents cannot save themselves or save us, that everyone who wades through time eventually gets dragged out to sea by the undertow – that, in short, we are all going.

So she became impulsive, scared by her inaction into perpetual action. When the Eagle confronted her with expulsion, maybe she blurted out Marya's name because it was the first that came to mind, because in that moment she didn't want to get expelled and couldn't think past that moment. She was scared, sure. But more importantly, maybe she'd been scared of being paralyzed by fear again.

"We are all going," McKinley said to his wife, and we sure are. There's your labyrinth of suffering. We are all going. Find your way out of that maze.

1 **assassinate sb.**: murder sb. for political reasons 10 **scrawny**: very thin
11 **convulse**: cause a sudden shaking movement in sb's body 21 **undertow** (n): *Sog* 24 **blurt sth. out**: say sth. suddenly and without thinking carefully enough
27 **paralyzed**: unable to feel or move

None of which I said out loud to her. Not then and not ever. We never said another word about it. Instead, it became just another worst day, albeit the worst of the bunch, and as night fell fast, we continued on, drinking and joking.

Later that night, after Alaska stuck her finger down her throat and made herself puke in front of all of us because she was too drunk to walk into the woods, I lay down in my sleeping bag. Lara was lying beside me, in her bag, which was almost touching mine. I moved my arm to the edge of my bag and pushed it so it slightly overlapped with hers. I pressed my hand against hers. I could feel it, although there were two sleeping bags between us. My plan, which struck me as very slick, was to pull my arm out of my sleeping bag and put it into hers, and then hold her hand. It was a good plan, but when I tried to actually get my arm out of the mummy bag, I flailed around like a fish out of water, and nearly dislocated my shoulder. She was laughing – and not with me, at me – but we still didn't speak. Having passed the point of no return, I slid my hand into her sleeping bag anyway, and she stifled a giggle as my fingers traced a line from her elbow to her wrist.

"That teekles," she whispered. So much for me being sexy.

"Sorry," I whispered.

"No, it's a nice teekle," she said, and held my hand. She laced her fingers in mine and squeezed. And then she rolled over and keessed me. I am sure that she tasted like stale booze, but I did not notice, and I'm sure I tasted like stale booze and cigarettes, but she didn't notice. We were kissing.

I thought: *This is good.*

I thought: *I am not bad at this kissing. Not bad at all.*

I thought: *I am clearly the greatest kisser in the history of the universe.*

3 **bunch** (n): number of things of the same type 12 **slick**: clever 14 **mummy**: *Mumie* 14 **flail around**: move around without control 15 **dislocate sth.**: put sth. (esp. a bone) out of its normal position 18 **stifle sth.**: suppress sth. 20 **teekle:** tickle 24 **stale**: no longer fresh

Suddenly she laughed and pulled away from me. She wiggled a hand out of her sleeping bag and wiped her face. "You slobbered on my nose," she said, and laughed.

I laughed, too, trying to give her the impression that my nose-slobbering kissing style was intended to be funny. "I'm sorry." To borrow the base system from Alaska, I hadn't hit more than five singles in my entire life, so I tried to chalk it up to inexperience. "I'm a bit new at this," I said.

"Eet was a nice slobbering," she said, laughed, and kissed me again. Soon we were entirely out of our sleeping bags, making out quietly. She lay on top of me, and I held her small waist in my hands. I could feel her breasts against my chest, and she moved slowly on top of me, her legs straddling me. "You feel nice," she said.

"You're beautiful," I said, and smiled at her. In the dark, I could make out the outline of her face and her large, round eyes blinking down at me, her eyelashes almost fluttering against my forehead.

"Could the two people who are making out please be quiet?" the Colonel asked loudly from his sleeping bag. "Those of us who are not making out are drunk and tired."

"Mostly. Drunk," Alaska said slowly, as if enunciation required great effort.

We had almost never talked, Lara and I, and we didn't get a chance to talk anymore because of the Colonel. So we kissed quietly and laughed softly with our mouths and our eyes. After so much kissing that it almost started to get boring, I whispered, "Do you want to be my girlfriend?" And she said, "Yes please," and smiled. We slept together in her sleeping bag, which felt a little crowded, to be honest, but was still nice. I had never felt another person against me as I slept. It was a fine end to the best day of my life.

2 **slobber**: *sabbern* 7 **chalk sth. up to sth. else**: consider that sth is caused by sth. else 20 **enunciation**: act of saying or pronouncing words clearly

one day before

THE NEXT MORNING, a term I use loosely since it was not yet dawn, the Colonel shook me awake. Lara was wrapped in my arms, folded into my body.

"We gotta go, Pudge. Time to roll up."

"Dude. Sleeping."

"You can sleep after we check in. IT'S TIME TO GO!" he shouted.

"All right. All right. No screaming. Head hurts." And it did. I could feel last night's wine in my throat and my head throbbed like it had the morning after my concussion. My mouth tasted like a skunk had crawled into my throat and died. I made an effort not to exhale near Lara as she groggily extricated herself from the sleeping bag.

We packed everything quickly, threw our empty bottles into the tall grass of the field – littering was an unfortunate necessity at the Creek, since no one wanted to throw an empty bottle of booze in a campus trash can – and walked away from the barn. Lara grabbed my hand and then shyly let go. Alaska looked like a train wreck, but insisted on pouring the last few sips of Strawberry Hill into her cold instant coffee before chucking the bottle behind her.

"Hair of the dog," she said.

"How ya doin'?" the Colonel asked her.

"I've had better mornings."

"Hungover?"

"Like an alcoholic preacher on Sunday morning."

"Maybe you shouldn't drink so much," I suggested.

"Pudge." She shook her head and sipped the cold coffee and wine. "Pudge, what you must understand about me is that I am a deeply unhappy person."

We walked side by side down the washed-out dirt road on our way back to campus. Just after we reached the bridge, Takumi stopped,

8 **throb**: *pochen, hämmern* 10 **skunk**: *Stinktier* 19 **chuck sth.** (infml): throw sth. carelessly 20 **hair of the dog** (infml): alcohol that you drink in order to make you feel better when you have drunk too much alcohol the night before 23 **hungover**: *verkatert*

said "uh-oh," got on his hands and knees, and puked a volcano of yellow and pink.

"Let it out," Alaska said. "You'll be fine."

He finished, stood up, and said, "I finally found something that can stop the fox. The fox cannot summit Strawberry Hill."

Alaska and Lara walked to their rooms, planning to check in with the Eagle later in the day, while Takumi and I stood behind the Colonel as he knocked on the Eagle's door at 9:00 A.M.

"Y'all are home early. Have fun?"

"Yes sir," the Colonel said.

"How's your mom, Chip?"

"She's doing well, sir. She's in good shape."

"She feed y'all well?"

"Oh yes sir," I said. "She tried to fatten me up."

"You need it. Y'all have a good day."

"Well, I don't think he suspected anything," the Colonel said on our way back to Room 43. "So maybe we actually pulled it off." I thought about going over to see Lara, but I was pretty tired, so I just went to bed and slept through my hangover.

It was not an eventful day. I should have done extraordinary things. I should have sucked the marrow out of life. But on that day, I slept eighteen hours out of a possible twenty-four.

the last day

THE NEXT MORNING, the first Monday of the new semester, the Colonel came out of the shower just as my alarm went off.

As I pulled on my shoes, Kevin knocked once and then opened the door, stepping inside.

"You're looking good," the Colonel said casually. Kevin now sported a crew cut, a small patch of short blue hair on each side of his head, just above the ear. His lower lip jutted out – the morning's

5 **summit sth.**: *etwas erklimmen* 21 **marrow**: *(Knochen)mark* 28 **crew cut**: *Bürstenschnitt*

first dip. He walked over to our COFFEE TABLE, picked up a can of Coke, and spit into it.

"You almost didn't get me. I noticed it in my conditioner and got right back in the shower. But I didn't notice it in my gel. It didn't show up in Jeff 's hair at all. But Longwell and me, we had to go with the Marine look. Thank God I have clippers."

"It suits you," I said, although it didn't. The short hair accentuated his features, specifically his too-close-together beady eyes, which did not stand up well to accentuation. The Colonel was trying hard to look tough – ready for whatever Kevin might do – but it's hard to look tough when you're only wearing an orange towel.

"Truce?"

"Well, your troubles aren't over, I'm afraid," the Colonel said, referring to the mailed-but-not-yet-received progress reports.

"A'ight. If you say so. We'll talk when it's over, I guess."

"I guess so," the Colonel said. As Kevin walked out, the Colonel said, "Take the can you spit in, you unhygienic shit." Kevin just closed the door behind him. The Colonel grabbed the can, opened the door, and threw it at Kevin – missing him by a good margin.

"Jeez, go easy on the guy."

"No truce yet, Pudge."

I spent that afternoon with Lara. We were very cutesy, even though we didn't know the first thing about each other and barely talked. But we made out. She grabbed my butt at one point, and I sort of jumped. I was lying down, but I did the best version of jumping that one can do lying down, and she said, "Sorry," and I said, "No, it's okay. It's just a little sore from the swan."

We walked to the TV room together, and I locked the door. We were watching *The Brady Bunch*, which she had never seen. The episode, where the Bradys visit the gold-mining ghost town and they all get locked up in the one-room jail by some crazy old gold panner

6 **clippers** (pl): machine for cutting hair 8 **beady**: (of eyes) small, round and bright 12 **truce**: *Waffenstillstand* 22 **cutesy** (infml): too nice in a way that is not realistic 27 **sore**: painful 31 **panner** (infml): person who searches for gold

with a scraggly white beard, was especially horrible, and gave us a lot to laugh about. Which is good, since we didn't have much to *talk* about.

Just as the Bradys were getting locked in jail, Lara randomly asked me, "Have you ever gotten a blow job?"

"Um, that's out of the blue," I said.

"The blue?"

"Like, you know, out of left field."

"Left field?"

"Like, in baseball. Like, out of nowhere. I mean, what made you think of that?"

"I've just never geeven one," she answered, her little voice dripping with seductiveness. It was so brazen. I thought I would explode. I never thought. I mean, from Alaska, hearing that stuff was one thing. But to hear her sweet little Romanian voice go so sexy all of the sudden ...

"No," I said. "I never have."

"Think it would be fun?"

DO I!?!?!?!?!?!?! "Um. yeah. I mean, you don't have to."

"I think I want to," she said, and we kissed a little, and then. And then with me sitting watching *The Brady Bunch*, watching Marcia Marcia Marcia up to her Brady antics, Lara unbuttoned my pants and pulled my boxers down a little and pulled out my penis.

"Wow," she said.

"What?"

She looked up at me, but didn't move, her face nanometers away from my penis. "It's weird."

"What do you mean *weird?*"

"Just beeg, I guess."

I could live with that kind of weird. And then she wrapped her hand around it and put it into her mouth.

And waited.

1 **scraggly** (infml): thin and growing in a way that is not even 5 **blow job** (sl): act of taking a man's penis in the mouth 6 **out of the blue**: unexpected
13 **seductiveness**: *Verführung* **brazen** ['breɪzən]: open and without shame
22 **antics**: *Mätzchen*

We were both very still. She did not move a muscle in her body, and I did not move a muscle in mine. I knew that at this point something else was supposed to happen, but I wasn't quite sure what.

She stayed still. I could feel her nervous breath. For minutes, for as long as it took the Bradys to steal the key and unlock themselves from the ghost-town jail, she lay there, stock-still with my penis in her mouth, and I sat there, waiting.

And then she took it out of her mouth and looked up at me quizzically.

"Should I do somethееng?"

"Um. I don't know," I said. Everything I'd learned from watching porn with Alaska suddenly exited my brain. I thought maybe she should move her head up and down, but wouldn't that choke her? So I just stayed quiet.

"Should I, like, bite?"

"Don't bite! I mean, I don't think. I think – I mean, that felt good That was nice. I don't know if there's something else."

"I mean, you deedn't –"

"Um. Maybe we should ask Alaska."

So we went to her room and asked Alaska. She laughed and laughed. Sitting on her bed, she laughed until she cried. She walked into the bathroom, returned with a tube of toothpaste, and showed us. In detail. Never have I so wanted to be Crest Complete.

Lara and I went back to her room, where she did exactly what Alaska told her to do, and I did exactly what Alaska said I would do, which was die a hundred little ecstatic deaths, my fists clenched, my body shaking. It was my first orgasm with a girl, and afterward, I was embarrassed and nervous, and so, clearly, was Lara, who finally broke the silence by asking, "So, want to do some homework?"

There was little to do on the first day of the semester, but she read for her English class. I picked up a biography of Argentinian revolutionary Che Guevara – whose face adorned a poster on the wall – that Lara's roommate had on her bookshelf, then I lay down

14 **choke sb.**: make sb. unable to breathe 24 **Crest Complete**: (brand name) toothpaste 33 **adorn sth.**: be on sth. to make it look more attractive

next to Lara on the bottom bunk. I began at the end, as I sometimes did with biographies I had no intention of reading all the way through, and found his last words without too much searching. Captured by the Bolivian army, Guevara said, “Shoot, coward. You are only going to kill a man.” I thought back to Simón Bolívar’s last words in García Márquez’s novel – “How will I ever get out of this labyrinth!” South American revolutionaries, it would seem, died with flair. I read the last words out loud to Lara. She turned on her side, placing her head on my chest.

“Why do you like last words so much?”

Strange as it might seem, I’d never really thought about why. “I don’t know,” I said, placing my hand against the small of her back. “Sometimes, just because they’re funny. Like in the Civil War, a general named Sedgwick said, ‘They couldn’t hit an elephant from this dis–’ and then he got shot.” She laughed. “But a lot of times, people die how they live. And so last words tell me a lot about who people were, and why they became the sort of people biographies get written about. Does that make sense?”

“Yeah,” she said.

“Yeah?” Just yeah?

“Yeah,” she said, and then went back to reading.

I didn’t know how to talk to her. And I was frustrated with trying, so after a little while, I got up to go.

I kissed her good-bye. I could do that, at least.

I picked up Alaska and the Colonel at our room and we walked down to the bridge, where I repeated in embarrassing detail the fellatio fiasco.

“I can’t believe she went down on you twice in one day,” the Colonel said.

“Only technically. Really just once,” Alaska corrected.

“Still. I mean. Still. Pudge got his hog smoked.”

“The poor Colonel,” Alaska said with a rueful smile. “I’d give you a pity blow, but I really am attached to Jake.”

27 **fellatio** [fe'leɪʃioʊ] (fml): oral sex 31 **hog** (sl): penis 31 **smoke sth.** (sl): *etwas lutschen* 32 **rueful**: *reuevoll, traurig*

"That's just creepy," the Colonel said. "You're only supposed to flirt with Pudge."

"But Pudge has a *giiirrrrlllfriend*." She laughed.

That night, the Colonel and I walked down to Alaska's room to celebrate our Barn Night success. She and the Colonel had been celebrating a lot the past couple days, and I didn't feel up to climbing Strawberry Hill, so I sat and munched on pretzels while Alaska and the Colonel drank wine from paper cups with flowers on them.

"We ain't drinkin' out the bottle tonight, hun," the Colonel said. "We classin' it up!"

"It's an old-time Southern drinking contest," Alaska responded. "We's a-gonna treat Pudge to an evening of real Southern livin': We go'n match each other Dixie cup for Dixie cup till the lesser drinker falls."

And that is pretty much what they did, pausing only to turn out the lights at 11:00 so the Eagle wouldn't drop by. They chatted some, but mostly they drank, and I drifted out of the conversation and ended up squinting through the dark, looking at the book spines in Alaska's Life Library. Even minus the books she'd lost in the mini-flood, I could have stayed up until morning reading through the haphazard stacks of titles. A dozen white tulips in a plastic vase were precariously perched atop one of the book stacks, and when I asked her about them, she just said, "Jake and my's anniversary," and I didn't care to continue that line of dialogue, so I went back to scanning titles, and I was just wondering how I could go about learning Edgar Allan Poe's last words (for the record: "Lord help my poor soul") when I heard Alaska say, "Pudge isn't even listening to us."

And I said, "I'm listening."

"We were just talking about Truth or Dare. Played out in seventh grade or still cool?"

7 **munch on sth.:** eat sth steadily and noisily 9 **hun**: (term of affection): honey 12 **treat sb. to sth.**: entertain sb. with sth. special 13 **Dixie cup** (brand name): *Plastikbecher* 18 **book spine**: *Buchrücken* 22 **perch (on) sth**: be placed on the top of sth. 23 **anniversary**: *Jahrestag* 30 **Truth or Dare**: party game

"Never played it," I said. "No friends in seventh grade."

"Well, that does it!" she shouted, a bit too loud given the late hour and also given the fact that she was openly drinking wine in the room. "Truth or Dare!"

"All right," I agreed, "but I'm not making out with the Colonel."

The Colonel sat slumped in the corner. "Can't make out. Too drunk."

Alaska started. "Truth or Dare, Pudge."

"Dare."

"Hook up with me."

So I did.

It was that quick. I laughed, looked nervous, and she leaned in and tilted her head to the side, and we were kissing. Zero layers between us. Our tongues dancing back and forth in each other's mouth until there was no her mouth and my mouth but only our mouths intertwined. She tasted like cigarettes and Mountain Dew and wine and Chap Stick. Her hand came to my face and I felt her soft fingers tracing the line of my jaw. We lay down as we kissed, she on top of me, and I began to move beneath her. I pulled away for a moment, to say, "What is going on here?" and she put one finger to her lips and we kissed again. A hand grabbed one of mine and she placed it on her stomach. I moved slowly on top of her and felt her arching her back fluidly beneath me.

I pulled away again. "What about Lara? Jake?" Again, she *sshed* me. "Less tongue, more lips," she said, and I tried my best. I thought the tongue was the whole point, but she was the expert.

"Christ," the Colonel said quite loudly. "That wretched beast, drama, draws nigh."

But we paid no attention. She moved my hand from her waist to her breast, and I felt cautiously, my fingers moving slowly under her shirt but over her bra, tracing the outline of her breasts and then cupping one in my hand, squeezing softly. "You're good at that," she

10 **hook up with sb.** (sl): (here) become intimate with sb. 16 **intertwine**: *verschlingen* 16 **Mountain Dew**: (brand name) type of lemonade 17 **Chap Stick**: (brand name) type of lip balm to prevent sore lips in cold weather

whispered. Her lips never left mine as she spoke. We moved together, my body between her legs.

"This is so fun," she whispered, "but I'm so sleepy. To be continued?" She kissed me for another moment, my mouth straining to stay near hers, and then she moved from beneath me, placed her head on my chest, and fell asleep instantly.

We didn't have sex. We never got naked. I never touched her bare breast, and her hands never got lower than my hips. It didn't matter. As she slept, I whispered, "I love you, Alaska Young."

Just as I was falling asleep, the Colonel spoke. "Dude, did you just make out with Alaska?"

"Yeah."

"This is going to end poorly," he said to himself.

And then I was asleep. That deep, can-still-taste-her-in-my-mouth sleep, that sleep that is not particularly restful but is difficult to wake from all the same. And then I heard the phone ring. I think. And I think, although I can't know, that I felt Alaska get up. I think I heard her leave. I think. How long she was gone is impossible to know.

But the Colonel and I both woke up when she returned, whenever that was, because she slammed the door. She was sobbing, like that post-Thanksgiving morning but worse.

"I have to get out of here!" she cried.

"What's wrong?" I asked.

"I forgot! God, how many times can I fuck up?" she said. I didn't even have time to wonder what she forgot before she screamed, "I JUST HAVE TO GO. HELP ME GET OUT OF HERE!"

"Where do you need to go?"

She sat down and put her head between her legs, sobbing. "Just please distract the Eagle right now so I can go. Please."

The Colonel and I, at the same moment, equal in our guilt, said, "Okay."

"Just don't turn on your lights," the Colonel said. "Just drive slow and don't turn on your lights. Are you sure you're okay?"

"Fuck," she said. "Just get rid of the Eagle for me," she said, her sobs childlike half screams. "God oh God, I'm so sorry."

4 **strain**: make an effort to do sth.

"Okay," the Colonel said. "Start the car when you hear the second string."

We left.

We did not say: *Don't drive. You're drunk.*

We did not say: *We aren't letting you in that car when you are upset.*

We did not say: *We insist on going with you.*

We did not say: *This can wait until tomorrow. Anything – everything – can wait.*

We walked to our bathroom, grabbed the three strings of leftover firecrackers from beneath the sink, and ran to the Eagle's. We weren't sure that it would work again.

But it worked well enough. The Eagle tore out of his house as soon as the first string of firecrackers started popping – he was waiting for us, I suppose – and we headed for the woods and got him in deeply enough that he never heard her drive away. The Colonel and I doubled back, wading through the creek to save time, slipped in through the back window of Room 43, and slept like babies.

2 **string**: (here) series of firecrackers

after

the day after

THE COLONEL SLEPT the not-restful sleep of the drunk, and I lay on my back on the bottom bunk, my mouth tingling and alive as if still kissing, and we would have likely slept through our morning classes had the Eagle not awoken us at 8:00 with three quick knocks. I rolled over as he opened the door, and the morning light rushed into the room.

"I need y'all to go to the gym," he said. I squinted toward him, the Eagle himself backlit into invisibility by the too bright sun. "Now," he added, and I knew it. We were done for. Caught. Too many progress reports. Too much drinking in too short a time. Why did they have to drink last night? And then I could taste her again, the wine and the cigarette smoke and the Chap Stick and Alaska, and I wondered if she had kissed me because she was drunk. *Don't expel me,* I thought. *Don't. I have just begun to kiss her.*

And as if answering my prayers, the Eagle said, "You're not in any trouble. But you need to go to the gym now."

I heard the Colonel rolling over above me. "What's wrong?"

"Something terrible has happened," the Eagle said, and then closed the door.

*

2 **tingle**: *kribbeln* 9 **be done for**: be caught and punished for doing sth. illegal

As he grabbed a pair of jeans lying on the floor, the Colonel said, “This happened a couple years ago. When Hyde’s wife died. I guess it’s the Old Man himself now. Poor bastard really *didn’t* have many breaths left.” He looked up at me, his half-open eyes bloodshot, and yawned.

“You look a little hungover,” I observed.

He closed his eyes. “Well, then I’m putting up a good front, Pudge, ’cause I’m actually a lot hungover.”

“I kissed Alaska.”

“Yeah. I wasn’t *that* drunk. Let’s go.”

We walked across the dorm circle to the gym. I sported baggy jeans, a sweatshirt with no shirt underneath, and a bad case of bedhead. All the teachers were in the dorm circle knocking on doors, but I didn’t see Dr. Hyde. I imagined him lying dead in his house, wondered who had found him, how they even knew he was missing before he failed to show up for class.

“I don’t see Dr. Hyde,” I told the Colonel.

“Poor bastard.”

The gym was half full by the time we arrived. A podium had been set up in the middle of the basketball court, close to the bleachers. I sat in the second row, with the Colonel directly in front of me. My thoughts were split between sadness for Dr. Hyde and excitement about Alaska, remembering the up-close sight of her mouth whispering, “To be continued?”

And it did not occur to me – not even when Dr. Hyde shuffled into the gym, taking tiny, slow steps toward the Colonel and me.

I tapped the Colonel on the shoulder and said, “Hyde’s here,” and the Colonel said, “Oh shit,” and I said, “What?” and he said, “Where’s Alaska?” and I said, “No,” and he said, “Pudge, is she here or not?” and then we both stood up and scanned the faces in the gym.

The Eagle walked up to the podium and said, “Is everyone here?”

“No,” I said to him. “Alaska isn’t here.”

4 **bloodshot**: (of eyes) red 7 **put up good front**: *eine gute Erscheinung machen*
11 **sport sth.**: wear sth.

The Eagle looked down. "Is everyone else here?"

"Alaska isn't here!"

"Okay, Miles. Thank you."

"We can't start without Alaska."

The Eagle looked at me. He was crying, noiselessly. Tears just rolled from his eyes to his chin and then fell onto his corduroy pants. He stared at me, but it was not the Look of Doom. His eyes blinking the tears down his face, the Eagle looked, for all the world, sorry.

"Please, sir," I said. "Can we please wait for Alaska?" I felt all of them staring at us, trying to understand what I now knew, but didn't quite believe.

The Eagle looked down and bit his lower lip. "Last night, Alaska Young was in a terrible accident." His tears came faster, then. "And she was killed. Alaska has passed away."

For a moment, everyone in the gym was silent, and the place had never been so quiet, not even in the moments before the Colonel ridiculed opponents at the free-throw stripe. I stared down at the back of the Colonel's head. I just stared, looking at his thick and bushy hair. For a moment, it was so quiet that you could hear the sound of not-breathing, the vacuum created by 190 students shocked out of air.

I thought: *It's all my fault.*

I thought: *I don't feel very good.*

I thought: *I'm going to throw up.*

I stood up and ran outside. I made it to a trash can outside the gym, five feet from the double doors, and heaved toward Gatorade bottles and half-eaten McDonald's. But nothing much came out. I just heaved, my stomach muscles tightening and my throat opening and a gasping, guttural *blech*, going through the motions of vomiting over and over again. In between gags and coughs, I sucked air in hard. Her mouth. Her dead, cold mouth. To not be continued. I knew she was drunk. Upset. Obviously you don't let someone drive

17 **free-throw stripe**: (in basketball) line from which a player throws a ball at the basket when he is given a free throw 29 **blech**: expression of disgust 30 **gag** (n): unpleasant feeling in your mouth and stomach

drunk and pissed off. *Obviously*. And Christ, Miles, what the hell is wrong with you? And then comes the puke, finally, splashing onto the trash. And here is whatever of her I had left in my mouth, here in this trash can. And then it comes again, more – and then okay, calm down, okay, seriously, she's not dead.

She's not dead. She's alive. She's alive somewhere. She's in the woods. Alaska is hiding in the woods and she's not dead, she's just hiding. She's just playing a trick on us. This is just an Alaska Young Prank Extraordinaire. It's Alaska being Alaska, funny and playful and not knowing when or how to put on the brakes.

And then I felt much better, because she had not died at all.

I walked back into the gym, and everyone seemed to be in various stages of disintegration. It was like something you see on TV, like a *National Geographic* special on funeral rituals. I saw Takumi standing over Lara, his hands on her shoulders. I saw Kevin with his crew cut, his head buried between his knees. A girl named Molly Tan, who'd studied with us for precalc, wailed, beating balled fists against her thighs. All these people I sort of knew and sort of didn't, and all of them disintegrating, and then I saw the Colonel, his knees tucked into his chest, lying on his side on the bleachers, Madame O'Malley sitting next to him, reaching toward his shoulder but not actually touching it. The Colonel was screaming. He would inhale, and then scream. Inhale. Scream. Inhale. Scream.

I thought, at first, that it was only yelling. But after a few breaths, I noticed a rhythm. And after a few more, I realized that the Colonel was saying words. He was screaming, "I'm so sorry."

Madame O'Malley grabbed his hand. "You've got nothing to be sorry for, Chip. There was nothing you could have done." But if only she knew.

And I just stood there, looking at the scene, thinking about her not dead, and I felt a hand on my shoulder and turned around to see the Eagle, and I said, "I think she's playing a dumb prank," and he said, "No, Miles, no, I'm sorry," and I felt the heat in my cheeks and

9 **extraordinaire**: being a good example of sth. 13 **disintegration**: act of falling apart 17 **wail**: make a long loud high cry because you are sad

said, “She’s really good. She could pull this off,” and he said, “I saw her. I’m sorry.”

“What happened?”

“Somebody was setting off firecrackers in the woods,” he said, and I closed my eyes tight, the ineluctable fact of the matter at hand: I had killed her. “I went out after them, and I guess she drove off campus. It was late. She was on I-65 just south of downtown. A truck had jackknifed, blocking both lanes. A police car had just gotten to the scene. She hit the cruiser without ever swerving. I believe she must have been very intoxicated. The police said they smelled alcohol.”

“How do you know?” I asked.

“I saw her, Miles. I talked to the police. It was instant. The steering wheel hit her chest. I’m so sorry.”

And I said, you saw her and he said yes and I said how did she look and he said, just a bit of blood coming out of her nose, and I sat down on the floor of the gym. I could hear the Colonel still screaming, and I could feel hands on my back as I hunched forward, but I could only see her lying naked on a metal table, a small trickle of blood falling out of her half-teardrop nose, her green eyes open, staring off into the distance, her mouth turned up just enough to suggest the idea of a smile, and she had felt so warm against me, her mouth soft and warm on mine.

The Colonel and I are walking back to our dorm room in silence. I am staring at the ground beneath me. I cannot stop thinking that she is dead, and I cannot stop thinking that she cannot possibly be dead. People do not just die. I can’t catch my breath. I feel afraid, like someone has told me they’re going to kick my ass after school and now it’s sixth period and I know full well what’s coming. It is so cold today – literally freezing – and I imagine running to the creek and diving in headfirst, the creek so shallow that my hands scrape against the rocks, and my body slides into the cold water, the shock

5 **ineluctable** [- - '- - -] (fml): that you cannot avoid 8 **jacknife** (v): form a V-shape 9 **cruiser** (AE): police car 9 **swerve**: change direction suddenly 10 **intoxicated**: under the influence of alcohol or drugs

of the cold giving way to numbness, and I would stay there, float down with that water first to the Cahaba River, then to the Alabama River, then to Mobile Bay and the Gulf of Mexico.

I want to melt into the brown, crunchy grass that the Colonel and I step on as we silently make our way back to our room. His feet are so large, too large for his short body, and the new generic tennis shoes he wears since his old ones were pissed in look almost like clown shoes. I think of Alaska's flip-flops clinging to her blue toes as we swung on the swing down by the lake. Will the casket be open? Can a mortician re-create her smile? I could still hear her saying it: "This is so fun, but I'm so sleepy. To be continued?"

Nineteenth-century preacher Henry Ward Beecher's last words were "Now comes the mystery." The poet Dylan Thomas, who liked a good drink at least as much as Alaska, said, "I've had eighteen straight whiskeys. I do believe that's a record," before dying. Alaska's favorite was playwright Eugene O'Neill: "Born in a hotel room, and – God damn it – died in a hotel room." Even car-accident victims sometimes have time for last words. Princess Diana said, "Oh God. What's happened?" Movie star James Dean said, "They've got to see us," just before slamming his Porsche into another car. I know so many last words. But I will never know hers.

I am several steps in front of him before I realize that the Colonel has fallen down. I turn around, and he is lying on his face. "We have to get up, Chip. We have to get up. We just have to get to the room."

The Colonel turns his face from the ground to me and looks me dead in the eye and says, "I. Can't. Breathe."

But he *can* breathe, and I know this because he is hyperventilating, breathing as if trying to blow air back into the dead. I pick him up, and he grabs onto me and starts sobbing, again saying, "I'm so sorry," over and over again. We have never hugged before, me and the Colonel, and there is nothing much to say, because he ought to be

1 **numbness** ['nvmnəs]: *Taubheit* 10 **mortician**: person whose job is to prepare the bodies of dead people for viewing before they are buried 29 **sob**: *schluchzen*

sorry, and I just put my hand on the back of his head and say the only true thing. "I'm sorry, too."

two days after

I DIDN'T SLEEP THAT NIGHT. Dawn was slow in coming, and even when it did, the sun shining bright through the blinds, the rickety radiator couldn't keep us warm, so the Colonel and I sat wordlessly on the couch. He read the almanac.

The night before, I'd braved the cold to call my parents, and this time when I said, "Hey, it's Miles," and my mom answered with, "What's wrong? Is everything okay?" I could safely tell her no, everything was not okay. My dad picked up the line then.

"What's wrong?" he asked.

"Don't yell," my mother said.

"I'm not yelling; it's just the phone."

"Well, talk quieter," she said, and so it took some time before I could say anything, and then once I could, it took some time to say the words in order – my friend Alaska died in a car crash. I stared at the numbers and messages scrawled on the wall by the phone.

"Oh, Miles," Mom said. "I'm so sorry, Miles. Do you want to come home?"

"No," I said. "I want to be here … I can't believe it," which was still partly true.

"That's just awful," my dad said. "Her poor parents." *Poor parent*, I thought, and wondered about her dad. I couldn't even imagine what my parents would do if I died. Driving drunk. God, if her father ever found out, he would disembowel the Colonel and me.

"What can we do for you right now?" my mom asked.

"I just needed you to pick up. I just needed you to answer the phone, and you did." I heard a sniffle behind me – from cold or grief, I didn't know – and told my parents, "Someone's waiting for the phone. I gotta go."

4 **rickety**: not strong 7 **brave sth.**: have to deal with sth. difficult
25 **disembowel sb.**: *jdm. den Bauch aufschlitzen* 28 **sniffle**: *Schniefen*

All night, I felt paralyzed into silence, terrorized. What was I so afraid of, anyway? The thing had happened. She was dead. She was warm and soft against my skin, my tongue in her mouth, and she was laughing, trying to teach me, make me better, promising to be continued. And now.

And now she was colder by the hour, more dead with every breath I took. I thought: *That is the fear: I have lost something important, and I cannot find it, and I need it. It is fear like if someone lost his glasses and went to the glasses store and they told him that the world had run out of glasses and he would just have to do without.*

Just before eight in the morning, the Colonel announced to no one in particular, "I think there are bufriedos at lunch today."

"Yeah," I said. "Are you hungry?"

"God no. But she named them, you know. They were called fried burritos when we got here, and Alaska started calling them bufriedos, and then everyone did, and then finally Maureen officially changed the name." He paused. "I don't know what to do, Miles."

"Yeah. I know."

"I finished memorizing the capitals," he said.

"Of the states?"

"No. That was fifth grade. Of the countries. Name a country."

"Canada," I said.

"Something hard."

"Um. Uzbekistan?"

"Tashkent." He didn't even take a moment to think. It was just there, at the tip of his tongue, as if he'd been waiting for me to say "Uzbekistan" all along. "Let's smoke."

We walked to the bathroom and turned on the shower, and the Colonel pulled a pack of matches from his jeans and struck a match against the matchbook. It didn't light. Again, he tried and failed, and again, smacking at the matchbook with a crescendoing fury until he finally threw the matches to the ground and screamed, "GODDAMN IT!"

31 **matchbook**: *Streichholzbrief* 31 **crescendo** (v): become larger or louder

"It's okay," I said, reaching into my pocket for a lighter.

"No, Pudge, it's not," he said, throwing down his cigarette and standing up, suddenly pissed. "Goddamn it! God, how did this happen? How could she be so stupid! She just never thought anything through. So goddamned impulsive. Christ. It is not okay. I can't believe she was so *stupid!*"

"We should have stopped her," I said.

He reached into the stall to turn off the dribbling shower and then pounded an open palm against the tile wall. "Yeah, I know we should have stopped her, damn it. I am shit sure keenly aware that we should have stopped her. But we shouldn't have *had* to. You had to watch her like a *three-year-old*. You do one thing wrong, and then she just dies. Christ! I'm losing it. I'm going on a walk."

"Okay," I answered, trying to keep my voice calm.

"I'm sorry," he said. "I feel so screwed up. I feel like I might die."

"You might," I said.

"Yeah. Yeah. I might. You never know. It's just. It's like. *POOF*. And you're gone."

I followed him into the room. He grabbed the almanac from his bunk, zipped his jacket, closed the door, and *POOF*. He was gone.

With morning came visitors. An hour after the Colonel left, resident stoner Hank Walsten dropped by to offer me some weed, which I graciously turned down. Hank hugged me and said, "At least it was instant. At least there wasn't any pain."

I knew he was only trying to help, but he didn't get it. There was pain. A dull endless pain in my gut that wouldn't go away even when I knelt on the stingingly frozen tile of the bathroom, dry-heaving.

And what is an "instant" death anyway? How long is an instant? Is it one second? Ten? The pain of those seconds must have been awful as her heart burst and her lungs collapsed and there was no air and no blood to her brain and only raw panic. What the hell is *instant?* Nothing is instant. Instant rice takes five minutes, instant

15 **screwed up** (infml): upset and anxious 26 **gut** (infml): person's stomach
27 **stingingly** (adv): *beißend, stechend*

pudding an hour. I doubt that an instant of blinding pain *feels* particularly instantaneous.

Was there time for her life to flash before her eyes? Was I there? Was Jake? And she promised, I remembered, she promised to be continued, but I knew, too, that she was driving north when she died, north toward Nashville, toward Jake. Maybe it hadn't meant anything to her, had been nothing more than another grand impulsivity. And as Hank stood in the doorway, I just looked past him, looking across the too-quiet dorm circle, wondering if it had mattered to her, and I can only tell myself that of course, yes, she had promised. To be continued.

Lara came next, her eyes heavy with swelling. "What happeened?" she asked me as I held her, standing on my tiptoes so I could place my chin on top of her head.

"I don't know," I said.

"Deed you see her that night?" she asked, speaking into my collarbone.

"She got drunk," I told her. "The Colonel and I went to sleep, and I guess she drove off campus." And that became the standard lie.

I felt Lara's fingers, wet with her tears, press against my palm, and before I could think better of it, I pulled my hand away. "I'm sorry," I said.

"Eet's okay," she said. "I'll be een my room eef you want to come by." I did not drop by. I didn't know what to say to her – I was caught in a love triangle with one dead side.

That afternoon, we all filed into the gym again for a town meeting. The Eagle announced that the school would charter a bus on Sunday to the funeral in Vine Station. As we got up to leave, I noticed Takumi and Lara walking toward me. Lara caught my eye and smiled wanly. I smiled back, but quickly turned and hid myself amid the mass of mourners filing out of the gym.

2 **instantaneous**: happening immediately 17 **collarbone**: *Schlüsselbein*
29 **wan**: looking pale and weak 31 **mourner**: person who attends a funeral of a friend or relative

I am sleeping, and Alaska flies into the room. She is naked, and intact. Her breasts, which I felt only very briefly and in the dark, are luminously full as they hang down from her body. She hovers inches above me, her breath warm and sweet against my face like a breeze passing through tall grass.

"Hi," I say. "I've missed you."

"You look good, Pudge."

"So do you."

"I'm so naked," she says, and laughs. "How did I get so *naked?*"

"I just want you to stay," I say.

"No," she says, and her weight falls dead on me, crushing my chest, stealing away my breath, and she is cold and wet, like melting ice. Her head is split in half and a pink-gray sludge oozes from the fracture in her skull and drips down onto my face, and she stinks of formaldehyde and rotting meat. I gag and push her off me, terrified.

I woke up falling, and landed with a thud on the floor. Thank God I'm a bottom-bunk man. I had slept for fourteen hours. It was morning. Wednesday, I thought. Her funeral Sunday. I wondered if the Colonel would get back by then, where he was. He *had* to come back for the funeral, because I could not go alone, and going with anyone other than the Colonel would amount to alone.

The cold wind buffeted against the door, and the trees outside the back window shook with such force that I could hear it from our room, and I sat in my bed and thought of the Colonel out there somewhere, his head down, his teeth clenched, walking into the wind.

four days after

IT WAS FIVE IN THE MORNING and I was reading a biography of the explorer Meriwether Lewis (of & Clark fame) and trying to stay awake when the door opened and the Colonel walked in.

3 **luminous**: shining in the dark 3 **hover**: stay in the air in one place 13 **sludge**: slime 13 **ooze from sth.**: *aus etwas (heraus)sickern* 15 **gag**: feel as if you have to vomit 16 **thud**: *dumpfer Schlag* 22 **buffet against sth.** [ˈbʌfət]: *etwas rütteln*

His pale hands shook, and the almanac he held looked like a puppet dancing without strings.

"Are you cold?" I asked.

He nodded, slipped off his sneakers, and climbed into my bed on the bottom bunk, pulling up the covers. His teeth chattered like Morse code.

"Jesus. Are you all right?"

"Better now. Warmer," he said. A small, ghost white hand appeared from beneath the comforter. "Hold my hand, will ya?"

"All right, but that's it. No kissing." The quilt shook with his laughter.

"Where have you been?"

"I walked to Montevallo."

"Forty miles?!"

"Forty-two," he corrected me. "Well. Forty-two there. Forty-two back. Eighty-two miles. No. Eighty-four. Yes. Eighty-four miles in forty-five hours."

"What the hell's in Montevallo?" I asked.

"Not much. I just walked till I got too cold, and then I turned around."

"You didn't sleep?"

"No! The dreams are terrible. In my dreams, she doesn't even look like herself anymore. I don't even remember what she looked like."

I let go of his hand, grabbed last year's yearbook, and found her picture. In the black-and-white photograph, she's wearing her orange tank top and cutoff jeans that stretch halfway down her skinny thighs, her mouth open wide in a frozen laugh as her left arm holds Takumi in a headlock. Her hair falls over her face just enough to obscure her cheeks.

"Right," the Colonel said. "Yeah. I was so tired of her getting upset for no reason. The way she would get sulky and make references to the freaking oppressive weight of tragedy or whatever but then never said what was wrong, never have any goddamned *reason* to be sad. And I just think you ought to have a *reason*. My girlfriend dumped

29 **in a headlock**: *im Schwitzkasten*

me, so I'm sad. I got caught smoking, so I'm pissed off. My head hurts, so I'm cranky. She never had a *reason*, Pudge. I was just so tired of putting up with her drama. And I just let her go. Christ."

Her moodiness had annoyed me, too, sometimes, but not that night. That night I let her go because she told me to. It was that simple for me, and that stupid.

The Colonel's hand was so little, and I grabbed it tight, his cold seeping into me and my warmth into him. "I memorized the populations," he said.

"Uzbekistan."

"Twenty-four million seven hundred fifty-five thousand five hundred and nineteen."

"Cameroon," I said, but it was too late. He was asleep, his hand limp in mine. I placed it back under the quilt and climbed up into his bed, a top-bunk man for this night at least. I fell asleep listening to his slow, even breaths, his stubbornness finally melting away in the face of insurmountable fatigue.

six days after

THAT SUNDAY, I got up after three hours of sleep and showered for the first time in a long while. I put on my only suit. I almost hadn't brought it, but my mom insisted that you never know when you're going to need a suit, and sure enough.

The Colonel did not own a suit, and by virtue of his stature could not borrow one from anyone at the Creek, so he wore black slacks and a gray button-down.

"I don't suppose I can wear the flamingo tie," he said as he pulled on black socks.

"It's a bit festive, given the occasion," I responded.

"Can't wear it to the opera," said the Colonel, almost smiling. "Can't wear it to a funeral. Can't use it to hang myself. It's a bit useless, as ties go." I gave him a tie.

*

17 **insurmountable**: that cannot be avoided 17 **fatigue**: tiredness 23 **slacks** (pl; AE): trousers 24 **button-down** (n): type of shirt 27 **festive**: *festlich*

The school had chartered buses to ferry students north to Alaska's hometown of Vine Station, but Lara, the Colonel, Takumi, and I drove in Takumi's SUV, taking the back roads so we didn't have to drive past the spot on the highway. I stared out the window, watching as the suburban sprawl surrounding Birmingham faded into the slow-sloping hills and fields of northern Alabama.

Up front, Takumi told Lara about the time Alaska got her boob honked over the summer, and Lara laughed. That was the first time I had seen her, and now we were coming to the last. More than anything, I felt the unfairness of it, the inarguable injustice of loving someone who might have loved you back but can't due to deadness, and then I leaned forward, my forehead against the back of Takumi's headrest, and I cried, whimpering, and I didn't even feel sadness so much as pain. It hurt, and that is not a euphemism. It hurt like a beating.

Meriwether Lewis's last words were, "I am not a coward, but I am so strong. So hard to die." I don't doubt that it is, but it cannot be much harder than being left behind. I thought of Lewis as I followed Lara into the A-frame chapel attached to the single-story funeral home in Vine Station, Alabama, a town every bit as depressed and depressing as Alaska had always made it out to be. The place smelled of mildew and disinfectant, and the yellow wallpaper in the foyer was peeling at the corners.

"Are y'all here for Ms. Young?" a guy asked the Colonel, and the Colonel nodded. We were led to a large room with rows of folding chairs populated by only one man. He knelt before a coffin at the front of the chapel. The coffin was closed. Closed. Never going to see her again. Can't kiss her forehead. Can't see her one last time. But I needed to, I needed to *see* her, and much too loud, I asked, "Why is it closed?" and the man, whose potbelly pushed out from his too-tight suit, turned around and walked toward me.

1 **ferry**: carry people from one place to another 5 **sprawl**: *Ausbreitung (von Häusern)* 7 **boob** (sl): female breast 8 **honk sth.**: *hupen*; (here) touch a female breast 10 **inarguable**: *unbestreitbar* 13 **whimper**: make low, weak crying noises 14 **euphemism**: *sprachliche Beschönigung* 22 **disinfectant**: *Desinfektionsmittel* 30 **potbelly**: *dicker Bauch*

"Her mother," he said. "Her mother had an open casket, and Alaska told me, 'Don't ever let them see me dead, Daddy,' and so that's that. Anyway, son, she's not in there. She's with the Lord."

And he put his hands on my shoulders, this man who had grown fat since he'd last had to wear a suit, and I couldn't believe what I had done to him, his eyes glittering green like Alaska's but sunk deep into dark sockets, like a green-eyed, still-breathing ghost, and don't no don't don't die, Alaska. Don't die. And I walked out of his embrace and past Lara and Takumi to her casket and knelt before it and placed my hands on the finished wood, the dark mahogany, the color of her hair. I felt the Colonel's small hands on my shoulders, and a tear dripped onto my head, and for a few moments, it was just the three of us – the buses of students hadn't arrived, and Takumi and Lara had faded away, and it was just the three of us – three bodies and two people – the three who knew what had happened and too many layers between all of us, too much keeping us from one another. The Colonel said, "I just want to save her so bad," and I said, "Chip, she's gone," and he said, "I thought I'd feel her looking down on us, but you're right. She's just gone," and I said, "Oh God, Alaska, I love you. I love you," and the Colonel whispered, "I'm so sorry, Pudge. I know you did," and I said, "No. Not past tense." She wasn't even a person anymore, just flesh rotting, but I loved her present tense. The Colonel knelt down beside me and put his lips to the coffin and whispered, "I am sorry, Alaska. You deserved a better friend."

Is it so hard to die, Mr. Lewis? Is that labyrinth really worse than this one?

seven days after

I SPENT THE NEXT DAY in our room, playing football on mute, at once unable to do nothing and unable to do anything much. It was Martin Luther King Day, our last day before classes started again, and I could

7 **socket**: *(hier) Augenhöhle*

think of nothing but having killed her. The Colonel spent the morning with me, but then he decided to go to the cafeteria for meat loaf.

"Let's go," he said.

"Not hungry."

"You have to eat."

"Wanna bet?" I asked without looking up from the game.

"Christ. Fine." He sighed and left, slamming the door behind him. *He's still very angry*, I found myself thinking with a bit of pity. No reason to be angry. Anger just distracts from the all-encompassing sadness, the frank knowledge that you killed her and robbed her of a future and a life. Getting pissed wouldn't fix it. Damn it.

"How's the meat loaf?" I asked the Colonel when he returned.

"About as you remember it. Neither meaty nor loafy." The Colonel sat down next to me. "The Eagle ate with me. He wanted to know if we set off the fireworks." I paused the game and turned to him. With one hand, he picked at one of the last remaining pieces of blue vinyl on our foam couch.

"And you said?" I asked.

"I didn't rat. Anyway, he said her aunt or something is coming tomorrow to clean out her room. So if there's anything that's ours, or anything her aunt wouldn't want to find … "

I turned back to the game and said, "I'm not up for it today."

"Then I'll do it alone," he answered. He turned and walked outside, leaving the door open, and the bitter remnants of the cold snap quickly overwhelmed the radiator, so I paused the game and stood up to close the door, and when I peeked around the corner to see if the Colonel had entered her room, he was standing there, just outside our door, and he grabbed onto my sweatshirt, smiled, and said, "I *knew* you wouldn't make me do that alone. I *knew* it." I shook my head and rolled my eyes but followed him down the sidewalk, past the pay phone, and into her room.

2–3 **meat loaf**: *Hackbraten* 10 **distract sb. from sth.**: take sb's attention away from sth. 10 **encompass**: *umfassen* 25 **remnant**: *Überrest* 26 **snap** (n): period of cold weather 27 **peek**: look at sth. quickly and secretly

I hadn't thought of her smell since she died. But when the Colonel opened the door, I caught the edge of her scent: wet dirt and grass and cigarette smoke, and beneath that the vestiges of vanilla-scented skin lotion. She flooded into my present, and only tact kept me from burying my face in the dirty laundry overfilling the hamper by her dresser. It looked as I remembered it: hundreds of books stacked against the walls, her lavender comforter crumpled at the foot of her bed, a precarious stack of books on her bedside table, her volcanic candle just peeking out from beneath the bed. It looked as I knew it would, but the smell, unmistakably her, shocked me. I stood in the center of the room, my eyes shut, inhaling slowly through my nose, the vanilla and the uncut autumn grass, but with each slow breath, the smell faded as I became accustomed to it, and soon she was gone again.

"This is unbearable," I said matter-of-factly, because it was. "God. These books she'll never read. Her Life's Library."

"Bought at garage sales and now probably destined for another one."

"Ashes to ashes. Garage sale to garage sale," I said.

"Right. Okay, down to business. Get anything her aunt wouldn't want to find," the Colonel said, and I saw him kneeling at her desk, the drawer beneath her computer pulled open, his small fingers pulling out groups of stapled papers. "Christ, she kept every paper she ever wrote. *Moby-Dick. Ethan Frome.*"

I reached between her mattress and box spring for the condoms I knew she hid for Jake's visits. I pocketed them, and then went over to her dresser, searching through her underwear for hidden bottles of liquor or sex toys or God knows what. I found nothing. And then I settled on the books, staring at them stacked on their sides, spines out, the haphazard collection of literature that was Alaska. There was one book I wanted to take with me, but I couldn't find it.

The Colonel was sitting on the floor next to her bed, his head bent toward the floor, looking under her bed frame. "She sure didn't leave any booze, did she?" he asked.

4 **tact**: sensitive behavior 8 **precarious**: (here) likely to fall

And I almost said, *She buried it in the woods out by the soccer field*, but I realized that the Colonel didn't know, that she never took him to the edge of the woods and told him to dig for buried treasure, that she and I had shared that alone, and I kept it for myself like a keepsake, as if sharing the memory might lead to its dissipation.

"Do you see *The General in His Labyrinth* anywhere?" I asked while scanning the titles on the book spines. "It has a lot of green on the cover, I think. It's a paperback, and it got flooded, so the pages are probably bloated, but I don't think she –" and then he cut me off with, "Yeah, it's right here," and I turned around and he was holding it, the pages fanned out like an accordion from Longwell, Jeff, and Kevin's prank, and I walked over to him and took it and sat down on her bed. The places she'd underlined and the little notes she'd written had all been blurred out by the soaking, but the book was still mostly readable, and I was thinking I would take it back to my room and try to read it even though it wasn't a biography when I flipped to that page, toward the back:

> He was shaken by the overwhelming revelation that the headlong race between his misfortunes and his dreams was at that moment reaching the finish line. The rest was darkness. "Damn it," he sighed. "How will I ever get out of this labyrinth!"

The whole passage was underlined in bleeding, water-soaked black ink. But there was another ink, this one a crisp blue, post-flood, and an arrow led from "How will I ever get out of this labyrinth!" to a margin note written in her loop-heavy cursive: *Straight & Fast*.

"Hey, she wrote something in here after the flood," I said. "But it's weird. Look. Page one ninety-two."

I tossed the book to the Colonel, and he flipped to the page and then looked up at me. "Straight and fast," he said.

5 **keepsake**: small object that reminds you of sb. 5 **dissipation**: process of disappearing 9 **bloat**: *(hier) aufquellen* 14 **blur**: *verschwimmen* 19 **misfortune**: bad luck 26 **loop-heavy**: *verschnörkelt*

"Yeah. Weird, huh? The way out of the labyrinth, I guess."

"Wait, how did it happen? What happened?"

And because there was only one it, I knew to what he was referring. "I told you what the Eagle told me. A truck jackknifed on the road. A cop car showed up to stop traffic, and she ran into the cop car. She was so drunk she didn't even swerve."

"So *drunk?* So *drunk?* The cop car would have had its lights on. Pudge, she ran into a cop car that had its lights on," he said hurriedly. "Straight and fast. Straight and fast. Out of the labyrinth."

"No," I said, but even as I said it, I could see it. I could see her drunk enough and pissed off enough. (About what – about cheating on Jake? About hurting me? About wanting me and not him? Still pissed about ratting out Marya?) I could see her staring down the cop car and aiming for it and not giving a shit about anyone else, not thinking of her promise to me, not thinking of her father or anyone, and that bitch, that bitch, she killed herself. But no. No. That was not her. No. She said *To be continued*. Of course. "No."

"Yeah, you're probably right," the Colonel said. He dropped the book, sat down on the bed next to me, and put his forehead in his hands. "Who drives six miles off campus to kill herself? Doesn't make any sense. But 'straight and fast.' Bit of an odd premonition, isn't it? And we still don't really know what happened, if you think about it. Where she was going, why. Who called. Someone called, right, or did I make –"

And the Colonel kept talking, puzzling it out, while I picked up the book and found my way to that page where the general's headlong race came to its end, and we were both stuck in our heads, the distance between us unbridgeable, and I could not listen to the Colonel, because I was busy trying to get the last hints of her smell, busy telling myself that of course she had not done it. It was me – I had done it, and so had the Colonel. He could try to puzzle his way out of it, but I knew better, knew that we could never be anything but wholly, unforgivably guilty.

21 **premonition:** feeling that sth (unpleasant) is going to happen

eight days after

TUESDAY – WE HAD SCHOOL for the first time. Madame O'Malley had a moment of silence at the beginning of French class, a class that was always punctuated with long moments of silence, and then asked us how we were feeling.

"Awful," a girl said.

"En français," Madame O'Malley replied. *"En français."*

Everything looked the same, but more still: the Weekday Warriors still sat on the benches outside the library, but their gossip was quiet, understated. The cafeteria clamored with the sounds of plastic trays against wooden tables and forks scraping plates, but any conversations were muted. But more than the noiselessness of everyone else was the silence where she should have been, the bubbling bursting storytelling Alaska, but instead it felt like those times when she had withdrawn into herself, like she was refusing to answer *how* or why questions, only this time for good.

The Colonel sat down next to me in religion class, sighed, and said, "You reek of smoke, Pudge."

"Ask me if I give a shit."

Dr. Hyde shuffled into class then, our final exams stacked underneath one arm. He sat down, took a series of labored breaths, and began to talk. "It is a law that parents should not have to bury their children," he said. "And someone should enforce it. This semester, we're going to continue studying the religious traditions to which you were introduced this fall. But there's no doubting that the questions we'll be asking have more immediacy now than they did just a few days ago. What happens to us after we die, for instance, is no longer a question of idle philosophical interest. It is a question we must ask about our classmate. And how to live in the shadow of grief is not something nameless Buddhists, Christians, and Muslims have to explore. The questions of religious thought have become, I suspect, personal."

9 **understated** (adj): *untertrieben* 9 **clamor**: have a lot of noise 22 **enforce sth.**: make sure that people obey sth. (e.g. a law) 25 **immediacy**: *unmittelbare Gegebenheit* 27 **idle**: not important 28 **grief**: great sadness

He shuffled through our exams, pulling one out from the pile before him. "I have here Alaska's final. You'll recall that you were asked what the most important question facing people is, and how the three traditions we're studying this year address that question. This was Alaska's question."

With a sigh, he grabbed hold of his chair and lifted himself out of it, then wrote on the blackboard: *How will we ever get out of this labyrinth of suffering? – A. Y.*

"I'm going to leave that up for the rest of the semester," he said. "Because everybody who has ever lost their way in life has felt the nagging insistence of that question. At some point we all look up and realize we are lost in a maze, and I don't want us to forget Alaska, and I don't want to forget that even when the material we study seems boring, we're trying to understand how people have answered that question and the questions each of you posed in your papers – how different traditions have come to terms with what Chip, in his final, called 'people's rotten lots in life.'"

Hyde sat down. "So, how are you guys doing?"

The Colonel and I said nothing, while a bunch of people who didn't know Alaska extolled her virtues and professed to be devastated, and at first, it bothered me. I didn't want the people she didn't know – and the people she didn't like – to be sad. They'd never cared about her, and now they were carrying on as if she were a sister. But I guess I didn't know her completely, either. If I had, I'd have known what she'd meant by "To be continued?" And if I had cared about her as I should have, as I thought I did, how could I have let her go?

So they didn't bother me, really. But next to me, the Colonel breathed slowly and deeply through his nose like a bull about to charge.

He actually rolled his eyes when Weekday Warrior Brooke Blakely, whose parents had received a progress report courtesy of Alaska, said, "I'm just sad I never told her I loved her. I just don't understand *why*."

*

11 **nagging** (adj): *nagend, bohrend* 20 **extol sb.'s virtues**: praise sb. very much
20 **profess**: declare

"That's such bullshit," the Colonel said as we walked to lunch. "As if Brooke Blakely gives two shits about Alaska."

"If Brooke Blakely died, wouldn't you be sad?" I asked.

"I guess, but I wouldn't bemoan the fact I never told her I *loved* her. I *don't* love her. She's an idiot."

I thought everyone else had a better excuse to grieve than we did – after all, they hadn't killed her – but I knew better than to try to talk to the Colonel when he was mad.

nine days after

"I'VE GOT A THEORY," the Colonel said as I walked in the door after a miserable day of classes. The cold had begun to let up, but word had not spread to whoever ran the furnaces, so the classrooms were all stuffy and overheated, and I just wanted to crawl into bed and sleep until the time came to do it all over again.

"Missed you in class today," I noted as I sat down on my bed. The Colonel sat at his desk, hunched over a notebook. I lay down on my back and pulled the covers up over my head, but the Colonel was undiscouraged.

"Right, well, I was busy coming up with the theory, which isn't terribly likely, admittedly, but it's plausible. So, listen. She kisses you. That night, someone calls. Jake, I imagine. They have a fight – about cheating or about something else – who knows. So she's upset, and she wants to go see him. She comes back to the room crying, and she tells us to help her get off campus. And she's freaked out, because, I don't know, let's say because if she can't go visit him, Jake will break up with her. That's just a hypothetical reason. So she gets off campus, drunk and all pissed off, and she's furious at herself over whatever it is, and she's driving along and sees the cop car and then in a flash everything comes together and the end to her labyrinthine mystery is staring her right in the face and she just does it, straight and fast, just aims at the cop car and never swerves, not because she's drunk but because she killed herself."

4 **bemoan sth.**: complain that you are not happy about sth. 10 **let up**: become less strong 11 **furnace** (AE): boiler, heater 17 **undiscouraged**: *nicht entmutigt*

"That's ridiculous. She wasn't thinking about Jake or fighting with Jake. *She was making out with me*. I tried to bring up the whole Jake thing, but she just shushed me."

"So who called her?"

I kicked off my comforter and, my fist balled, smashed my hand against the wall with each syllable as I said, "I! DON'T! KNOW! And you know what, it doesn't matter. She's dead. Is the brilliant Colonel going to figure out something that's gonna make her less freaking dead?" But it did matter, of course, which is why I kept pounding at our cinder-block walls and why the questions had floated beneath the surface for a week. Who'd called? What was wrong? Why did she leave? Jake had not gone to her funeral. Nor had he called us to say he was sorry, or to ask us what happened. He had just disappeared, and of course, I had wondered. I had wondered if she had any intention of keeping her promise that we would be continued. I had wondered who called, and why, and what made her so upset. But I'd rather wonder than get answers I couldn't live with.

"Maybe she was driving there to break up with Jake, then," the Colonel said, his voice suddenly edgeless. He sat down on the corner of my bed.

"I don't know. I don't really want to know."

"Yeah, well," he said. "I want to know. Because if she knew what she was doing, Pudge, she made us accomplices. And I hate her for that. I mean, God, look at us. We can't even talk to anyone anymore. So listen, I wrote out a game plan: *One*. Talk to eyewitnesses. *Two*. Figure out how drunk she was. *Three*. Figure out where she was going, and why."

"I don't want to talk to Jake," I said halfheartedly, already resigned to the Colonel's incessant planning."If he knows, I definitely don't want to talk to him. And if he doesn't, I don't want to pretend like it didn't happen."

3 **shush sb.**: tell sb. to be quiet 5 **comforter** (AE): type of thick cover for a bed 19 **edgeless**: expressionless 23 **accomplice** [ə'kɑːmpləs]: person who helps another to commit a crime 28 **halfhearted**: *halbherzig* 29 **incessant**: never stopping

The Colonel stood up and sighed. "You know what, Pudge? I feel bad for you. I do. I know you kissed her, and I know you're broken up about it. But honestly, shut up. If Jake knows, you're not gonna make it any worse. And if he doesn't, he won't find out. So just stop worrying about your goddamned self for one minute and think about your dead friend. Sorry. Long day."

"It's fine," I said, pulling the covers back over my head. "It's fine," I repeated. And, whatever. It *was* fine. It had to be. I couldn't afford to lose the Colonel.

thirteen days after

BECAUSE OUR MAIN SOURCE of vehicular transportation was interred in Vine Station, Alabama, the Colonel and I were forced to walk to the Pelham Police Department to search for eyewitnesses. We left after eating dinner in the cafeteria, the night falling fast and early, and trudged up Highway 119 for a mile and a half before coming to a single-story stucco building situated between a Waffle House and a gas station.

Inside, a long desk that rose to the Colonel's solar plexus separated us from the police station proper, which seemed to consist of three uniformed officers sitting at three desks, all of them talking on the phone.

"I'm Alaska Young's brother," the Colonel announced brazenly. "And I want to talk to the cop who saw her die."

A pale, thin man with a reddish blond beard spoke quickly into the phone and then hung up."I seen 'er," he said. "She hit mah cruiser."

"Can we talk to you outside?" the Colonel asked.

"Yup."

The cop grabbed a coat and walked toward us, and as he approached, I could see the blue veins through the translucent skin of his face. For a cop, he didn't seem to get out much. Once outside, the Colonel lit a cigarette.

10 **inter sb.** [- '-]: bury sb. 14 **trudge** (v): walk slowly 15 **single-story**: *einstöckig* 15 **stucco**: *Stuck* 21 **brazen** ['breɪzən]: *unverschämt* 24 **mah**: my 28 **translucent**: allowing light to pass through

"You nineteen?" the cop asked. In Alabama, you can get married at eighteen (fourteen with Mom and Dad's permission), but you have to be nineteen to smoke.

"So fine me. I just need to know what you saw."

"Ah most always work from six t' midnight, but I was coverin' the graveyard shift. We got a call 'bout a jackknifed truck, and I's only about a mile away, so I headed over, and I'd just pulled up. I's still in mah cruiser, and I seen out the corner a' my eye the headlights, and my lights was on and I turned the siren on, but the lights just kept comin' straight at me, son, and I got out quick and run off and she just barreled inta me. I seen plenty, but I ain't never seen that. She didn't tarn. She didn't brake. She jest hit it. I wa'n't more than ten feet from the cruiser when she hit it. I thought I'd die, but here ah am."

For the first time, the Colonel's theory seemed plausible. She didn't hear *the siren?* She didn't see *the lights?* She was sober enough to kiss well, I thought. Surely she was sober enough to swerve.

"Did you see her face before she hit the car? Was she asleep?" the Colonel asked.

"That I cain't tell ya. I didn't see 'er. There wa'n't much time."

"I understand. She was dead when you got to the car?" he asked.

"I – I did everything I could. Ah run right up to her, but the steerin' wheel – well, ah reached in there, thought if ah could git that steerin' wheel loose, but there weren't no gettin' her outta that car alive. It fairly well crushed her chest, see."

I winced at the image. "Did she say anything?" I asked.

"She was passed on, son," he said, shaking his head, and my last hope of last words faded.

"Do you think it was an accident?" the Colonel asked as I stood beside him, my shoulders slouching, wanting a cigarette but nervous to be as audacious as him.

5 **ah most**: I mostly 6 **graveyard shift**: hours between midnight and dawn
11 **barrel** (v; infml): move very fast in a particular direction 12 **tarn**: turn
16 **swerve**: change direction suddenly 24 **chest**: top part of the front of the body
26 **be passed on**: be dead 29 **slouch**: *Schultern hängen lassen* 30 **audacious** (fml): willing to take risks

"Ah been an officer here twenty-six years, and ah've seen more drunks than you'n count, and ah ain't never seen someone so drunk they cain't swerve. But ah don't know. The coroner said it was an accident, and maybe it was. That ain't my field, y'know. I s'pose that's 'tween her and the Lord now."

"How drunk was she?" I asked. "Like, did they test her?"

"Yeah. Her BAL was point twenty-four. That's drunk, certainly. That's a powerful drunk."

"Was there anything in the car?" the Colonel asked. "Anything, like, unusual that you remember?"

"I remember them brochures from colleges – places in Maine and Ohia and Texas – I thought t' myself that girl must be from Culver Crick and that was mighty sad, see a girl like that lookin' t' go t' college. That's a goddamned shame. And they's flowers. They was flowers in her backseat. Like, from a florist. Tulips."

Tulips? I thought immediately of the tulips Jake had sent her.

"Were they white?" I asked.

"They sure was," the cop answered. Why would she have taken his tulips with her? But the cop wouldn't have an answer for that one.

"Ah hope y'all find out whatever y'all's lookin' for. I have thought it over some, 'cause I never seen nothing like that before. Ah've thought hard on it, wondered if I'da started up the cruiser real quick and drove it off, if she'da been all right. There mightn't've been time. No knowing now. But it don't matter, t' my mind, whether it were an accident or it weren't. It's a goddamned shame either way."

"There was nothing you could have done," the Colonel said softly. "You did your job, and we appreciate it."

"Well. Thanks. Y'all go 'long now, and take care, and let me know if ya have any other questions. This is mah card if you need anything."

The Colonel put the card in his fake leather wallet, and we walked toward home.

"White tulips," I said. "Jake's tulips. Why?"

"One time last year, she and Takumi and I were at the Smoking Hole, and there was this little white daisy on the bank of the creek, and all of a sudden she just jumped waist-deep into the water and

7 **BAL**: blood alcohol level 22 **I'da**: I'd have

waded across and grabbed it. She put it behind her ear, and when I asked her about it, she told me that her parents always put white flowers in her hair when she was little. Maybe she wanted to die with white flowers."

"Maybe she was going to return them to Jake," I said.

"Maybe. But that cop just shit sure convinced me that it might have been a suicide."

"Maybe we should just let her be dead," I said, frustrated. It seemed to me that nothing we might find out would make anything any better, and I could not get the image of the steering wheel careening into her chest out of my mind, her chest "fairly well crushed" while she sucked for a last breath that would never come, and no, this was not making anything better. "What if she *did* do it?" I asked the Colonel. "We're not any less guilty. All it does is make her into this awful, selfish bitch."

"Christ, Pudge. Do you even remember the person she actually was? Do you remember how she *could* be a selfish bitch? That was part of her, and you used to know it. It's like now you only care about the Alaska you made up."

I sped up, walking ahead of the Colonel, silent. And he couldn't know, because he wasn't the last person she kissed, because he hadn't been left with an unkeepable promise, because he wasn't me. *Screw this*, I thought, and for the first time, I imagined just going back home, ditching the Great Perhaps for the old comforts of school friends. Whatever their faults, I'd never known my school friends in Florida to die on me.

After a considerable distance, the Colonel jogged up to me and said, "I just want it to be normal again," he said. "You and me. Normal. Fun. Just, normal. And I feel like if we knew –"

"Okay, fine," I cut him off. "Fine. We'll keep looking."

The Colonel shook his head, but then he smiled. "I have always appreciated your enthusiasm, Pudge. And I'm just going to go ahead and pretend you still have it until it comes back. Now let's go home and find out why people off themselves."

11 **careen**: *(hier) rasen* 26 **die on me**: *vor mir sterben* 34 **off yourself** (infml): kill yourself

fourteen days after

WARNING SIGNS OF SUICIDE the Colonel and I found on the Web:

- Previous suicide attempts
- Verbally threatening suicide
- Giving away prized possessions
- Collecting and discussing methods of suicide
- Expressions of hopelessness and anger at oneself and/or the world
- Writing, talking, reading, and drawing about death and/or depression
- Suggesting that the person would not be missed if s/he were gone
- Self-injury
- Recent loss of a friend or family member through death or suicide
- Sudden and dramatic decline in academic performance
- Eating disorders, sleeplessness, excessive sleeping, chronic headaches
- Use (or increased use) of mind-altering substances
- Loss of interest in sex, hobbies, and other activities previously enjoyed

Alaska displayed two of those warning signs. She had lost, although not recently, her mother. And her drinking, always pretty steady, had definitely increased in the last month of her life. She did talk about dying, but she always seemed to be at least half kidding.

"I make jokes about death all the time," the Colonel said. "I made a joke last week about hanging myself with my tie. And I'm not gonna off myself. So that doesn't count. And she didn't give anything away, and she sure as hell didn't lose interest in sex. One would have to like sex an awful lot to make out with your scrawny ass."

"Funny," I said.

2 **previous**: *vorherig, vorausgehend* 4 **prized**: very valuable to sb. 16 **eating disorder**: *Essstörung* 18 **alter sth.**: change sth. 29 **scrawny**: very thin in a way that is not attractive

"I know. God, I'm a genius. And her grades were good. And I don't recall her talking about killing herself."

"Once, with the cigarettes, remember? 'You smoke to enjoy it. I smoke to die.' "

"That was a *joke*."

But when prodded by the Colonel, maybe to prove to him that I could remember Alaska as she really was and not just as I wanted her to be, I kept returning the conversation to those times when she would be mean and moody, when she didn't feel like answering *how, when, why, who,* or *what* questions. "She could seem so *angry,*" I thought aloud.

"What, and I can't?" the Colonel retorted. "I'm plenty angry, Pudge. And you haven't been the picture of placidity of late, either, and you aren't going to off yourself. Wait, are you?"

"No," I said. And maybe it was only because Alaska couldn't hit the brakes and I couldn't hit the accelerator. Maybe she just had an odd kind of courage that I lacked, but no.

"Good to know. So yeah, she was up and down – from fire and brimstone to smoke and ashes. But partly, this year at least, it was the whole Marya thing. Look, Pudge, she obviously wasn't thinking about killing herself when she was making out with you. After that, she was asleep until the phone rang. So she decided to kill herself at some point between that ringing phone and crashing, or it was an accident."

"But why wait until you're six miles off campus to die?" I asked.

He sighed and shook his head. "She did like being mysterious. Maybe she wanted it like this." I laughed then, and the Colonel said, "What?"

"I was just thinking – *Why do you run head-on into a cop car with its lights on?* and then I thought, *Well, she hated authority figures*."

The Colonel laughed. "Hey, look at that. Pudge made a funny!"

It felt almost normal, and then my distance from the event itself seemed to evaporate and I found myself back in the gym, hearing

6 **prod sb.**: try to make sb do sth, esp. when they are unwilling 12 **retort**: reply quickly in an angry way 13 **placidity**: *Gelassenheit* 13 **of late** (fml): recently 19 **brimstone** (old use): *Schwefel* 33 **evaporate**: gradually become less

the news for the first time, the Eagle's tears dripping onto his pants, and I looked over at the Colonel and thought of all the hours we'd spent on this foam couch in the past two weeks – everything she'd ruined. Too pissed off to cry, I said, "This is only making me hate her. I don't want to hate her. And what's the point, if that's all it's making me do?" Still refusing to answer *how* and *why* questions. Still insisting on an aura of mystery.

I leaned forward, head between my knees, and the Colonel placed a hand on my upper back. "The point is that there are always answers, Pudge." And then he pushed air out between his pursed lips and I could hear the angry quiver in his voice as he repeated, "There are *always* answers. We just have to be smart enough. The Web says that suicides usually involve carefully thought-out plans. So clearly she did not commit suicide." I felt embarrassed to be still falling apart two weeks later when the Colonel could take his medicine so stoically, and I sat up.

"Okay, fine" I answered. "It wasn't suicide."

"Although it sure doesn't make sense as an accident," the Colonel said.

I laughed. "We sure are making progress."

We were interrupted by Holly Moser, the senior I knew primarily from viewing her nude self-portraits over Thanksgiving with Alaska. Holly hung with the Weekday Warriors, which explains why I'd previously said about two words to her in my life, but she just came in without knocking and said that she'd had a mystical indicator of Alaska's presence.

"I was in the Waffle House, and suddenly all the lights went off, except for, like, the light over my booth, which started flashing. It would be like on for a second and then off for a while and then on for a couple of seconds and then off. And I realized, you know, it was Alaska. I think she was trying to talk to me in Morse code. But, like, I don't know Morse code. She probably didn't know that. Anyway, I thought you guys should know."

11 **quiver**: *Beben, Zittern* 16 **stoical**: being able to suffer pain or trouble without complaining 28 **booth**: (here) place to sit in a restaurant which consists of two long seats with a table between them

"Thanks," I said curtly, and she stood for a while, looking at us, her mouth opening as if to speak, but the Colonel was staring at her through half-closed eyes, his jaw jutting out and his distaste uncontained. I understood how he felt: I didn't believe in ghosts who used Morse code to communicate with people they'd never liked. And I disliked the possibility that Alaska would give someone else peace but not me.

"God, people like that shouldn't be allowed to live," he said after she left.

"It was pretty stupid."

"It's not just stupid, Pudge. I mean, as if Alaska would talk to Holly Moser. God! I can't stand these fake grievers. Stupid bitch."

I almost told him that Alaska wouldn't want him to call *any* woman a bitch, but there was no use fighting with the Colonel.

twenty days after

IT WAS SUNDAY, and the Colonel and I decided against the cafeteria for dinner, instead walking off campus and across Highway 119 to the Sunny Konvenience Kiosk, where we indulged in a well-balanced meal of two oatmeal cream pies apiece. Seven hundred calories. Enough energy to sustain a man for half a day. We sat on the curb in front of the store, and I finished dinner in four bites.

"I'm going to call Jake tomorrow, just so you know. I got his phone number from Takumi."

"Fine," I said.

I heard a bell jangle behind me and turned toward the opening door.

"Y'all's loitering," said the woman who'd just sold us dinner.

"We're eating," the Colonel answered.

The woman shook her head and ordered, as if to a dog, "Git."

1 **curt**: abrupt and rude 3 **jaw**: *Kiefer* 3 **jut out**: stick out 4 **uncontained**: *unverhohlen* 12 **griever**: sb. who is very sad because sb. else died 17 **indulge in sth.**: allow yourself to have or do sth that you like 18 **apiece**: each 19 **sustain sb.**: provide enough of what sb. needs in order to live 19 **curb**: *Bordkante* 26 **loiter**: hang around

So we walked behind the store and sat by the stinking, fetid Dumpster.

"Enough with the *fine*'s already, Pudge. That's ridiculous. I'm going to call Jake, and I'm going to write down everything he says, and then we're going to sit down together and try and figure out what happened."

"No. You're on your own with that. I don't want to know what happened between her and Jake."

The Colonel sighed and pulled a pack of Pudge Fund cigarettes of his jeans pocket. "Why not?"

"Because I don't want to! Do I have to provide you with an in-depth analysis of every decision I make?"

The Colonel lit the cigarette with a lighter I'd paid for and took a drag. "Whatever. It needs to be figured out, and I need your help to do it, because between the two of us we knew her pretty well. So that's that."

I stood up and stared down at him sitting smugly, and he blew a thin stream of smoke at my face, and I'd had enough. "I'm tired of following orders, asshole! I'm not going to sit with you and discuss the finer points of her relationship with Jake, goddamn it. I can't say it any clearer: *I don't want to know* about them. I *already know* what she told me, and that's all I need to know, and you can be a condescending prick as long as you'd like, but I'm not going to sit around and chat with you about how goddamned much she loved Jake! Now give me my cigarettes." The Colonel threw the pack on the ground and was up in a flash, a fistful of my sweater in his hand, trying but failing to pull me down to his height.

"You don't even care about her!" he shouted. "All that matters is you and your precious fucking fantasy that you and Alaska had this goddamned secret love affair and she was going to leave Jake for you and you'd live happily ever after. But she kissed a lot of guys, Pudge. And if she were here, we both know that she would still be Jake's girlfriend and that there'd be nothing but drama between the two of you – not love, not sex, just you pining after her and her like, 'You're

1 **fetid**: stinking 2 **Dumpster**: (brand name) large metal container for rubbish
34 **pine after sb.**: think about and miss sb. very much

cute, Pudge, but I love Jake.' If she loved you so much, why did she leave you that night? And if you loved her so much, why'd you help her go? I was drunk. What's your excuse?"

The Colonel let go of my sweater, and I reached down and picked up the cigarettes. Not screaming, not through clenched teeth, not with the veins pulsing in my forehead, but calmly. Calmly. I looked down at the Colonel and said, "Fuck you."

The vein-pulsing screaming came later, after I had jogged across Highway 119 and through the dorm circle and across the soccer field and down the dirt road to the bridge, when I found myself at the Smoking Hole. I picked up a blue chair and threw it against the concrete wall, and the clang of plastic on concrete echoed beneath the bridge as the chair fell limply on its side, and then I lay on my back with my knees hanging over the precipice and screamed. I screamed because the Colonel was a self-satisfied, condescending bastard, and I screamed because he was right, for I did want to believe that I'd had a secret love affair with Alaska. Did she love me? Would she have left Jake for me? Or was it just another impulsive Alaska moment? It was not enough to be the last guy she kissed. I wanted to be the last one she loved. And I knew I wasn't. I knew it, and I hated her for it. I hated her for not caring about me. I hated her for leaving that night, and I hated myself, too, not only because I let her go but because if I had been enough for her, she wouldn't have even wanted to leave. She would have just lain with me and talked and cried, and I would have listened and kissed at her tears as they pooled in her eyes.

I turned my head and looked at one of the little blue plastic chairs on its side. I wondered if there would ever be a day when I didn't think about Alaska, wondered whether I should hope for a time when she would be a distant memory – recalled only on the anniversary of her death, or maybe a couple of weeks after, remembering only after having forgotten.

I knew that I would know more dead people. The bodies pile up. Could there be a space in my memory for each of them, or would I forget a little of Alaska every day for the rest of my life?

Once, early on in the year, she and I had walked down to the Smoking Hole, and she jumped into Culver Creek with her flip-flops still on. She stepped across the creek, picking her steps carefully over the mossy rocks, and grabbed a waterlogged stick from the creek bank. As I sat on the concrete, my feet dangling toward the water, she overturned rocks with the stick and pointed out the skittering crawfish.

"You boil 'em and then suck the heads out," she said excitedly. "That's where all the good stuff is – the heads."

She taught me everything I knew about crawfish and kissing and pink wine and poetry. She made me different.

I lit a cigarette and spit into the creek. "You can't just make me different and then leave," I said out loud to her. "Because I was fine before, Alaska. I was fine with just me and last words and school friends, and you can't just make me different and then die." For she had embodied the Great Perhaps – she had proved to me that it was worth it to leave behind my minor life for grander maybes, and now she was gone and with her my faith in perhaps. I could call everything the Colonel said and did "fine." I could try to pretend that I didn't care anymore, but it could never be true again. You can't just make yourself matter and then die, Alaska, because now I am irretrievably different, and I'm sorry I let you go, yes, but you made the choice. You left me Perhapsless, stuck in your goddamned labyrinth. And now I don't even know if you chose the straight and fast way out, if you left me like this on purpose. And so I never knew you, did I? I can't remember, because I never knew.

And as I stood up to walk home and make my peace with the Colonel, I tried to imagine her in that chair, but I could not remember whether she crossed her legs. I could still see her smiling at me with half of *Mona Lisa*'s smirk, but I couldn't picture her hands well enough to see her holding a cigarette. I needed, I decided, to really know her, because I needed more to remember. Before I could begin the shameful process of forgetting the how and the why of her living and dying, I needed to learn it: *How. Why. When. Where. What.*

4 **mossy**: *moosig* 4 **waterlogged**: *voll gesogen* 7 **skitter**: run or move very quickly and lightly 7 **crawfish**: *Flusskrebs* 21 **irretrievable**: that you can never get back

At Room 43, after quickly offered and accepted apologies, the Colonel said, "We've made a tactical decision to push back calling Jake. We're going to pursue some other avenues first."

twenty-one days after

AS DR. HYDE shuffled into class the next morning, Takumi sat down next to me and wrote a note on the edge of his notebook. *Lunch at McInedible*, it read.

I scribbled *Okay* on my own notebook and then turned to a blank page as Dr. Hyde started talking about Sufism, the mystical sect of Islam. I'd only scanned through the reading – I'd been studying only enough not to fail – but in my scanning, I'd come across great last words. This poor Sufi dressed in rags walked into a jewelry store owned by a rich merchant and asked him, "Do you know how you're going to die?" The merchant answered, "No. No one knows how they're going to die." And the Sufi said, "I do."

"How?" asked the merchant.

And the Sufi lay down, crossed his arms, said, "Like this," and died, whereupon the merchant promptly gave up his store to live a life of poverty in pursuit of the kind of spiritual wealth the dead Sufi had acquired.

But Dr. Hyde was telling a different story, one that I'd skipped. "Karl Marx famously called religion 'the opiate of the masses.' Buddhism, particularly as it is popularly practiced, promises improvement through karma. Islam and Christianity promise eternal paradise to the faithful. And that is a powerful opiate, certainly, the hope of a better life to come. But there's a Sufi story that challenges the notion that people believe only because they need an opiate. Rabe'a al-Adiwiyah, a great woman saint of Sufism, was seen running through the streets of her hometown, Basra, carrying a torch in one hand and a bucket of water in the other. When someone asked her

1 **apology**: word or statement saying sorry for sth. 3 **pursue sth.**: (here) investigate sth. 3 **avenue**: (here) path, direction 21 **opiate**: drug containing opium 23 **karma**: (in Buddhism and Hinduism) the sum of sb.'s good and bad actions in one of their lives, believed to decide what will happen to them in the next life

what she was doing, she answered, 'I am going to take this bucket of water and pour it on the flames of hell, and then I am going to use this torch to burn down the gates of paradise so that people will not love God for want of heaven or fear of hell, but because He is God.'"

A woman so strong she burns heaven and drenches hell. *Alaska would have liked this Rabe'a woman*, I wrote in my notebook. But even so, the afterlife mattered to me. Heaven and hell and reincarnation. As much as I wanted to know how Alaska had died, I wanted to know where she was now, if anywhere. I liked to imagine her looking down on us, still aware of us, but it seemed like a fantasy, and I never really *felt* it – just as the Colonel had said at the funeral that she wasn't there, wasn't anywhere. I couldn't honestly imagine her as anything but dead, her body rotting in Vine Station, the rest of her just a ghost alive only in our remembering. Like Rabe'a, I didn't think people should believe in God because of heaven and hell. But I didn't feel a need to run around with a torch. You can't burn down a made-up place.

After class, as Takumi picked through his fries at McInedible, eating only the crunchiest, I felt the total loss of her, still reeling from the idea that she was not only gone from this world but from all of them.

"How have you been?" I asked.

"Uh," he said, a mouth full of fries, "nah good. You?"

"Not good." I took a bite of cheeseburger. I'd gotten a plastic stock car with my Happy Meal, and it sat overturned on the table. I spun the wheels.

"I miss her," Takumi said, pushing away his tray, uninterested in the remaining soggy fries.

"Yeah. I do, too. I'm sorry, Takumi," and I meant it in the largest possible way. I was sorry we ended up like this, spinning wheels at a McDonald's. Sorry the person who had brought us together now lay

4 **for want of**: (here) in order to go to 6 **drench sth.**: make sth. completely wet
8 **reincarnation**: belief that after sb.'s death their soul lives again in a new body
20 **reel from sth.**: feel very shocked or upset about sth. 29 **soggy**: *matschig*

dead between us. I was sorry I let her die. *Sorry I haven't talked to you because you couldn't know the truth about the Colonel and me, and I hated being around you and having to pretend that my grief is this uncomplicated thing – pretending that she died and I miss her instead of that she died because of me.*

"Me too. You're not dating Lara anymore, are you?"

"I don't think so."

"Okay. She was kind of wondering."

I had been ignoring her, but by then she had begun to ignore me back, so I figured it was over, but maybe not. "Well," I told Takumi, "I just can't – I don't know, man. That's pretty complicated."

"Sure. She'll understand. Sure. All good."

"Okay."

"Listen, Pudge. I – ah, I don't know. It sucks, huh?"

"Yeah."

twenty-seven days after

SIX DAYS LATER, four Sundays after the last Sunday, the Colonel and I were trying to shoot each other with paintball guns while turning 900s in a half pipe. "We need booze. And we need to borrow the Eagle's Breathalyzer."

"*Borrow* it? Do you know where it is?"

"Yeah. He's never made you take one?"

"Um. No. He thinks I'm a nerd."

"You *are* a nerd, Pudge. But you're not gonna let a detail like that keep you from drinking." Actually, I hadn't drunk since that night, and didn't feel particularly inclined to ever take it up ever again.

Then I nearly elbowed the Colonel in the face, swinging my arms wildly as if contorting my body in the right ways mattered as much as pressing the right buttons at the right moments – the same video-game-playing delusion that had always gripped Alaska. But the

17–18 **turn 900s**: *(beim Skaten) zweieinhalb Umdrehungen* 18 **half pipe**: *(beim Skaten) Halbröhre* 19 **breathalyser**: device used by the police to measure the amount of alcohol in a driver's breath 22 **nerd**: person who is boring, stupid and not fashionable 25 **inclined to do sth.**: wanting to do sth. 27 **contort**: *verrenken, verdrehen*

Colonel was so focused on the game he didn't even notice. "Do you have a plan for how, exactly, we're going to steal the Breathalyzer from *inside the Eagle's house?*"

The Colonel looked over at me and said, "Do you suck at this game?" and then, without turning back to the screen, shot my skater in the balls with a blue paint blast. "But first, we gotta get some liquor, because the ambrosia's sour and my booze connection is –"

"*POOF.* Gone," I finished.

When I opened his door, Takumi was sitting at his desk, boxy headphones surrounding his entire head, bouncing his head to the beat. He seemed oblivious to us. "Hey," I said. Nothing. "Takumi!" Nothing. "TAKUMI!" He turned around and pulled off his headphones. I closed the door behind me and said, "You got any alcohol?"

"Why?" he asked.

"Uh, because we want to get drunk?" the Colonel answered.

"Great. I'll join you."

"Takumi," the Colonel said. "This is – we need to do this alone."

"No. I've had enough of that shit." Takumi stood up, walked into his bathroom, and came out with a Gatorade bottle filled with clear liquid. "I keep it in the medicine cabinet," Takumi said. "On account of how it's medicine." He pocketed the bottle and then walked out of the room, leaving the door open behind him. A moment later, he peeked his head back in and, brilliantly mimicking the Colonel's bossy bass voice, said, "Christ, you comin' or what?"

"Takumi," the Colonel said. "Okay. Look, what we're doing is a little dangerous, and I don't want you caught up in it. Honestly. But, listen, we'll tell you everything starting tomorrow."

"I'm tired of all this secret shit. She was my friend, too."

"Tomorrow. Honestly."

He pulled the bottle out of his pocket and tossed it to me. "Tomorrow," he said.

6 **paint blast**: *Treffer mit einer Farbkugel* 11 **oblivious to sth.**: not aware of sth. 23 **mimick sb.**: copy the way sb. speaks or behaves 24 **bossy**: always telling people what to do

"I don't really want him to know," I said as we walked back to the room, the Gatorade bottle stuffed in the pocket of my sweatshirt. "He'll hate us."

"Yeah, well, he'll hate us more if we keep pretending he doesn't exist," the Colonel answered.

Fifteen minutes later, I stood at the Eagle's doorstep.

He opened the door with a spatula in hand, smiled, and said, "Miles, come in. I was just making an egg sandwich. Want one?"

"No thanks," I said, following the Eagle into his kitchen.

My job was to keep him out of his living room for thirty seconds so the Colonel could get the Breathalyzer undetected. I coughed loudly to let the Colonel know the coast was clear. The Eagle picked up his egg sandwich and took a bite. "To what do I owe the pleasure of your visit?" he asked.

"I just wanted to tell you that the Colonel – I mean, Chip Martin – he's my roommate, you know, he's having a tough time in Latin."

"Well, he's not attending the class, from what I understand, which can make it very difficult to learn the language." He walked toward me. I coughed again, and backpedaled, the Eagle and I tangoing our way toward his living room.

"Right, well, he's up all night every night thinking about Alaska," I said, standing up straight and tall, trying to block the Eagle's view of the living room with my none-too-wide shoulders. "They were very close, you know."

"I know that –" he said, and in the living room, the Colonel's sneakers squeaked against the hardwood floor. The Eagle looked at me quizzically and sidestepped me. I quickly said, "Is that burner on?" and pointed toward the frying pan.

The Eagle wheeled around, looked at the clearly not-on burner, then dashed into the living room.

7 **spatula**: cooking tool 11 **undetected**: not noticed by anyone 12 **the coast was clear**: there was no visible danger 19 **backpedal** (here): walk backwards 27 **quizzical**: showing that you are slightly surprised or amused 29 **wheel** (here): turn quickly

Empty. He turned back to me. "Are you up to something, Miles?"

"No, sir. Honestly. I just wanted to talk about Chip."

He arched his eyebrows, skeptical. "Well, I understand that this is a devastating loss for Alaska's close friends. It's just awful. There's no comfort to this grief, is there?"

"No sir."

"I'm sympathetic to Chip's troubles. But school is important. Alaska would have wanted, I'm sure, for Chip's studies to continue unimpeded."

I'm sure, I thought. I thanked the Eagle, and he promised me an egg sandwich at some point in the future, which made me nervous that he would just show up at our room one afternoon with an egg sandwich in hand to find us *A.* illegally smoking while the Colonel *B.* illegally drank milk and vodka out of a gallon jug.

Halfway across the dorm circle, the Colonel ran up to me. "That was smooth, with the 'Is that burner on?' If you hadn't pulled that, I was toast. Although I guess I'll have to start going to Latin. Stupid Latin."

"Did you get it?" I asked.

"Yeah," he said. "Yeah. God, I hope he doesn't go looking for it tonight. Although, really, he could never suspect anything. Why would someone *steal a Breathalyzer?*"

At two o'clock in the morning, the Colonel took his sixth shot of vodka, grimaced, then frantically motioned with his hand toward the bottle of Mountain Dew I was drinking. I handed it to him, and he took a long pull on it.

"I don't think I'll be able to go to Latin tomorrow," he said. His words were slightly slurred, as if his tongue were swollen.

"One more," I pleaded.

4 **arch sth.**: form sth. into a curved shape 5 **devastating** (adj): extremely shocking to a person 8 **sympathetic to sb.**: showing that you understand and care about sb.'s problems 10 **unimpeded** (fml): with nothing stopping sb./sth. 18 **be toast**: be likely to get into bad trouble 25 **grimace**: make a sign of displeasure with your face 29 **slur**: *undeutlich sprechen* 30 **plead**: beg

"Okay. This is it, though." He poured a sip of vodka into a Dixie cup, swallowed, pursed his lips, and squeezed his hands into tight little fists. "*Oh God*, this is bad. It's so much better with milk. This better be point two-four."

"We have to wait for fifteen minutes after your last drink before we test it," I said, having downloaded instructions for the Breathalyzer off the Internet. "Do you feel drunk?"

"If drunk were cookies, I'd be Famous Amos."

We laughed. "Chips Ahoy! would have been funnier," I said.

"Forgive me. Not at my best."

I held the Breathalyzer in my hand, a sleek, silver gadget about the size of a small remote control. Beneath an LCD screen was a small hole. I blew into it to test it: 0.00, it read. I figured it was working.

After fifteen minutes, I handed it to the Colonel. "Blow really hard onto it for at least two seconds," I said.

He looked up at me. "Is that what you told Lara in the TV room? Because, see, Pudge, they only *call* it a blow job."

"Shut up and blow," I said.

His cheeks puffed out, the Colonel blew into the hole hard and long, his face turning red.

.16. "Oh no," the Colonel said. "Oh God."

"You're two-thirds of the way there," I said encouragingly.

"Yeah, but I'm like three-fourths of the way to puking."

"Well, obviously it's possible. *She* did it. C'mon! You can outdrink a girl, can't you?"

"Give me the Mountain Dew," he said stoically.

And then I heard footsteps outside. Footsteps. We'd waited till 1:00 to turn on the lights, figuring everyone would be long asleep – it was a school night after all – but footsteps, shit, and as the Colonel looked at me confused, I grabbed the Breathalyzer from him and stuffed it between the foam cushions of the couch and grabbed the

1 **sip** (n): small amount of a drink 8, 9 **Famous Amos, Chips Ahoy!**: types of biscuit (brand name) 11 **sleek**: *glatt* 20 **puffed out**: breathing quickly and with difficulty 25 **outdrink sb.** (infml): *jdm. unter den Tisch trinken*

Dixie cup and the Gatorade bottle of vodka and stashed them behind the COFFEE TABLE, and in one motion I grabbed a cigarette from a pack and lit it, hoping the smell of smoke would cover up the smell of booze. I puffed the cigarette without inhaling, trying to smoke up the room, and I was almost back to the couch when the three quick knocks came against the door and the Colonel looked at me, his eyes wide, his suddenly unpromising future flashing before his eyes, and I whispered, "Cry," as the Eagle turned the knob.

The Colonel hunched forward, his head between his knees and his shoulders shaking, and I put my arm around him as the Eagle came in.

"I'm sorry," I said before the Eagle could say anything. "He's having a tough night."

"Are you *smoking?*" the Eagle asked. *"In your room? Four hours after lights-out?"*

I dropped the cigarette into a half-empty Coke can. "I'm sorry, sir. I'm just trying to stay awake with him."

The Eagle walked up toward the couch, and I felt the Colonel start to rise, but I held his shoulders down firmly, because if the Eagle smelled the Colonel's breath we were done for sure. "Miles," the Eagle said. "I understand that this is a difficult time for you. But you will respect the rules of this school, or you will matriculate someplace else. I'll see you in Jury tomorrow. Is there anything I can do for you, Chip?"

Without looking up, the Colonel answered in a quivering, tear-soaked voice, "No, sir. I'm just glad I have Miles."

"Well, I am, too," the Eagle said. "Perhaps you should encourage him to live within the confines of our rules, lest he risk his place on this campus."

"Yessir," the Colonel said.

"Y'all can leave your lights on until you're ready to go to bed. I'll see you tomorrow, Miles."

7 **unpromising**: not likely to be successful 22 **matriculate**: officially become a student 25 **quivering** (adj): shaking slightly 25–26 **tear-soaked**: *tränenerstickt* 28 **confines** (pl): limits or borders 28 **lest**: *dass nicht*

"Good night, sir," I said, imagining the Colonel sneaking the Breathalyzer back into the Eagle's house while I got harangued at Jury. As the Eagle closed the door behind him, the Colonel shot up, smiling at me, and still nervous that the Eagle might be outside, whispered, "That was a thing of beauty."

"I learned from the best," I said. "Now drink."

An hour later, the Gatorade bottle mostly empty, the Colonel hit .24.

"Thank you, Jesus!" he exclaimed, and then added, "This is awful. This is not fun drunk."

I got up and cleared the COFFEE TABLE out of the way so the Colonel could walk the length of the room without hitting any obstacles, and said, "Okay, can you stand?"

The Colonel pushed his arms into the foam of the couch and began to rise, but then fell backward onto the couch, lying on his back. "Spinning room," he observed. "Gonna puke."

"Don't puke. That will ruin everything."

I decided to give him a field sobriety test, like the cops do. "Okay. Get over here and try to walk a straight line." He rolled off the couch and fell to the floor, and I caught him beneath his armpits and held him up. I positioned him in between two tiles of the linoleum floor. "Follow that line of tiles. Walk straight, toe to heel." He raised one leg and immediately leaned to the left, his arms windmilling. He took a single unsteady step, sort of a waddle, as his feet were seemingly unable to land directly in front of each other. He regained his balance briefly, then took a step backward and landed on the couch. "I fail," he said matter-of-factly.

"Okay, how's your depth perception?"

"My what perwhatshun?"

"Look at me. Is there one of me? Are there two of me? Could you accidentally drive into me if I were a cop car?"

2 **harangue sb.**: *(hier) jdm. eine Strafpredigt halten* 18 **field sobriety test**: *Fahrtüchtigkeitstest* 21 **tile**: *Fliese* 22 **toe to heel**: *Zehe an Ferse* 24 **waddle**: *watscheln* 28 **depth perception:** *(hier) 3D Wahrnehmung*

"Everything's very spinny, but I don't think so. This is bad. Was she really like this?"

"Apparently. Could you drive like this?"

"Oh God no. No. No. She was really drunk, huh."

"Yeah."

"We were really stupid."

"Yeah."

"I'm spinning. But no. No cop car. I can *see*."

"So there's your evidence."

"Maybe she fell asleep. I feel awfully sleepy."

"We'll find out," I said, trying to play the role that the Colonel had always played for me.

"Not tonight," he answered. "Tonight, we're gonna throw up a little, and then we are going to sleep through our hangover."

"Don't forget about Latin."

"Right. Fucking Latin."

twenty-eight days after

THE COLONEL MADE IT to Latin the next morning – "I feel awesome right now, because I'm still drunk. But God help me in a couple of hours" – and I took a French test for which I had studied *un petit peu*. I did all right on the multiple choice (which-verb-tense-makes-sense-here type questions), but the essay question, *In* Le Petit Prince, *what is the significance of the rose?* threw me a bit.

Had I read *The Little Prince* in English or French, I suspect this question might have been quite easy. Unfortunately, I'd spent the evening getting the Colonel drunk. So I answered, *Elle symbolise l'amour* ("It symbolizes love"). Madame O'Malley had left us with an entire page to answer the question, but I figured I'd covered it nicely in three words.

I'd kept up in my classes well enough to get B-minuses and not worry my parents, but I didn't really care much anymore. *The*

22 **throw sb.**: (here) make sb. feel confused or surprised

significance of the rose? I thought. *Who gives a shit? What's the significance of the white tulips?* There was a question worth answering.

After I'd gotten a lecture and ten work hours at Jury, I came back to Room 43 to find the Colonel telling Takumi everything – well, everything except the kiss. I walked in to the Colonel saying, "So we helped her go."

"You set off the fireworks," he said.

"How'd you know about the fireworks?"

"I've been doing a bit of investigating," Takumi answered. "Well, anyway, that was dumb. You shouldn't have done it. But we all let her go, really," he said, and I wondered what the hell he meant by that, but I didn't have time to ask before he said to me, "So you think it was suicide?"

"Maybe," I said. "I don't see how she could have hit the cop by accident unless she was asleep."

"Maybe she was going to visit her father," Takumi said. "Vine Station is on the way."

"Maybe," I said. "Everything's a maybe, isn't it?"

The Colonel reached in his pocket for a pack of cigarettes. "Well, here's another one: *Maybe* Jake has the answers," he said. "We've exhausted other strategies, so I'm calling him tomorrow, okay?"

I wanted answers now, too, but not to some questions. "Yeah, okay," I said. "But listen – don't tell me anything that's not relevant. I don't want to know anything unless it's going to help me know where she was going and why."

"Me neither, actually," Takumi said. "I feel like maybe some of that shit should stay private."

The Colonel stuffed a towel under the door, lit a cigarette, and said, "Fair enough, kids. We'll work on a need-to-know basis."

twenty-nine days after

AS I WALKED HOME from classes the next day, I saw the Colonel sitting on the bench outside the pay phone, scribbling into a notebook balanced on his knees as he cradled the phone between his ear and shoulder.

I hurried into Room 43, where I found Takumi playing the racing game on mute. "How long has he been on the phone?" I asked.

"Dunno. He was on when I got here twenty minutes ago. He must have skipped Smart Boy Math. Why, are you scared Jake's gonna drive down here and kick your ass for letting her go?"

"Whatever," I said, thinking, *This is precisely why we shouldn't have told him*. I walked into the bathroom, turned on the shower, and lit a cigarette. Takumi came in not long after.

"What's up?" he said.

"Nothing. I just want to know what happened to her."

"Like you really want to know the truth? Or like you want to find out that she fought with him and was on her way to break up with him and was going to come back here and fall into your arms and you were going to make hot, sweet love and have genius babies who memorized last words *and* poetry?"

"If you're pissed at me, just say so."

"I'm not pissed at you for letting her go. But I'm tired of you acting like you were the only guy who ever wanted her. Like you had some monopoly on liking her," Takumi answered. I stood up, lifted the toilet seat, and flushed my unfinished cigarette.

I stared at him for a moment, and then said, "I kissed her that night, and I've got a monopoly on that."

"What?" he stammered.

"I kissed her."

His mouth opened as if to speak, but he said nothing. We stared at each other for a while, and I felt ashamed of myself for what amounted to bragging, and finally I said, "I – look, you know how

3 **cradle sth.**: *(hier) etwas halten* 8 **Smart Boy Math**: educational software
24 **flush sth.**: *etwas herunterspülen* 31 **brag**: talk too proudly about sth. you have done

she was. She wanted to do something, and she did it. I was probably just the guy who happened to be there."

"Yeah. Well, I was never that guy," he said. "I – well, Pudge, God knows I can't blame you."

"Don't tell Lara."

He was nodding as we heard the three quick knocks on the front door that meant the Eagle, and I thought, *Shit, caught twice in a week*, and Takumi pointed into the shower, and so we jumped in together and pulled the curtain shut, the too-low showerhead spitting water onto us from rib cage down. Forced to stand closer together than seemed entirely necessary, we stayed there, silent, the sputtering shower slowly soaking our T-shirts and jeans for a few long minutes, while we waited for the steam to lift the smoke into the vents. But the Eagle never knocked on the bathroom door, and eventually Takumi turned off the shower. I opened the bathroom door a crack and peeked out to see the Colonel sitting on the foam couch, his feet propped up on the COFFEE TABLE, finishing Takumi's NASCAR race. I opened the door and Takumi and I walked out, fully clothed and dripping wet.

"Well, there's something you don't see every day," the Colonel said nonchalantly.

"What the hell?" I asked.

"I knocked like the Eagle to scare you." He smiled. "But shit, if y'all need privacy, just leave a note on the door next time."

Takumi and I laughed, and then Takumi said, "Yeah, Pudge and I were getting a little testy, but man, ever since we showered together, Pudge, I feel really close to you."

"So how'd it go?" I asked. I sat down on the COFFEE TABLE, and Takumi plopped down on the couch next to the Colonel, both of us wet and vaguely cold but more concerned with the Colonel's talk with Jake than with getting dry.

10 **rib cage**: *Brustkorb* 14 **eventually**: finally 15 **crack**: (here) narrow opening 17 **NASCAR**: National Association for Stock Car Auto Racing 26 **testy**: easily annoyed 29 **plop down**: sit or lie down heavily

"It was interesting. Here's what you need to know: He gave her those flowers, like we thought. They didn't fight. He just called because he had promised to call at the exact moment of their eight-month anniversary, which happened to be three-oh-two in the A.M., which – let's agree – is a little ridiculous, and I guess somehow she heard the phone ringing. So they talked about nothing for like five minutes, and then completely out of nowhere, she freaked out."

"Completely out of nowhere?" Takumi asked.

"Allow me to consult my notes." The Colonel flipped through his notebook. "Okay. Jake says, 'Did you have a nice anniversary?' and then Alaska says, 'I had a *splendid* anniversary,' " and I could hear in the Colonel's reading the excitement of her voice, the way she leaped onto certain words like *splendid* and *fantastic* and *absolutely*. "Then it's quiet, then Jake says, 'What are you doing?' and Alaska says, 'Nothing, just doodling,' and then she says, 'Oh God.'And then she says, 'Shit shit shit' and starts sobbing, and told him she had to go but she'd talk to him later, but she didn't say she was driving to see him, and Jake doesn't think she was. He doesn't know where she was going, but he says she always asked if she could come up and see him, and she didn't ask, so she must not have been coming. Hold on, lemme find the quote." He flipped a page in the notebook. "Okay, here: 'She said she'd talk to me later, not that she'd *see* me.' "

"She tells me 'To be continued' and tells him she'll talk to him later," I observed.

"Yes. Noted Planning for a future. Admittedly inconsistent with suicide. So then she comes back into her room screaming about forgetting something. And then her headlong race comes to its end. So no answers, really."

"Well, we know where she wasn't going."

"Unless she was feeling particularly impulsive," Takumi said. He looked at me. "And from the sound of things, she was feeling rather impulsive that night."

The Colonel looked over at me curiously, and I nodded.

5 **ridiculous**: silly, absurd 11 **splendid**: excellent, very good 15 **doodle**: *kritzeln* 21 **lemme** = let me 25 **inconsistent**: *widersprüchlich* 27 **headlong** (adj): *(hier) unbesonnen*

"Yeah," Takumi said. "I know."

"Okay, then. And you were pissed, but then you took a shower with Pudge and it's all good. Excellent. So, so that night …" the Colonel continued.

And we tried to resurrect the conversation that last night as best we could for Takumi, but neither of us remembered it terribly well, partly because the Colonel was drunk and I wasn't paying attention until she brought up Truth or Dare. And, anyway, we didn't know how much it might mean. Last words are always harder to remember when no one knows that someone's about to die.

"I mean," the Colonel said, "I think she and I were talking about how much I adored skateboarding on the computer but how it would never even occur to me to try and step on a skateboard in real life, and then she said, 'Let's play Truth or Dare' and then you fucked her."

"Wait, you *fucked* her? *In front of the Colonel?*" Takumi cried.

"I didn't fuck her."

"Calm down, guys," the Colonel said, throwing up his hands. "It's a euphemism."

"For what?" Takumi asked.

"Kissing."

"Brilliant euphemism." Takumi rolled his eyes. "Am I the only one who thinks that might be significant?"

"Yeah, that never occurred to me before," I deadpanned. "But now I don't know. She didn't tell Jake. It couldn't have been that important."

"Maybe she was racked with guilt," he said.

"Jake said she seemed normal on the phone before she freaked out," the Colonel said. "But it must have been that phone call. Something happened that we aren't seeing." The Colonel ran his hands through his thick hair, frustrated. "Christ, something. Something inside of her. And now we just have to figure out what that was."

5 **resurrect sth.**: (here) bring sth. back to life 27 **racked with**: *gequält von*

"So we just have to read the mind of a dead person," Takumi said. "Easy enough."

"Precisely. Want to get shitfaced?" the Colonel asked.

"I don't feel like drinking," I said.

The Colonel reached into the foam recesses of the couch and pulled out Takumi's Gatorade bottle. Takumi didn't want any either, but the Colonel just smirked and said, "More for me," and chugged.

thirty-seven days after

THE NEXT WEDNESDAY, I ran into Lara after religion class – literally. I'd seen her, of course. I'd seen her almost every day – in English or sitting in the library whispering to her roommate, Katie. I saw her at lunch and dinner at the cafeteria, and I probably would have seen her at breakfast, if I'd ever gotten up for it. And surely, she saw me as well, but we hadn't, until that morning, looked at each other simultaneously.

By now, I assumed she'd forgotten me. After all, we only dated for about a day, albeit an eventful one. But when I plowed right into her left shoulder as I hustled toward precalc, she spun around and looked up at me. Angry, and not because of the bump. "I'm sorry," I blurted out, and she just squinted at me like someone about to either fight or cry, and disappeared silently into a classroom. First two words I'd said to her in a month.

I wanted to want to talk to her. I knew I'd been awful – *Imagine*, I kept telling myself, *if you were Lara, with a dead friend and a silent ex-boyfriend* – but I only had room for one true want, and she was dead, and I wanted to know the how and why of it, and Lara couldn't tell me, and that was all that mattered.

14 **simultaneously**: happening at the same time 16 **plow into sb.** (AE): (here) crash into sb. because you are not paying enough attention 17 **hustle**: (here) move very fast 17 **spin around (spun – spun)**: turn around quickly

forty-five days after

FOR WEEKS, the Colonel and I had relied on charity to support our cigarette habit – we'd gotten free or cheap packs from everyone from Molly Tan to the once-crew-cutted Longwell Chase. It was as if people wanted to help and couldn't think of a better way. But by the end of February, we ran out of charity. Just as well, really. I never felt right taking people's gifts, because they did not know that we'd loaded the bullets and put the gun in her hand.

So after our classes, Takumi drove us to Coosa "We Cater to Your Spiritual Needs" Liquors. That afternoon, Takumi and I had learned the disheartening results of our first major precalc test of the semester. Possibly because Alaska was no longer available to teach us precalc over a pile of McInedible french fries and possibly because neither of us had really studied, we were both in danger of getting progress reports sent home.

"The thing is that I just don't find precalc very interesting," Takumi said matter-of-factly.

"It might be hard to explain that to the director of admissions at Harvard," the Colonel responded.

"I don't know," I said. "I find it pretty compelling."

And we laughed, but the laughs drifted into a thick, pervasive silence, and I knew we were all thinking of her, dead and laughless, cold, no longer Alaska. The idea that Alaska didn't exist still stunned me every time I thought about it. *She's rotting underground in Vine Station, Alabama*, I thought, but even that wasn't quite it. Her body was there, but she was nowhere, nothing, *POOF*.

The times that were the most fun seemed always to be followed by sadness now, because it was when life started to feel like it did when she was with us that we realized how utterly, totally gone she was.

I bought the cigarettes. I'd never entered Coosa Liquors, but it was every bit as desolate as Alaska described. The dusty wooden

1 **rely on sb./sth.**: need or depend on sb./sth. 10 **disheartening** (adj): making sb. lose hope 19 **compelling** (adj): *(hier) überzeugend* 20 **pervasive**: *überall vorhanden* 22 **stun sb.**: shock sb. so much that they cannot think clearly 31 **desolate** ['desələt]: (of a place) empty and depressing

floor creaked as I made my way to the counter, and I saw a large barrel filled with brackish water that purported to contain LIVE BAIT, but in fact contained a veritable school of dead, floating minnows. The woman behind the counter smiled at me with all four of her teeth when I asked her for a carton of Marlboro Lights.

"You go t'Culver Creek?" she asked me, and I did not know whether to answer truthfully, since no high-school student was likely to be nineteen, but she grabbed the carton of cigarettes from beneath her and put it on the counter without asking for an ID, so I said, "Yes, ma'am."

"How's school?" she asked.

"Pretty good," I answered.

"Heard y'all had a death up there."

"Yes'm," I say.

"I's awful sorry t' hear it."

"Yes'm."

The woman, whose name I did not know because this was not the sort of commercial establishment to waste money on name tags, had one long, white hair growing from a mole on her left cheek. It wasn't disgusting, exactly, but I couldn't stop glancing at it and then looking away.

Back in the car, I handed a pack of cigarettes to the Colonel.

We rolled down the windows, although the February cold bit at my face and the loud wind made conversation impossible. I sat in my quarter of the car and smoked, wondering why the old woman at Coosa Liquors didn't just pull that one hair out of her mole. The wind blew through Takumi's rolled-down window in front of me and against my face. I scooted to the middle of the backseat and looked up at the Colonel sitting shotgun, smiling, his face turned to the wind blowing in through his window.

1 **creak**: *knarren* 2 **bait**: *Köder* 3 **veritable**: *wahrhaftig* 3 **minnow**: small freshwater fish 19 **mole**: small dark brown mark on the skin

forty-six days after

I DIDN'T WANT TO TALK TO LARA, but the next day at lunch, Takumi pulled the ultimate guilt trip. "How do you think Alaska would feel about this shit?" he asked as he stared across the cafeteria at Lara. She was sitting three tables away from us with her roommate, Katie, who was telling some story, and Lara smiled whenever Katie laughed at one of her own jokes. Lara scooped up a forkful of canned corn and held it above her plate, moving her mouth to it and bowing her head toward her lap as she took the bite from the fork – a quiet eater.

"She could talk to *me*," I told Takumi.

Takumi shook his head. His open mouth gooey with mashed potatoes, he said, "Yuh ha' to." He swallowed. "Let me ask you a question, Pudge. When you're old and gray and your grandchildren are sitting on your knee and look up at you and say, 'Grandpappy, who gave you your first blow job?' do you want to have to tell them it was some girl you spent the rest of high school ignoring? No!" He smiled. "You want to say, 'My dear friend Lara Buterskaya. Lovely girl. Prettier than your grandma by a wide margin.' " I laughed. So yeah, okay. I had to talk to Lara.

After classes, I walked over to Lara's room and knocked, and then she stood in the doorway, looking like, *What? What now? You've done the damage you could, Pudge,* and I looked past her, into the room I'd only entered once, where I learned that kissing or no, I couldn't talk to her – and before the silence could get too uncomfortable, I talked. "I'm sorry," I said.

"For what?" she asked, still looking toward me but not quite at me.

"For ignoring you. For everything," I said.

"You deedn't have to be my boyfriend." She looked so pretty, her big eyes blinking fast, her cheeks soft and round, and still the roundness could only remind me of Alaska's thin face and her high cheekbones. But I could live with it – and, anyway, I had to. "You could have just been my friend," she said.

"I know. I screwed up. I'm sorry."

"Don't forgive that asshole," Katie cried from inside the room.

"I forgeeve you." Lara smiled and hugged me, her hands tight around the small of my back. I wrapped my arms around her shoulders and smelled violets in her hair.

"*I* don't forgive you," Katie said, appearing in the doorway. And although Katie and I were not well acquainted, she felt comfortable enough to knee me in the balls. She smiled then, and as I crumpled into a bow, Katie said, "*Now* I forgive you."

Lara and I took a walk to the lake – sans Katie – and we talked. We talked – about Alaska and about the past month, about how she had to miss me *and* miss Alaska, while I only had to miss Alaska (which was true enough). I told her as much of the truth as I could, from the firecrackers to the Pelham Police Department and the white tulips.

"I loved her," I said, and Lara said she loved her, too, and I said, "I know, but that's why. I loved her, and after she died I couldn't think about anything else. It felt, like, dishonest. Like cheating."

"That's not a good reason," she said.

"I know," I answered.

She laughed softly. "Well, good then. As long as you know." I knew I wasn't going to erase that anger, but we were talking.

As darkness spread that evening, the frogs croaked and a few newly resurrected insects buzzed about campus, and the four of us – Takumi, Lara, the Colonel, and I – walked through the cold gray light of a full moon to the Smoking Hole.

"Hey, Colonel, why do you call eet the Smoking Hole?" Lara asked. "Eet's, like, a tunnel."

"It's like fishing hole," the Colonel said. "Like, if we fished, we'd fish here. But we smoke. I don't know. I think Alaska named it." The Colonel pulled a cigarette out of his pack and threw it into the water.

"What the hell?" I asked.

"For her," he said.

7 **balls** (infml): *Hoden* 7 **crumple**: *(hier) sich krümmen*

I half smiled and followed his lead, throwing in a cigarette of my own. I handed Takumi and Lara cigarettes, and they followed suit. The smokes bounced and danced in the stream for a few moments, and then they floated out of sight.

I was not religious, but I liked rituals. I liked the idea of connecting an action with remembering. In China, the Old Man had told us, there are days reserved for grave cleaning, where you make gifts to the dead. And I imagined that Alaska would want a smoke, and so it seemed to me that the Colonel had begun an excellent ritual.

The Colonel spit into the stream and broke the silence. "Funny thing, talking to ghosts," he said. "You can't tell if you're making up their answers or if they are really talking to you."

"I say we make a list," Takumi said, steering clear of introspective talk. "What kind of proof do we have of suicide?" The Colonel pulled out his omnipresent notebook.

"She never hit the brakes," I said, and the Colonel started scribbling.

And she was awfully upset about something, although she'd been awfully upset without committing suicide many times before. We considered that maybe the flowers were some kind of memorial to herself – like a funeral arrangement or something. But that didn't seem very Alaskan to us. She was cryptic, sure, but if you're going to plan your suicide down to the flowers, you probably have a plan as to how you're actually going to die, and Alaska had no way of knowing a police car was going to present itself on I-65 for the occasion.

And the evidence suggesting an accident?

"She was really drunk, so she could have thought she wasn't going to hit the cop, although I don't know how," Takumi said.

"She could have fallen asleep," Lara offered.

"Yeah, we've thought about that," I said. "But I don't think you keep driving straight if you fall asleep."

2 **follow suit**: act or behave in the way that sb else has just done 13 **steer clear of sth.**: (here) avoid (talking about) sth. because it may cause problems
15 **omnipresent** (fml) present everywhere 22 **cryptic**: mysterious

"I can't think of a way to find out that does not put our lives in considerable danger," the Colonel deadpanned. "Anyway, she didn't show warning signs of suicide. I mean, she didn't talk about wanting to die or give away her stuff or anything."

"That's two. Drunk and no plans to die," Takumi said. This wasn't going anywhere. Just a different dance with the same question. What we needed wasn't more thinking. We needed more evidence.

"We have to find out where she was going," the Colonel said.

"The last people she talked to were me, you, and Jake," I said to him. "And we don't know. So how the hell are we going to find out?"

Takumi looked over at the Colonel and sighed. "I don't think it would help, to know where she was going. I think that would make it worse for us. Just a gut feeling."

"Well, *my* gut wants to know," Lara said, and only then did I realize what Takumi meant the day we'd showered together – I may have kissed her, but I really *didn't* have a monopoly on Alaska; the Colonel and I weren't the only ones who cared about her, and weren't alone in trying to figure out how she died and why.

"Well, regardless," said the Colonel, "we're at a dead end. So one of you think of something to do. Because I'm out of investigative tools."

He flicked his cigarette butt into the creek, stood up, and left. We followed him. Even in defeat, he was still the Colonel.

fifty-one days after

THE INVESTIGATION STALLED, I took to reading for religion class again, which seemed to please the Old Man, whose pop quizzes I'd been failing consistently for a solid six weeks. We had one that Wednesday morning: *Share an example of a Buddhist koan.* A koan is like a riddle that's supposed to help you toward enlightenment in Zen Buddhism.

14 **gut feeling**: *Bauchgefühl* 20 **regardless**: *(hier) ungeachtet (der Tatsache)* 25 **stall**: stop making progress 26 **pop quiz** (AE): short test that is given to students without any warning 27 **consistent**: happening in the same way for a period of time

For my answer, I wrote about this guy Banzan. He was walking through the market one day when he overheard someone ask a butcher for his best piece of meat. The butcher answered, "Everything in my shop is the best. You cannot find a piece of meat that is not the best." Upon hearing this, Banzan realized that there is no best and no worst, that those judgments have no real meaning because there is only what is, and *poof*, he reached enlightenment. Reading it the night before, I'd wondered if it would be like that for me – if in one moment, I would finally understand her, know her, and understand the role I'd played in her dying. But I wasn't convinced enlightenment struck like lightning.

After we'd passed our quizzes, the Old Man, sitting, grabbed his cane and motioned toward Alaska's fading question on the blackboard. "Let's look at one sentence on page ninety-four of this very entertaining introduction to Zen that I had you read this week. 'Everything that comes together falls apart,'" the Old Man said. "Everything. The chair I'm sitting on. It was built, and so it will fall apart. I'm gonna fall apart, probably before this chair. And you're gonna fall apart. The cells and organs and systems that make you you – they came together, grew together, and so must fall apart. The Buddha knew one thing science didn't prove for millennia after his death: Entropy increases. Things fall apart."

We are all going, I thought, and it applies to turtles and turtlenecks, Alaska the girl and Alaska the place, because nothing can last, not even the earth itself. The Buddha said that suffering was caused by desire, we'd learned, and that the cessation of desire meant the cessation of suffering. When you stopped wishing things wouldn't fall apart, you'd stop suffering when they did.

Someday no one will remember that she ever existed, I wrote in my notebook, and then, *or that I did*. Because memories fall apart, too. And then you're left with nothing, left not even with a ghost but with its shadow. In the beginning, she had haunted me, haunted my

11 **lightning**: *Blitz* 22 **entropy**: *Maß für die Unordnung eines Systems*
23 **turtleneck**: *Rollkragen* 27 **cessation**: stopping of sth. 32 **haunt sb.**: *jdm. verfolgen, nicht mehr aus dem Sinn gehen*

dreams, but even now, just weeks later, she was slipping away, falling apart in my memory and everyone else's, dying again.

The Colonel, who had driven the Investigation from the start, who had cared about what happened to her when I only cared if she loved me, had given up on it, answerless. And I didn't like what answers I had: She hadn't even cared enough about what happened between us to tell Jake; instead, she had just talked cute with him, giving him no reason to think that minutes before, I'd tasted her boozy breath. And then something invisible snapped inside her, and that which had come together commenced to fall apart.

And maybe that was the only answer we'd ever have. She fell apart because that's what happens. The Colonel seemed resigned to that, but if the Investigation had once been his idea, it was now the thing that held me together, and I still hoped for enlightenment.

sixty-two days after

THE NEXT SUNDAY, I slept in until the late-morning sunlight slivered through the blinds and found its way to my face. I pulled the comforter over my head, but the air got hot and stale, so I got up to call my parents.

"Miles!" my mom said before I even said hello. "We just got caller identification."

"Does it magically know it's me calling from the pay phone?"

She laughed. "No, it just says 'pay phone' and the area code. So I deduced. How are you?" she asked, a warm concern in her voice.

"I'm doing okay. I kinda screwed up some of my classes for a while, but I'm back to studying now, so it should be fine," I said, and that was mostly true.

"I know it's been hard on you, buddy," she said. "Oh! Guess who your dad and I saw at a party last night? Mrs. Forrester. Your fourth-grade teacher! Remember? She remembered you *perfectly*, and spoke very highly of you, and we just talked" – and while I was pleased to

7 **talk cute** (infml): *Süßholz raspeln* 15 **sliver**: *splittern* 19–20 **caller identification**: *Rufnummernerkennung* 23 **deduce sth.**: *etwas ableiten* 23 **concern**: (here) worry

know that Mrs. Forrester held my fourth-grade self in high regard, I only half listened as I read the scribbled notes on the white-painted pine wall on either side of the phone, looking for any new ones I might be able to decode (*Lacy's – Friday, 10* were the when and where of a Weekday Warrior party, I figured) – "and we had dinner with the Johnstons last night and I'm afraid that Dad had too much wine. We played charades and he was just *awful*." She laughed, and I felt so tired, but someone had dragged the bench away from the pay phone, so I sat my bony butt down on the hard concrete, pulling the silver cord of the phone taut and preparing for a serious soliloquy from my mom, and then down below all the other notes and scribbles, I saw a drawing of a flower. Twelve oblong petals around a filled-in circle against the daisy-white paint, and daisies, white daisies, and I could hear her saying, *What do you see, Pudge? Look*, and I could see her sitting drunk on the phone with Jake talking about nothing and *What are you doing?* and she says, *Nothing, just doodling, just doodling*. And then, *Oh God*.

"Miles?"

"Yeah, sorry, Mom. Sorry. Chip's here. We gotta go study. I gotta go."

"Will you call us later, then? I'm sure Dad wants to talk to you."

"Yeah, Mom; yeah, of course. I love you, okay? Okay, I gotta go."

"I think I found something!" I shouted at the Colonel, invisible beneath his blanket, but the urgency in my voice and the promise of something, anything, found, woke the Colonel up instantly, and he jumped from his bunk to the linoleum. Before I could say anything, he grabbed yesterday's jeans and sweatshirt from the floor, pulled them on, and followed me outside.

"Look." I pointed, and he squatted down beside the phone and said, "Yeah. She drew that. She was always doodling those flowers."

1 **hold sb. in high regard**: have a good opinion of sb. 4 **decode sth.**: find the meaning of sth. 7 **charades**: party game 9 **concrete**: *(hier) Beton* 10 **taut** [tɑːt]: stretched tightly 10 **soliloquy** [sə'lɪləkwi]: monologue 12 **oblong** (adj): *rechteckig* 12 **petal**: *Blütenblatt* 24 **urgency**: expression that sth. needs to be dealt with immediately

"And 'just doodling,' remember? Jake asked her what she was doing and she said 'just doodling,' and *then* she said 'Oh God' and freaked out. She looked at the doodle and remembered something."

"Good memory, Pudge," he acknowledged, and I wondered why the Colonel wouldn't just get excited about it.

"And then she freaked out," I repeated, "and went and got the tulips while we were getting the fireworks. She saw the doodle, remembered whatever she'd forgotten, and then freaked out."

"Maybe," he said, still staring at the flower, trying perhaps to see it as she had. He stood up finally and said, "It's a solid theory, Pudge," and reached up and patted my shoulder, like a coach complimenting a player. "But we still don't know what she forgot."

sixty-nine days after

A WEEK AFTER THE DISCOVERY of the doodled flower, I'd resigned myself to its insignificance – I wasn't Banzan in the meat market after all – and as the maples around campus began to hint of resurrection and the maintenance crew began mowing the grass in the dorm circle again, it seemed to me we had finally lost her.

The Colonel and I walked into the woods down by the lake that afternoon and smoked a cigarette in the precise spot where the Eagle had caught us so many months before. We'd just come from a town meeting, where the Eagle announced the school was going to build a playground by the lake in memory of Alaska. She did like swings, I guess, but a *playground?* Lara stood up at the meeting – surely a first for her – and said they should do something funnier, something Alaska herself would have done.

Now, by the lake, sitting on a mossy, half-rotten log, the Colonel said to me, "Lara was right. We should do something for her. A prank. Something she would have loved."

"Like, a memorial prank?"

10 **solid**: strong 14 **insignificance**: *Bedeutungslosigkeit* 16 **maintenance**: *(hier) Wartung*

"Exactly. The Alaska Young Memorial Prank. We can make it an annual event. Anyway, she came up with this idea last year. But she wanted to save it to be our senior prank. But it's good. It's really good. It's historic."

"Are you going to tell me?" I asked, thinking back to the time when he and Alaska had left me out of prank planning for Barn Night.

"Sure," he said. "The prank is entitled 'Subverting the Patriarchal Paradigm.'" And he told me, and I have to say, Alaska left us with the crown jewel of pranks, the *Mona Lisa* of high-school hilarity, the culmination of generations of Culver Creek pranking. And if the Colonel could pull it off, it would be etched in the memory of everyone at the Creek, and Alaska deserved nothing less. Best of all, it did not, technically, involve any expellable offenses.

The Colonel got up and dusted the dirt and moss off his pants. "I think we owe her that."

And I agreed, but still, she owed us an explanation. If she was up there, down there, out there, somewhere, maybe she would laugh. And maybe – just maybe – she would give us the clue we needed.

eighty-three days after

TWO WEEKS LATER, the Colonel returned from spring break with two notebooks filled with the minutiae of prank planning, sketches of various locations, and a forty-page, two-column list of problems that might crop up and their solutions. He calculated all times to a tenth of a second, and all distances to the inch, and then he recalculated, as if he could not bear the thought of failing her again. And then on that Sunday, the Colonel woke up late and rolled over. I was reading *The Sound and the Fury*, which I was supposed to have read in mid-February, and I looked up as I heard the rustling in the bed, and the

8 **subvert sth.**: *etwas untergraben, etwas umstoßen* 8 **patriarchal** [ˌpeɪtriˈɑrkl]: ruled or controlled by men 9 **paradigm** [ˈperədaɪm]: typical example or pattern of sth. 10 **hilarity**: state of great amusement 12 **etch in the memory**: *sich ins Gedächtnis einprägen* 21 **minutiae** [maɪˈnuːʃiaɪ]: very small details 27 **The Sound and the Fury**: novel (1929) by William Faulkner

Colonel said, "Let's get the band back together." And so I ventured out into the overcast spring and woke up Lara and Takumi, then brought them back to Room 43. The Barn Night crew was intact – or as close as it ever would be – for the Alaska Young Memorial Prank.

The three of us sat on the couch while the Colonel stood in front of us, outlining the plan and our parts in it with an excitement I hadn't seen in him since Before. When he finished, he asked, "Any questions?"

"Yeah," Takumi said. "Is that seriously going to work?"

"Well, first we gotta find a stripper. And second Pudge has to work some magic with his dad."

"All right, then," Takumi said. "Let's get to work."

eighty-four days after

EVERY SPRING, Culver Creek took one Friday afternoon off from classes, and all the students, faculty, and staff were required to go to the gym for Speaker Day. Speaker Day featured two speakers – usually small-time celebrities or small-time politicians or small-time academics, the kind of people who would come and speak at a school for the measly three hundred bucks the school budgeted. The junior class picked the first speaker and the seniors the second, and anyone who had ever attended a Speaker Day agreed that they were torturously boring. We planned to shake Speaker Day up a bit.

All we needed to do was convince the Eagle to let "Dr. William Morse," a "friend of my dad's" and a "preeminent scholar of deviant sexuality in adolescents," be the junior class's speaker.

So I called my dad at work, and his secretary, Paul, asked me if everything was all right, and I wondered why everyone, *everyone*, asked me if everything was all right when I called at any time other than Sunday morning.

"Yeah, I'm fine."

2 **overcast** (adj): covered with clouds 16 **small-time**: not very important
18 **measly** (adj): very small in size or quantity 23 **preeminent**: important
23 **deviant** ['di:viənt]: different from what most people consider to be normal and acceptable

My dad picked up. "Hey, Miles. Is everything all right?"

I laughed and spoke quietly into the phone, since people were milling about. "Yeah, Dad. Everything is fine. Hey, remember when you stole the school bell and buried it in the cemetery?"

"Greatest Culver Creek prank ever," he responded proudly.

"It was, Dad. It *was*. So listen, I wonder if you'd help out with the new greatest Culver Creek prank ever."

"Oh, I don't know about that, Miles. I don't want you getting in any trouble."

"Well, I won't. The whole junior class is planning it. And it's not like anyone is going to get hurt or anything. Because, well, remember Speaker Day?"

"*God* that was boring. That was almost worse than class."

"Yeah, well, I need you to pretend to be our speaker. Dr. William Morse, a professor of psychology at the University of Central Florida and an expert in adolescent understandings of sexuality."

He was quiet for a long time, and I looked down at Alaska's last daisy and waited for him to ask what the prank was, and I would have told him, but I just heard him breathe slowly into the phone, and then he said, "I won't even ask. *Hmm.*" He sighed. "Swear to God you'll never tell your mother."

"I swear to God." I paused. It took me a second to remember the Eagle's real name. "Mr. Starnes is going to call you in about ten minutes."

"Okay, my name is Dr. William Morse, and I'm a psychology professor, and – adolescent sexuality?"

"Yup. You're the best, Dad."

"I just want to see if you can top me," he said, laughing.

Although it killed the Colonel to do it, the prank could not work without the assistance of the Weekday Warriors – specifically junior-class president Longwell Chase, who by now had grown his silly surfer mop back. But the Warriors loved the idea, so I met Longwell in his room and said, "Let's go."

3 **mill about**: *herumlaufen*

Longwell Chase and I had nothing to talk about and no desire to pretend otherwise, so we walked silently to the Eagle's house. The Eagle came to the door before we even knocked. He cocked his head a little when he saw us, looking confused – and, indeed, we made an odd couple, with Longwell's pressed and pleated khaki pants and my I-keep-meaning-to-do-laundry blue jeans.

"The speaker we picked is a friend of Miles's dad," Longwell said. "Dr. William Morse. He's a professor at a university down in Florida, and he studies adolescent sexuality."

"Aiming for controversy, are we?"

"Oh no," I said. "I've met Dr. Morse. He's interesting, but he's not controversial. He just studies the, uh, the way that adolescents' understanding of sex is still changing and growing. I mean, he's opposed to premarital sex."

"Well. What's his phone number?" I gave the Eagle a piece of paper, and he walked to a phone on the wall and dialed. "Yes, hello. I'm calling to speak with Dr. Morse? … Okay, thanks … Hello, Dr. Morse. I have Miles Halter here in my home, and he tells me … great, wonderful … Well, I was wondering" – the Eagle paused, twisting the cord around his finger – "wondering, I guess, whether you – just so long as you understand that these are impressionable young people. We wouldn't want explicit discussions. … Excellent. Excellent. I'm glad you understand. … You, too, sir. See you soon!" The Eagle hung up the phone, smiling, and said, "Good choice! He seems like a very interesting man."

"Oh yeah," Longwell said very seriously. "I think he will be extraordinarily interesting."

one hundred two days after

MY FATHER PLAYED Dr. William Morse on the phone, but the man playing him in real life went by the name of Maxx with two x's, except that his name was actually Stan, except on Speaker Day his name was, obviously, Dr. William Morse. He was a veritable

10 **controversy**: *(hier) Auseinandersetzung* 14 **premarital** [priːˈmærɪtəl]: before marriage

existential identity crisis, a male stripper with more aliases than a covert CIA agent.

The first four "agencies" the Colonel called turned us down. It wasn't until we got to the *B*'s in the "Entertainment" section of the Yellow Pages that we found Bachelorette Parties R Us. The owner of the aforementioned establishment liked the idea a great deal, but, he said, "Maxx is gonna love that. But no nudity. Not in front of the kids." We agreed – with some reluctance.

To ensure that none of us would get expelled, Takumi and I collected five dollars from every junior at Culver Creek to cover "Dr. William Morse's" appearance fee, since we doubted the Eagle would be keen on paying him after witnessing the, uh, speech. I paid the Colonel's five bucks. "I feel that I have earned your charity," he said, gesturing to the spiral notebooks he'd filled with plans.

As I sat through my classes that morning, I could think of nothing else. Every junior in the school had known for two weeks, and so far not even the faintest rumor had leaked out. But the Creek was rife with gossips – particularly the Weekday Warriors, and if just one person told one friend who told one friend who told one friend who told the Eagle, everything would fall apart.

The Creek's don't-rat ethos withstood the test nicely, but when Maxx/Stan/Dr. Morse didn't shown up by 11:50 that morning, I thought the Colonel would lose his shit. He sat on the bumper of a car in the student parking lot, his head bowed, his hands running through his thick mop of dark hair over and over again, as if he were trying to find something in there. Maxx had promised to arrive by 11:40, twenty minutes before the official start of Speaker Day, giving him time to learn the speech and everything. I stood next to the Colonel,

2 **covert**: secret or hidden 2 **CIA = Central Intelligence Agency**: *US Geheimdienst* 6 **aforementioned**: mentioned before 8 **reluctance**: unwillingness to do sth. 13 **charity** (here): act of giving money to people who are in need 17 **leak out**: become known to other people 17–18 **rife with sth.**: full of sth. bad or unpleasant 21 **ethos**: *(hier) Geist, Überzeugung* 21 **withstand sth.**: *etwas standhalten* 23 **lose your shit** (sl): get very angry as a result of sb.'s stupid behavior

worried but quiet, waiting. We'd sent Takumi to call "the agency" and learn the whereabouts of "the performer."

"Of all the things I thought could go wrong, this was not one of them. We have no solution for this."

Takumi ran up, careful not to speak to us until he was near. Kids were starting to file into the gym. Late late late late. We asked so little of our performer, really. We had written his speech. We had planned everything for him. All Maxx had to do was show up with his outfit on. And yet …

"The agency," said Takumi, "says the performer is on his way."

"On his way?" the Colonel said, clawing at his hair with a new vigor. "On his way? He's *already* late."

"They said he should be –" and then suddenly our worries disappeared as a blue minivan rounded the corner toward the parking lot, and I saw a man inside wearing a suit.

"That'd better be Maxx," the Colonel said as the car parked. He jogged up to the front door.

"I'm Maxx," the guy said upon opening the door.

"I am a nameless and faceless representative of the junior class," the Colonel answered, shaking Maxx's hand. He was thirtyish, tan and wide-shouldered, with a strong jaw and a dark, close-cropped goatee.

We gave Maxx a copy of his speech, and he read through it quickly.

"Any questions?" I asked.

"Uh, yeah. Given the nature of this event, I think y'all should pay me in advance."

He struck me as very articulate, even professorial, and I felt a supreme confidence, as if Alaska had found the best male stripper in central Alabama and led us right to him.

Takumi popped the trunk of his SUV and grabbed a paper grocery bag with $320 in it. "Here you go, Maxx," he said. "Okay, Pudge here is going to sit down there with you, because you are friends with Pudge's dad. That's in the speech. But, uh, we're hoping that if you

21 **close-cropped**: cut very short   22 **goatee**: small beard

get interrogated when this is all over, you can find it in your heart to say that the whole junior class called on a conference call to hire you, because we wouldn't want Pudge here to get in any trouble."

He laughed. "Sounds good to me. I took this gig because I thought it was hilarious. Wish *I'd* thought of this in high school."

As I walked into the gym, Maxx/Dr. William Morse at my side, Takumi and the Colonel trailing a good bit behind me, I knew I was more likely to get busted than anyone else. But I'd been reading the Culver Creek Handbook pretty closely the last couple weeks, and I reminded myself of my two-pronged defense, in the event I got in trouble: *1*. There is not, technically, a rule against paying a stripper to dance in front of the school. 2. It cannot be proven that I was responsible for the incident. It can only be proven that I brought a person onto campus who I presumed to be an expert on sexual deviancy in adolescence and who turned out to be an actual sexual deviant.

I sat down with Dr. William Morse in the middle of the front row of bleachers. Some ninth graders sat behind me, but when the Colonel walked up with Lara a moment later, he politely told them, "Thanks for holding our seats," and ushered them away. As per the plan, Takumi was in the supply room on the second floor, connecting his stereo equipment to the gym's loudspeakers. I turned to Dr. Morse and said, "We should look at each other with great interest and talk like you're friends with my parents."

He smiled and nodded his head. "He is a great man, your father. And your mother – so beautiful." I rolled my eyes, a bit disgusted. Still, I liked this stripper fellow. The Eagle came in at noon on the nose, greeted the senior-class speaker – a former Alabama state attorney general – and then came over to Dr. Morse, who stood with great aplomb and half bowed as he shook the Eagle's hand – maybe *too* formal – and the Eagle said, "We're certainly very glad to

1 **interrogate sb.**: ask sb. a lot of questions 4 **gig**: short-term entertainment job 5 **hilarious**: extremely funny 10 **two-pronged**: *(hier) zweigleisig* 27–28 **on the nose**: exactly 28–29 **state attorney general**: *Generalstaatsanwalt* 30 **with aplomb**: in a confident and successful way, often in a difficult situation

have you here," and Maxx replied, "Thank you. I hope I don't disappoint."

I wasn't worried about getting expelled. I wasn't even worried about getting the Colonel expelled, although maybe I should have been. I was worried that it wouldn't work because Alaska hadn't planned it. Maybe no prank worthy of her could be pulled off without her.

The Eagle stood behind the podium.

"This is a day of historic significance at Culver Creek. It was the vision of our founder Phillip Garden that you, as students and we, as faculty, might take one afternoon a year to benefit from the wisdom of voices outside the school, and so we meet here annually to learn from them, to see the world as others see it. Today, our juniorclass speaker is Dr. William Morse, a professor of psychology at the University of Central Florida and a widely respected scholar. He is here today to talk about teenagers and sexuality, a topic I'm sure you'll find considerably interesting. So please help me welcome Dr. Morse to the podium."

We applauded. My heart beat in my chest like it wanted to applaud, too. As Maxx walked up to the podium, Lara leaned down to me and whispered, "He *ees* really hot."

"Thank you, Mr. Starnes." Maxx smiled and nodded to the Eagle, then straightened his papers and placed them on the podium. Even *I* almost believed he was a professor of psychology. I wondered if maybe he was an actor supplementing his income.

He read directly from the speech without looking up, but he read with the confident, airy tone of a slightly snooty academic. "I'm here today to talk with you about the fascinating subject of teenage sexuality. My research is in the field of sexual linguistics, specifically the way that young people discuss sex and related questions. So, for instance, I'm interested in why my saying the word *arm* might not

6 **pull sth. off** (infml): succeed in doing sth difficult 10 **founder**: person who starts an organization 15 **scholar** ['skɑːlər]: person who knows a lot about a particular subject 25 **supplement sth.**: add sth. to sth. else in order to improve it 27 **airy**: *(hier) lässig, ungezwungen* 27 **snooty** (AE infml): *versnobt* 29 **linguistics**: scientific study of language

make you laugh, but my saying the word *vagina* might." And, indeed, there were some nervous twitters from the audience. "The way young people speak about one another's bodies says a great deal about our society. In today's world, boys are much more likely to objectify girls' bodies than the other way around. Boys will say amongst themselves that so-and-so has a nice rack, while girls will more likely say that a boy is cute, a term that describes both physical and emotional characteristics. This has the effect of turning girls into mere objects, while boys are seen by girls as whole people –"

And then Lara stood up, and in her delicate, innocent accent, cut Dr. William Morse off. "You're so hot! I weesh you'd shut up and take off your clothes."

The students laughed, but all of the teachers turned around and looked at her, stunned silent. She sat down.

"What's your name, dear?"

"Lara," she said.

"Now, Lara," Maxx said, looking down at his paper to remember the line, "what we have here is a very interesting case study – a female objectifying me, a male. It's so unusual that I can only assume you're making an attempt at humor."

Lara stood up again and shouted, "I'm not keeding! Take off your clothes."

He nervously looked down at the paper, and then looked up at all of us, smiling. "Well, it is certainly important to subvert the patriarchal paradigm, and I suppose this is a way. All right, then," he said, stepping to the left of the podium. And then he shouted, loud enough that Takumi could hear him upstairs, "This one's for Alaska Young."

As the fast, pumping bass of Prince's "Get Off" started from the loudspeakers, Dr. William Morse grabbed the leg of his pants with one hand and the lapel of his coat with the other, and the Velcro parted and his stage costume came apart, revealing Maxx with two *x*'s, a stunningly muscular man with an eight-pack in his stomach

2 **twitter**: *(hier) kichern* 6 **rack** (sl): breasts 18 **case study**: *Fallstudie* 31 **lapel**: *Revers* 31 **Velcro**: *Klettband*

and bulging pec muscles, and Maxx stood before us, smiling, wearing only briefs that were surely tighty, but not whitey – black leather.

His feet in place, Maxx swayed his arms to the music, and the crowd erupted with laughter and deafening, sustained applause – the largest ovation by a good measure in Speaker Day history. The Eagle was up in a flash, and as soon as he stood, Maxx stopped dancing, but he flexed his pec muscles so that they jumped up and down quickly in time to the music before the Eagle, not smiling but sucking his lips in as if not smiling required effort, indicated with a thumb that Maxx should go on home, and Maxx did.

My eyes followed Maxx out the door, and I saw Takumi standing in the doorway, fists raised in the air in triumph, before he ran back upstairs to cut the music. I was glad he'd gotten to see at least a bit of the show.

Takumi had plenty of time to get his equipment out, because the laughing and talking went on for several minutes while the Eagle kept repeating, "Okay. Okay. Let's settle down now. Settle down, y'all. Let's settle down."

The senior-class speaker spoke next. He blew. And as we left the gym, nonjuniors crowded around us, asking, "Was it you?" and I just smiled and said no, for it had not been me, or the Colonel or Takumi or Lara or Longwell Chase or anyone else in that gym. It had been Alaska's prank through and through. The hardest part about pranking, Alaska told me once, is not being able to confess. But I could confess on her behalf now. And as I slowly made my way out of the gym, I told anyone who would listen, "No. It wasn't us. It was Alaska."

The four of us returned to Room 43, aglow in the success of it, convinced that the Creek would never again see such a prank, and it didn't even occur to me that I might get in trouble until the Eagle opened the door to our room and stood above us, and shook his head disdainfully.

"I know it was y'all," said the Eagle.

1 **pec** (infml): muscle in the upper chest 2 **briefs** (AE): men's underpants
5 **ovation**: enthusiastic clapping 19 **he blew** (sl): he was not interesting
28 **aglow**: (here) shining with happiness 32 **disdainful**: *verächtlich*

We looked at him silently. He often bluffed. Maybe he was bluffing.

"Don't ever do anything like that again," he said. "But, Lord, 'subverting the patriarchal paradigm' – it's like she wrote the speech." He smiled and closed the door.

one hundred fourteen days after

A WEEK AND A HALF LATER, I walked back from my afternoon classes, the sun bearing down on my skin in a constant reminder that spring in Alabama had come and gone in a matter of hours, and now, early May, summer had returned for a six-month visit, and I felt the sweat dribble down my back and longed for the bitter winds of January. When I got to my room, I found Takumi sitting on the couch, reading my biography of Tolstoy.

"Uh, hi," I said.

He closed the book and placed it beside him and said, "January 10."

"What?" I asked.

"January 10. That date ring a bell?"

"Yeah, it's the day Alaska died." Technically, she died three hours into January 11, but it was still, to us anyway, Monday night, January 10.

"Yeah, but something else, Pudge. January 9. Alaska's mom took her to the zoo."

"Wait. No. How do you know that?"

"She told us at Barn Night. Remember?"

Of course I didn't remember. If I could remember numbers, I wouldn't be struggling toward a C-plus in precalc.

"Holy shit," I said as the Colonel walked in.

"What?" the Colonel asked.

"January 9, 1997," I told him. "Alaska liked the bears. Her mom liked the monkeys." The Colonel looked at me blankly for a moment

17 **ring a bell**: sound familiar

and then took his backpack off and slung it across the room in a single motion.

"Holy shit," he said. "WHY THE HELL DIDN'T I THINK OF THAT!"

Within a minute, the Colonel had the best solution either of us would ever come up with. "Okay. She's sleeping. Jake calls, and she talks to him, and she's doodling, and she looks at her white flower, and 'Oh God my mom liked white flowers and put them in my hair when I was little,' and then she flips out. She comes back into her room and starts screaming at us that she forgot – forgot about her mom, of course – so she takes the flowers, drives off campus, on her way to – what?" He looked at me. "What? Her mom's grave?"

And I said, "Yeah, probably. Yeah. So she gets into the car, and she just wants to get to her mom's grave, but there's this jackknifed truck and the cops there, and she's drunk and pissed off and she's in a hurry, so she thinks she can squeeze past the cop car, and she's not even thinking straight, but she has to get to her mom, and she thinks she can get past it somehow and *POOF*."

Takumi nods slowly, thinking, and then says, "Or, she gets into the car with the flowers. But she's already missed the anniversary. She's probably thinking that she screwed things up with her mom again – first she doesn't call 911, and now she can't even remember the freaking anniversary. And she's furious and she hates herself, and she decides, 'That's it, I'm doing it,' and she sees the cop car and there's her chance and she just floors it."

The Colonel reached into his pocket and pulled out a pack of cigarettes, tapping it upside down against the COFFEE TABLE. "Well," he said. "That clears things up nicely."

one hundred eighteen days after

SO WE GAVE UP. I'd finally had enough of chasing after a ghost who did not want to be discovered. We'd failed, maybe, but some mysteries aren't meant to be solved. I still did not know her as I

25 **floor it**: *(hier) das Gaspedal bis zum Anschlag durchdrücken*

wanted to, but I never could. She made it impossible for me. And the accicide, the suident, would never be anything else, and I was left to ask, *Did I help you toward a fate you didn't want, Alaska, or did I just assist in your willful self-destruction?* Because they are different crimes, and I didn't know whether to feel angry at her for making me part of her suicide or just to feel angry at myself for letting her go.

But we knew what could be found out, and in finding it out, she had made us closer – the Colonel and Takumi and me, anyway. And that was it. She didn't leave me enough to discover her, but she left me enough to rediscover the Great Perhaps.

"There's one more thing we should do," the Colonel said as we played a video game together with the sound on – just the two of us, like in the first days of the Investigation.

"There's nothing more we can do."

"I want to drive through it," he said. "Like she did."

We couldn't risk leaving campus in the middle of the night like she had, so we left about twelve hours earlier, at 3:00 in the afternoon, with the Colonel behind the wheel of Takumi's SUV. We asked Lara and Takumi to come along, but they were tired of chasing ghosts, and besides, finals were coming.

It was a bright afternoon, and the sun bore down on the asphalt so that the ribbon of road before us quivered with heat. We drove a mile down Highway 119 and then merged onto I-65 northbound, heading toward the accident scene and Vine Station.

The Colonel drove fast, and we were quiet, staring straight ahead. I tried to imagine what she might have been thinking, trying again to see through time and space, to get inside her head just for a moment. An ambulance, lights and sirens blaring, sped past us, going in the opposite direction, toward school, and for an instant, I felt a nervous excitement and thought, *It could be someone I know.* I almost wished it was someone I knew, to give new form and depth to the sadness I still felt.

2 **accicide, suident**: combination of the words "accident" and "suicide"

The silence broke: "Sometimes I liked it," I said. "Sometimes I liked it that she was dead."

"You mean it felt good?"

"No. I don't know. It felt … pure."

"Yeah," he said, dropping his usual eloquence. "Yeah. I know. Me, too. It's natural. I mean, it must be natural."

It always shocked me when I realized that I wasn't the only person in the world who thought and felt such strange and awful things.

Five miles north of school, the Colonel moved into the left lane of the interstate and began to accelerate. I gritted my teeth, and then before us, broken glass glittered in the blare of the sun like the road was wearing jewelry, and that spot must be the spot. He was still accelerating.

I thought: *This would not be a bad way to go.*

I thought: *Straight and fast. Maybe she just decided at the last second.*

And *POOF* we are through the moment of her death. We are driving through the place that she could not drive through, passing onto asphalt she never saw, and we are not dead. We are not dead! We are breathing and we are crying and now slowing down and moving back into the right lane.

We got off at the next exit, quietly, and, switching drivers, we walked in front of the car. We met and I held him, my hands balled into tight fists around his shoulders, and he wrapped his short arms around me and squeezed tight, so that I felt the heaves of his chest as we realized over and over again that we were still alive. I realized it in waves and we held on to each other crying and I thought, *God we must look so lame*, but it doesn't much matter when you have just now realized, all the time later, that you are still alive.

5 **eloquence**: *Redegewandtheit*

one hundred nineteen days after

THE COLONEL AND I threw ourselves into school once we gave up, knowing that we'd both need to ace our finals to achieve our GPA goals (I wanted a 3.0 and the Colonel wouldn't settle for even a 3.98). Our room became Study Central for the four of us, with Takumi and Lara over till all hours of the night talking about *The Sound and the Fury* and meiosis and the Battle of the Bulge. The Colonel taught us a semester's worth of precalc, although he was too good at math to teach it very well – "Of course it makes sense. Just trust me. Christ, it's not that hard" – and I missed Alaska.

And when I could not catch up, I cheated. Takumi and I shared copies of Cliffs Notes for *Things Fall Apart* and *A Farewell to Arms* ("These things are just too damned *long*!" he exclaimed at one point).

We didn't talk much. But we didn't need to.

one hundred twenty-two days after

A COOL BREEZE had beaten back the onslaught of summer, and on the morning the Old Man gave us our final exams, he suggested we have class outside. I wondered why we could have *an entire class* outside when I'd been kicked out of class last semester for merely *glancing* outside, but the Old Man wanted to have class outside, so we did. The Old Man sat in a chair that Kevin Richman carried out for him, and we sat on the grass, my notebook at first perched awkwardly in my lap and then against the thick green grass, and the bumpy ground did not lend itself to writing, and the gnats hovered. We were too close to the lake for comfortable sitting, really, but the Old Man seemed happy.

"I have here your final exam. Last semester, I gave you nearly two months to complete your final paper. This time, you get two weeks." He paused. "Well, nothing to be done about that, I guess." He

6 **meiosis** [maɪˈoʊsɪs]: *Meiose, Reduktionsteilung* 6 **Battle of the Bulge**: battle in Second World War in Belgium 11 **Things Fall Apart**: novel (1958) by Chinua Achebe 11 **Farewell to Arms**: novel (1929) by Ernest Hemingway 15 **onslaught** [ˈɑːnslɔːt] strong or violent attack

laughed. "To be honest, I just decided once and for all to use this paper topic last night. It rather goes against my nature. Anyway, pass these around." When the pile came to me, I read the question:

> How will you – you personally – ever get out of this labyrinth of suffering? Now that you've wrestled with three major religious traditions, apply your newly enlightened mind to Alaska's question.

After the exams had been passed out, the Old Man said, "You need not specifically discuss the perspectives of different religions in your essay, so no research is necessary. Your knowledge, or lack thereof, has been established in the quizzes you've taken this semester. I am interested in how you are able to fit the uncontestable fact of suffering into your understanding of the world, and how you hope to navigate through life in spite of it.

"Next year, assuming my lungs hold out, we'll study Taoism, Hinduism, and Judaism together –" The Old Man coughed and then started to laugh, which caused him to cough again. "Lord, maybe I won't last. But about the three traditions we've studied this year, I'd like to say one thing. Islam, Christianity, and Buddhism each have founder figures – Muhammad, Jesus, and the Buddha, respectively. And in thinking about these founder figures, I believe we must finally conclude that each brought a message of radical hope. To seventh-century Arabia, Muhammad brought the promise that anyone could find fulfillment and everlasting life through allegiance to the one true God. The Buddha held out hope that suffering could be transcended. Jesus brought the message that the last shall be first, that even the tax collectors and lepers – the outcasts – had cause for hope. And so that is the question I leave you with in this final: What is your cause for hope?"

*

12 **uncontestable**: *unbestreitbar* 20 **respectively**: *in dieser Reihenfolge*
24 **allegiance** [ə'li:dʒəns]: *Treue, Ergebenheit* 26 **transcend sth.**: be or go beyond the usual limits of sth. 27 **tax collector**: *Steuereinnehmer* 27 **leper**: *Leprakranke(r), Aussätzige(r)*

Back at Room 43, the Colonel was smoking in the room. Even though I still had one evening left of washing dishes in the cafeteria to work off my smoking conviction, we didn't much fear the Eagle. We had fifteen days left, and if we got caught, we'd just have to start senior year with some work hours. "So how will we ever get out of this labyrinth, Colonel?" I asked.

"If only I knew," he said.

"That's probably not gonna get you an A."

"Also it doesn't do much to put my soul to rest."

"Or hers," I said.

"Right. I'd forgotten about her." He shook his head. "That keeps happening."

"Well, you have to write *something*," I argued.

"After all this time, it still seems to me like straight and fast is the only way out – but I choose the labyrinth. The labyrinth blows, but I choose it."

one hundred thirty-six days after

TWO WEEKS LATER, I still hadn't finished my final for the Old Man, and the semester was just twenty-four hours from ending. I was walking home from my final test, a difficult but ultimately (I hoped) successful battle with precalculus that would win me the B-minus I so richly desired. It was genuinely hot out again, warm like she was. And I felt okay. Tomorrow, my parents would come and load up my stuff, and we'd watch graduation and then go back to Florida. The Colonel was going home to his mother to spend the summer watching the soybeans grow, but I could call him long-distance, so we'd be in touch plenty. Takumi was going to Japan for the summer, and Lara was again to be driven home via green limo. I was just thinking that it was all right not to know quite where Alaska was and quite where she was going that night, when I opened the door to my room and noticed a folded slip of paper on the linoleum floor.

3 **conviction**: fact of having been found guilty 25 **soybean**: *Sojabohne*

It was a single piece of lime green stationery. At the top, it read in calligraphy:

From the Desk of ... Takumi Hikohito

Pudge/Colonel:

I am sorry that I have not talked to you before. I am not staying for graduation. I leave for Japan tomorrow morning. For a long time, I was mad at you. The way you cut me out of everything hurt me, and so I kept what I knew to myself. But then even after I wasn't mad anymore, I still didn't say anything, and I don't even really know why. Pudge had that kiss, I guess. And I had this secret.

You've mostly figured this out, but the truth is that I saw her that night. I'd stayed up late with Lara and some people, and then I was falling asleep and I heard her crying outside my back window. It was like 3:15 that morning, maybe, and I walked out there and saw her walking through the soccer field. I tried to talk to her, but she was in a hurry. She told me that her mother was dead eight years that day, and that she always put flowers on her mother's grave on the anniversary, but she forgot that year. She was out there looking for flowers, but it was too early – too wintry. That's how I knew about January 10. I still have no idea whether it was suicide.

She was so sad, and I didn't know what to say or do. I think she counted on me to be the one person who would always say and do the right things to help her, but I couldn't. I just thought she was looking for flowers. I didn't know she was going to go. She was drunk, just trashed drunk, and I really didn't think she would drive or anything. I thought she would just cry herself to sleep and then drive to visit her mom the next day or something. She walked away, and then I heard a car start. I don't know what I was thinking.

2 **calligraphy**: beautiful handwriting 28 **trashed drunk**: *sturzbetrunken*

So I let her go, too. And I'm sorry. I know you loved her. It was hard not to.

Takumi

I ran out of the room, like I'd never smoked a cigarette, like I ran with Takumi on Barn Night, across the dorm circle to his room, but Takumi was gone. His bunk was bare vinyl; his desk empty; an outline of dust where his stereo had been. He was gone, and I did not have time to tell him what I had just now realized: that I forgave him, and that she forgave us, and that we had to forgive to survive in the labyrinth. There were so many of us who would have to live with things done and things left undone that day. Things that did not go right, things that seemed okay at the time because we could not see the future. If only we could see the endless string of consequences that result from our smallest actions. But we can't know better until knowing better is useless.

And as I walked back to give Takumi's note to the Colonel, I saw that I would never know. I would never know her well enough to know her thoughts in those last minutes, would never know if she left us on purpose. But the not-knowing would not keep me from caring, and I would always love Alaska Young, my crooked neighbor, with all my crooked heart.

I got back to Room 43, but the Colonel wasn't home yet, so I left the note on the top bunk and sat down at the computer, and I wrote my way out of the labyrinth:

Before I got here, I thought for a long time that the way out of the labyrinth was to pretend that it did not exist, to build a small, self-sufficient world in a back corner of the endless maze and to pretend that I was not lost, but home. But that only led to a lonely life accompanied only by the last words of the already-dead, so I came here looking for a Great Perhaps, for real friends and a more-than-minor life. And then I screwed

27 **self-sufficient**: *nicht auf fremde Hilfe angewiesen*

up and the Colonel screwed up and Takumi screwed up and she slipped through our fingers. And there's no sugarcoating it: She deserved better friends.

When she fucked up, all those years ago, just a little girl terrified into paralysis, she collapsed into the enigma of herself. And I could have done that, but I saw where it led for her. So I still believe in the Great Perhaps, and I can believe in it in spite of having lost her.

Because I will forget her, yes. That which came together will fall apart imperceptibly slowly, and I will forget, but she will forgive my forgetting, just as I forgive her for forgetting me and the Colonel and everyone but herself and her mom in those last moments she spent as a person. I know now that she forgives me for being dumb and scared and doing the dumb and scared thing. I know she forgives me, just as her mother forgives her. And here's how I know:

I thought at first that she was just dead. Just darkness. Just a body being eaten by bugs. I thought about her a lot like that, as something's meal. What was her – green eyes, half a smirk, the soft curves of her legs – would soon be nothing, just the bones I never saw. I thought about the slow process of becoming bone and then fossil and then coal that will, in millions of years, be mined by humans of the future, and how they would heat their homes with her, and then she would be smoke billowing out of a smokestack, coating the atmosphere. I still think that, sometimes, think that maybe "the afterlife" is just something we made up to ease the pain of loss, to make our time in the labyrinth bearable. Maybe she was just matter, and matter gets recycled.

But ultimately I do not believe that she was only matter. The rest of her must be recycled, too. I believe now that we are greater than the sum of our parts. If you take Alaska's genetic

2 **sugarcoat sth.**: make sth. unpleasant seem less unpleasant than it is
5 **enigma**: mystery 10 **imperceptible**: very small and therefore unable to be seen or felt 25 **billow**: (of smoke) rise and move in a large mass 25 **smokestack**: a tall chimney

code and you add her life experiences and the relationships she had with people, and then you take the size and shape of her body, you do not get her. There is something else entirely. There is a part of her greater than the sum of her knowable parts. And that part has to go somewhere, because it cannot be destroyed.

Although no one will ever accuse me of being much of a science student, one thing I learned from science classes is that energy is never created and never destroyed. And if Alaska took her own life, that is the hope I wish I could have given her. Forgetting her mother, failing her mother and her friends and herself – those are awful things, but she did not need to fold into herself and self-destruct. Those awful things are survivable, because we *are* as indestructible as we believe ourselves to be. When adults say, "Teenagers think they are invincible" with that sly, stupid smile on their faces, they don't know how right they are. We need never be hopeless, because we can never be irreparably broken. We think that we are invincible because we are. We cannot be born, and we cannot die. Like all energy, we can only change shapes and sizes and manifestations. They forget that when they get old. They get scared of losing and failing. But that part of us greater than the sum of our parts cannot begin and cannot end, and so it cannot fail.

So I know she forgives me, just as I forgive her. Thomas Edison's last words were: "It's very beautiful over there." I don't know where there is, but I believe it's somewhere, and I hope it's beautiful.

14 **indestructible**: that cannot be destroyed 18 **irreparable**: that cannot be repaired

some last words on last words

LIKE PUDGE HALTER, I am fascinated by last words. For me, it began when I was twelve years old. Reading a history textbook, I came across the dying words of President John Adams: "Thomas Jefferson still survives." (Incidentally, he didn't. Jefferson had died earlier that same day, July 4, 1826; Jefferson's last words were "This is the Fourth?")

I can't say for sure why I remain interested in last words or why I've never stopped looking for them. It is true that I really loved John Adams's last words when I was twelve. But I also really loved this girl named Whitney. Most loves don't last. (Whitney sure didn't. I can't even remember her last name.) But some do.

Another thing that I can't say for sure is that all of the last words quoted in this book are definitive. Almost by definition, last words are difficult to verify. Witnesses are emotional, time gets conflated, and the speaker isn't around to clear up any controversy. I have tried to be accurate, but it is not surprising that there is debate over the two central quotes in *Looking for Alaska*.

SIMÓN BOLÍVAR

"How will I ever get out of this labyrinth!"

In reality, "How will I ever get out of this labyrinth!" were probably not Simón Bolívar's last words (although he did, historically, say them). His last words may have been "José! Bring the luggage. They do not want us here." The significant source for "How will I ever get out of this labyrinth!" is also Alaska's source, Gabriel García Márquez's *The General in His Labyrinth.*

FRANÇOIS RABELAIS

"I go to seek a Great Perhaps."

François Rabelais is credited with four alternate sets of last words. *The Oxford Book of Death* cites his last words as: (a) "I go to seek a Great Perhaps"; (b) (after receiving extreme unction) "I am greasing my boots for the last journey"; (c) "Ring down the curtain; the farce is played out"; (d) (wrapping himself in his domino, or hooded cloak) *"Beati qui in Domino moriuntur."* The last one, incidentally, is a pun,* but because the pun is in Latin, it is now rarely quoted. Anyway, I dismiss (d) because it's hard to imagine a dying François Rabelais having the energy to make a physically demanding pun, *in Latin*. (c) is the most common citation, because it's funny, and everyone's a sucker for funny last words.

I still maintain that Rabelais' last words were "I go to seek a Great Perhaps," partly because Laura Ward's nearly authoritative book *Famous Last Words* agrees with me, and partly because I believe in them. I was born into Bolívar's labyrinth, and so I must believe in the hope of Rabelais' Great Perhaps.

For more information and source notes on the other quotes in the book, please visit my Web site: *www.sparksflyup.com.*

* It means both "Blessed are they who die in the Lord" and "Blessed are they who die wearing a cloak."

Information about the Author

John Green was born in 1977 in Indianapolis, Indiana, but he grew up in Florida. He attended Indian Springs School, a boarding school near Birmingham, Alabama, which served as a model for Culver Creek school in *Looking for Alaska.* He graduated from Kenyon College in 2000 with a double major in English and Religious Studies.

Green lived for several years in Chicago and New York City, where he worked as a book reviewer.

Looking for Alaska (2005) was Green's first novel and received many prizes. He has written a few novels since, including *An Abundance of Katherines* (2006).

He now lives in Indianapolis.